W9-AKY-556

PRAISE FOR *THE OUTSIDER TEST FOR FAITH*

"This is the greatest book Loftus has ever produced. It's without question a must-read for believers and any atheists who want to debate them. Superbly argued, air tight, and endlessly useful, this should be everyone's first stop in the god debate. Loftus meets every objection and proves the Outsider Test for Faith is the core of every case against religious belief and the one argument you can't honestly get around. It takes religion on at its most basic presuppositions, forcing the believer into a dilemma from which there is no escape: either abandon your faith or admit you don't believe in being logically consistent. After reading it and sincerely applying its principles, anyone who really wants to be rational will be on the road to atheism in no time."

—Richard Carrier, author of *Proving History:*
Bayes's Theorem and the Quest for the Historical Jesus

"A bold book based on a simple premise: the unexamined faith is not worth believing. Of course, every Christian apologist gives lip service to this premise and claims to have given the tenets of faith a full and fair hearing. Loftus shows just how cheap and hollow such talk usually is. He demands that believers examine their own faith with all of the rigor and skepticism that they direct towards other faiths. To those who condemn the beliefs of others while elevating their own dogmas, Loftus' message could come straight from the Gospel: remove the beam from your own eye before you seek to remove the speck from another's."

—Keith Parsons, author of *God and the Burden of Proof*

"Perhaps the most intractable argument against Loftus's Outsider Test for Faith is some version of 'I can't do it. I can't get far enough outside my emotions and beliefs to examine my own religion like I would any other.' As a psychologist I find that credible. We all have a very imperfect and fragmentary ability to see ourselves as others see us. But this in no way undermines Loftus's foundational argument that the outsider test should be the gold standard."

—Dr. Valerie Tarico, psychologist
and author of *Trusting Doubt*

"John Loftus will be remembered a century from now for his Outsider Test for Faith."

—Frank Zindler, former president of American Atheists
and editor of *American Atheist Magazine*

"When an evangelical minister can ask tough questions about religion and leave the faith, then so can you. John Loftus is the religious believer's genuine friend, respecting your intelligence enough to show you how religions really work. His new book questions every religion with the same challenge: What reasons could it really have for claiming to possesses the unique truth? When the façades of familiarity and unquestionability are ripped away, exposing faith's weaknesses to both insiders and outsiders, can any religion pass this test?"

—John Shook, author of *The God Debates*

The Outsider Test for

FAITH

The Outsider Test for

FAITH

How to Know
Which Religion Is True

JOHN W. LOFTUS

Prometheus Books

59 John Glenn Drive
Amherst, New York 14228–2119

Published 2013 by Prometheus Books

The Outsider Test for Faith: How to Know Which Religion Is True. Copyright © 2013 by John W. Loftus. All rights reserved. No part of this publication may be reproduced, stored in a retrieval system, or transmitted in any form or by any means, digital, electronic, mechanical, photocopying, recording, or otherwise, or conveyed via the Internet or a website without prior written permission of the publisher, except in the case of brief quotations embodied in critical articles and reviews.

Prometheus Books recognizes the following trademark
mentioned within the text: Carnival Sage®

Cover image © Clive Tooth/Shutterstock.com
Cover design by Jacqueline Nasso Cooke

Inquiries should be addressed to
Prometheus Books
59 John Glenn Drive
Amherst, New York 14228–2119
VOICE: 716–691–0133
FAX: 716–691–0137
WWW.PROMETHEUSBOOKS.COM

17 16 15 14 13   5 4 3 2 1

Library of Congress Cataloging-in-Publication Data

Loftus, John W.
    The outsider test for faith : how to know which religion is true / by John W. Loftus.
        p. cm.
    Includes bibliographical references and index.
    ISBN 978–1–61614–737–2 (pbk. : alk. paper)
    ISBN 978–1–61614–738–9 (ebook)
    1. Religion—Controversial literature. I. Title.

BL2775.3.L635 2013
200—dc23
                                                              2012044552

Printed in the United States of America on acid-free paper

CONTENTS

INTRODUCTION

The problem this book addresses is the massive amount of worldwide religious diversity, why it exists, and how to solve it, if it can be solved at all. The goal is to help readers know how to tell which religion is true, if any of them are. My claim is that if we keep on doing the same things, we will get the same results. So far nothing has worked because believers have not considered what their faith looks like to an outsider, a nonbeliever in their particular religion. So why keep on doing the same things? I see no reason why we should. This book presents a sustained case that the only way to settle this problem is with the *Outsider Test for Faith* (OTF).

The Outsider Test for Faith (OTF) is just one of several arguments I use in my books to demonstrate that the predisposition of skepticism is warranted when examining the evidence for a religious set of beliefs. I argue that skepticism offers the only way for believers to rationally test their faith. There is overwhelming, undeniable, and noncontroversial evidence for the basis of the test in extant sociological, neurological, anthropological, and psychological data.

My focus in this book is on Christianity, especially evangelicalism, best represented by the Evangelical Theological Society and the Evangelical Philosophical Society. This is my target audience. The OTF does not just apply to my target audience though. It applies to anyone with religious faith. I am pleased to note that Thomas Riskas utilizes the OTF quite heavily in his book *Deconstructing Mormonism: An Analysis and Assessment of the Mormon Faith* (Cranford, NJ: American Atheist Press, 2011). I'd like to see more books like this written—books that critically examine other religious faiths with the OTF just as I have done with Christianity.

I have been hammered from all sides by Christian apologists about the outsider test for several years. On the one hand, there are Christians who reject the test as faulty or unfair in some way. I suspect their initial gut reaction is to argue against it because the person proposing this test is an atheist. Since anything an atheist proposes to test religion must be "wrong," they try to find fault with it. However, as we shall see, the great Catholic apologist G. K. Chesterton proposed something like it before I ever did. Or perhaps believers just realize their faith won't pass the test. If their faith could pass the test, they would be the first ones pushing it on everyone else.

On the other hand, there are Christians, like Chesterton, who assert that their faith passes the test. Why can't they agree? Against believers who think the test is unfair or faulty, I argue that they fail to understand what it is. Against believers who think their faith passes the test, I argue that they don't really understand what it demands of them. But in the end I thank them, for they have helped me fine-tune the test for this book.

Inside these pages is my final understanding about the test. If someone finds any inconsistency with something I say in this book when compared with my previous writings or blog posts, then I have either learned from my critics how to better express myself or I have changed my mind, and that's a good thing. I've written this book as if it is the only one my readers have ever read from me, just in case that's the case. So sometimes you'll find me using the exact words I used in my previous books.

In the first chapter I offer my argument on behalf of the Outsider Test for Faith. It includes all the essential ingredients of my case. I have written the first chapter in such a way that it could be included in any future relevant college-level anthology for discussion purposes, should an editor think it worthy. If this happens, then the present book can help instructors present the pro and con arguments in class discussion. In later chapters I expand and defend the argument presented in the first chapter, so there will be some repetition. In chapter 2, I look at the fact of religious diversity and argue that it entails that one's culturally adopted religious faith is probably false because of the sociological (or demographic) facts alone. In chapter 3, I argue for religious dependency, that one's culturally adopted religious faith is overwhelmingly dependent on brain biology, cultural conditions, and irrational thinking patterns, and that it is therefore probably false. In chapter 4, I share in greater detail what the outsider perspective requires, and I also consider some alternative tests for faith. In chapter 5, I answer objections to the fact of religious dependency, which is largely the crucial premise in my case. In chapters 6 through 8, I answer objections that the outsider test is self-defeating, that it has hidden faith assumptions, and that it unfairly targets religion. In the last two chapters, I argue that Christianity fails the outsider test and that the real problem of religious diversity is faith itself.

For illustrative purposes Adam Smith created the maps showing the distributions of modern science and world religions included in the appendix of this book, for which I am grateful. To see these maps in color, do a search on my blog for "World Distribution of Religion and Science" (http://debunkingchristianity.blogspot.com/2013/01/world-distribution-of-religion-and.html).

John W. Loftus

1
WHAT IS THE OUTSIDER TEST FOR FAITH?

O n February 11, 2006, I first proposed the Outsider Test for Faith (OTF) in response to an argument by Christian apologists. I think this is instructive. There is nothing quite like discussing and debating the issues that divide us. We learn from doing so. Most of the time it helps me understand how to make a better case against Christianity, as it did on that day. Although I am a former Christian, I was repeatedly told I couldn't understand the Christian faith because I was not a believer, not an insider. The Christian apologists cited the apostle Paul, who insisted the "wisdom of the world" is foolishness to God to such a degree that nonbelievers "cannot understand" the things of God because his wisdom is "discerned only through the Spirit" (1 Cor. 1:17–25, 3:18–20). Paul claimed that nonbelievers had become "vain in their reasonings" and that, by "professing themselves to be wise, they became fools" (Rom. 1:21–22).

As I reflected on this I asked myself a few questions. How do reasonable people first become believers, or insiders, if from the outside they can't understand Christianity? Anselm, a twelfth-century Christian philosopher and theologian, argued that "faith seeks understanding." So which comes first, faith or understanding? If, as a nonbelieving outsider, I cannot understand the Christian faith, then how does God expect me to reasonably come to faith in the first place? What is faith? How do we reasonably get it unless understanding precedes faith? Christians will reply that faith is a gift, but why is that gift mostly given to people who are raised in Christian households in Christianized cultures? Does God dole out his gift of

saving faith differently to individuals on different sides of geographical or national boundaries? Why is it that other religious faiths are
given "by other gods" to people separated into geographically distinct parts of the planet? Have the gods agreed where on earth they
should each reign over the lives of human beings? Since there are
many religious faiths, how does anyone rationally choose to be on
the *inside* of any of them if from the *outside* they don't have any plausibility? Why do believers all seem to judge outsiders as ignorant,
unenlightened, misguided, deceived, and lacking in understanding?
Why is it that different believers within their culturally inherited religions cannot settle their own differences?

I also thought about my experience as a Christian believer. I was
raised a Catholic in my younger years. My religious ancestry stretches
back through my father to my great-great-grandfather, who, as a
Catholic, probably immigrated to America during the Irish Potato
Famine that lasted from about 1845 to 1852. During the famine
approximately one million Irish people died and a million more
immigrated to America, causing the population of Ireland to fall
by between 20 and 25 percent. My mother, however, was raised a
Presbyterian. When my parents got married the Catholic Church
required that couples raise their children as Catholics, so my mother
acquiesced to my father's inherited faith. This is how I came to be
raised as a Catholic, just like my father, his father, his father, and his
father before him.

There was a certain amount of religious conflict between my
maternal and fraternal grandparents, since staunch Catholics and
Presbyterians disagreed about which Christian sect was true. This
religious conflict has a long history that has been largely forgotten
by Christians today. But a lot of blood was spilt between these two
Christianities in Europe during the sixteenth and seventeenth centuries, and animosity between them lasted for centuries afterward. My
grandparents on my mother's side outlived my grandparents on my
father's side, so after my father's parents had both died (his mother
in 1971), it gave my mother the freedom to explore her Protestant

faith again, and she did. I was seventeen at the time. And guess what? Even though I was raised a Catholic, I ended up accepting the faith of the evangelical church she attended.

I inherited my religious faith, first from my father and then later from my mother. This is not surprising in the least. It's what we would expect. Richard E. Petty and John T. Cacioppo are experts on persuasive psychology who have documented this phenomenon: "Since most of the information that children have about the world comes directly from their parents, it is not surprising that children's beliefs, and thus their attitudes, are initially very similar to their parents." They claim that "social psychologists have well documented that children tend to share their parents' racial prejudices, religious preferences, and political party affiliations."[1]

As children we were all raised as believers. Whatever our parents told us we believed. If they said Santa Claus or the Tooth Fairy or the Easter Bunny existed, then we believed what they said until we were told otherwise. If they had told us Allah or Zeus or Baal or Poseidon or Thor or Odin existed, we would have believed them. We learn our religion on our Mamas' knees, so to speak, usually surrounded by a culture of people who believe in the same religious tradition. So Catholics will raise Catholics. Evangelicals will raise evangelicals. Pentecostals will raise Pentecostals. Orthodox Jews will raise Orthodox Jews. Mormons will raise Mormons. Militant Muslims will raise militant Muslims. Pantheists will raise pantheists. Polytheists will raise polytheists. Scientologists will raise Scientologists. Polygamists will raise polygamists. Snake handlers will raise snake handlers. As children, we cannot believe differently. We don't know not to believe what our parents tell us. The problem is that, since our parents were never told by their parents that their inherited faith was false, they passed it down to us. And, if we continue to believe, we will in turn pass it down to our children. We can even locate specific geographical boundary lines between different religious faiths around the globe.

At some point along the line, as we become adults, we need to critically examine what we were taught to believe as children. That's why doubt is the adult attitude and skepticism is a learned virtue. We must learn to question. As we do, we eventually become thinking adults. But the strange thing is that even as adults we do not usually question our religious faiths. They just seem too obvious to us. They have become too ingrained within us. They are usually part of the culture we live in. We see no need to question them. They are such a part of who we are that, for many of us, like me, it takes a personal crisis to do what we should have been doing all along, critically examining the religion that was handed down to us.

As a believer, I thought I had rationally investigated my faith, but I did it from the inside, as an insider, with the presumption that my culturally inherited religious faith was true. Eventually, however, even from an insider's perspective I couldn't continue to believe. So for me, like other ex-Christians, Christianity failed the *Insider Test for Faith*. Now, from the outside, it makes no sense at all. Christians are on the inside. I am now on the outside. Christians see things from the inside. I see things from the outside. From the inside, it seems true. From the outside, it seems, well, bizarre. Only when one is on the inside, as an adherent of a particular religious faith, can one see. But from the outside, the adherents of a different faith seem blind.

THE OUTSIDER TEST FOR FAITH

There is a great deal of discussion among Christian apologists about background-knowledge factors that play a significant role in assessing the truth of Christianity, given the improbability of miracles like the virgin birth and the resurrection of Jesus, difficulties in explaining such things as the barbaric nature of Yahweh in the Old Testament, and doctrinal improbabilities regarding the trinity, the incarnation, the atonement, and the goodness of God in the face of massive and ubiquitous human and animal suffering. These background factors help Christian believers answer objections to their faith, since any particular intractable difficulty can be assessed in light of the sum total of what they believe. What they fail to think seriously about is the most important background factor of all for cognitively assessing the truth of their religious faith: one's familial, sociological, and cultural background. Believers also ignore the scientific findings that the human mind is a belief engine and that people are not really rational about religious faith.

When it comes to assessing the truth claims of Christian theism (or religion in general) the biggest question of all is whether we should approach the available evidence through the eyes of faith, as an insider, or with the eyes of skepticism, as an outsider, a non-believer. Complete neutrality, as sort of a blank-slate-type condition, while desirable, is practically impossible, since the cultural glasses we use to see the available evidence are often already religious, and they're already there prior to looking at the evidence. So I argue that we need some sort of objective, unbiased, non-double-standard type of test in order to investigate what we were taught to believe.

My argument is as follows:

(1) People who are located in distinct geographical areas around the globe overwhelmingly adopt and justify a wide diversity of religious faiths due to their particular upbringing and shared cultural heritage, and most of these faiths are mutually exclusive. This is the *Religious Diversity Thesis* (RDVT). The sociological facts are easy to come by. If we were raised in Thailand we would probably be Buddhists. If we were raised in Saudi Arabia we'd probably be Muslims. If we were raised in Mexico we'd probably be Catholics. The main thing religious diversity shows us is that not every religious faith can possibly be true. In fact, given the number of mutually exclusive religious faiths in the world, each of which claims exclusive access to religious truth, it's highly likely, given the odds alone, that the one we inherited in our respective culture is false. This is a problem that believers must take seriously. It cries out for a good explanation.

(2) The best explanation for (1) is that adopting and justifying one's religious faith is not a matter of independent rational judgment. Rather, to an overwhelming degree, one's religious faith is

causally dependent on brain processes, cultural conditions, and irrational thinking patterns. This is the *Religious Dependency Thesis* (RDPT).

From brain biology we know that humans have inherited from our animal ancestors an innate capacity for detecting patterns (like faces) in random data and for seeing personal agency behind random forces in nature. In the animal world, where any hesitation in fleeing from a predator could lead to being eaten alive, these senses of *patternicity* and *agenticity* (as they are called) are beneficial for survival. Human beings transformed these survival mechanisms into seeing divine beings active behind the scenes, orchestrating such natural and human-made phenomena as thunderstorms, droughts, victory or defeat in war, births of sons, bumper crops, and so forth.[2] Anthropological data have shown us that we overwhelmingly adopt what our respective cultures teach us and that we are unable to see our own cultural biases because we are completely immersed in our inherited culture. Culture has an overwhelming impact on what we think and believe.[3] From conclusive psychological studies we have learned that people, all of us, have a very strong tendency toward believing what we prefer to believe and toward justifying those beliefs. Once our minds are made up, it is very hard to change them. We will even take lack of evidence as evidence for what we believe. Almost shockingly, these studies have shown us that encountering information that goes against our point of view can actually make us more convinced that we were right to begin with.[4]

From (1) and (2) it follows that:

(3) It is highly likely that any given religious faith is false and quite possible that they could all be false. At best there can be only one religious faith that is true. At worst, they could all be false. The sociological facts, along with our brain biology, anthropological (or cultural) data, and psychological studies, lead us to this highly likely conclusion.

So I propose that:

(4) The only way to rationally test one's culturally adopted reli-

gious faith is from the perspective of an outsider, a nonbeliever, with the same level of reasonable skepticism believers already use when examining the other religious faiths they reject. This expresses the Outsider Test for Faith (OTF).

The OTF is based on the same kind of data that cultural relativists use when arguing that, because moral practices and beliefs do in fact vary from culture to culture as well as at different times in history, morality is not the result of independent rational judgment but rather is causally dependent on cultural conditions. All we have to do is insert the phrase *religious faith* in place of the word *morality*, with one caveat. I'm not arguing that all religious faiths are false because of religious diversity or that they are completely dependent on one's cultural upbringing. I'm merely arguing that believers should be skeptical of their own culturally inherited faith because it is overwhelmingly the case that one's faith is dependent on one's cultural upbringing.[5]

The OTF is a self-diagnostic test to aid honest believers in examining their inherited religious faith. It is for believers who, upon becoming adults, wish to test their inherited faith. Learning a religion upon Mama's knee is an unreliable way to gain the "correct" religious faith, since a wide diversity of religions are taught to children in the same exact way, only one of which, at most, can be true. The odds are that the religious faith you were taught to believe is false, given the number of faiths handed down by parents in separate geographical regions around the globe.

I want people to see the OTF as a solution to the problem of religious diversity, a problem that needs a solution. No other methods have worked before. If people cannot find solutions to problems within a business, they hire solution specialists who offer ways to solve them. Mediators find ways to bring people together by offering ways they can see their differences in a better light. That's what the OTF does. The goal is to offer a fair test to find out which religion is true, if there is one. To be a fair and objective test it must allow that any conclusion could result, and the OTF does just that. The OTF grants that a religious faith can be reasonable and asks believers to test their faith with it, just as it grants that nonbelief can be reasonable and asks nonbelievers to consider the religious options available. It also grants the possibility that one particular religious faith could pass the test, just as it grants the possibility that none of them might pass it. It offers the only objective non–double standard for doing so.

Believers can respond to the OTF in four ways: (1) object to (or mitigate) the facts of the RDVT and the RDPT that form the basis for the test; (2) object to the OTF by arguing that it is faulty or unfair in some relevant manner; (3) along with objections (1) and/or (2), provide a better alternative to reasonably judge between religions; or (4) subject their religion to the test, as it has been described here, in which case it either (a) passes or (b) fails intellectual muster. It's that simple. If, in the end, believers can neither find fault with the OTF nor propose a better alternative, and if they find that no religion can pass the test, then that's not the fault of the test. Rather, the problem is with the religious faith(s) being tested.

One way to look at the OTF is to see it as involving three separate stages. The first stage involves establishing the sociological, biological, cultural, and psychological data that form the basis of the test. The second stage involves demonstrating that the OTF is required by these facts and that it offers the only way for believers to rationally test their faith. The third stage involves believers and nonbelievers using the OTF as a basis for arguments about which religious faith is true, if there is one.

Some believers may largely agree with the basis for the test, the first stage, but disagree with the second stage, the test itself, by finding fault with it and proposing what they consider a better test. But as you would guess, I think both of the first two stages in my whole case are unassailable, based on sound reasoning from the scientific data. Other believers may agree with the first and second stages but go on to argue in the third stage that their particular faith passes the outsider test. At that point believers have agreed to the standard of the test itself, and that's a good thing. For then we have a foundation for all future debates about religion. In the absence of accepting the test, believers and nonbelievers are condemned to talking past one another.

As a nonbeliever, I use the outsider test, in the third stage, to argue against religion in general and Christianity in particular. I suspect that if believers are willing to take the challenge of the OTF, they will find that their faith fails the test, and they will be forced to abandon it like I did mine. I argue that religious faiths do not pass the OTF. I argue that by its very nature faith cannot pass the OTF because faith is always unreasonable. I argue that the problem is faith itself. With faith as a foundation, anything can be believed, so informed people should reject faith altogether. Faith-based reasoning is belief in search of the facts. Faith, as I argue, is an irrational leap over the probabilities. Probabilities about such a matter are all that matter. We should think exclusively in terms of them.

Again, it is possible that there could be a religion that passes the test. That's to be determined based on the test itself. But I argue, in the third stage, that because of the nature of faith, no faith passes the outsider test. Sufficient evidence just doesn't exist for any faith. Christianity, for instance, could have passed the outsider test if God had provided the evidence needed to justify belief. But I argue he didn't do so. Given the fact that those of countless contradictory religious faiths believe and defend what they were raised to believe, and most of them are certain about their faith, until one of them steps up to the plate and offers something more by way of evidence than the other faiths, it's not reasonable to have faith in any of them.

That I use the OTF in this way does not undercut it at all, since a believer could argue for the test exactly as I do and then, in the third stage, argue that his or her particular faith passes the test. So someone cannot be skeptical of the OTF simply because I use it to argue against religious faith. For the first two stages can be justified independently of my conclusions in the third stage.

THE PERSPECTIVE OF AN OUTSIDER

What does the OTF require when it comes to *reasonable skepticism?* Every rational adult knows what it's like to be a skeptic or to doubt something. Since we all know how to be skeptics, we must distinguish between two types of skepticism, only one of which is a reasonable and informed one. There is a kind of skepticism that is born of faith. Faith-based skepticism causes believers to doubt other religious faiths simply because they believe that theirs is the true one. Since theirs is the true faith, the others must therefore be false. This same type of faith-based skepticism causes believers to doubt scientific findings whenever those findings undercut or discredit their faith in some way. This type of skepticism caused many believers to doubt that the sun was the center of the solar system in Galileo's day. It also causes Mormons to doubt the DNA evidence showing that Native Americans are not descendants from Semitic peoples.[6] This type of faith-based skepticism should be avoided as much as possible, if not altogether, if believers truly want to know the truth about their religion. Faith-based skepticism, because it refuses to question its own premise (i.e., faith), cannot help us solve the problem of religious diversity. It has a proven track record of not helping people reasonably examine their respective faiths. It has a proven track record that runs counter to the progress of science itself.

The other type of skepticism is born of science. It's a reasonable skepticism that demands sufficient evidence before accepting some claim as true. Even people of faith utilize scientific findings in every area of their lives (except those rare findings that directly undercut or discredit their respective faiths). So we all know what it's like to trust science, too. Since we all know how to be skeptics and we all know how to trust science, at the very minimum skeptics acknowledge that the scientific findings supportive of the RDVT and the RDPT are trustworthy, even though this means they should be skeptical of their faith. *The reasonable or informed skeptic is therefore someone who understands the force of the RDVT and the RDPT, and, at a very minimum, initially presumes when examining one's own religious faith that it is probably false.*[7] Unfortunately, believers who do not understand the problem, or refuse to face it head on, cannot be helped.

This *informed skepticism* becomes the default adult attitude when examining any religion, including one's own. It's an attitude, a skeptical attitude. It's a reasonable attitude that reasonable people should adopt. The extent of skepticism warranted depends on (1) the number of people who disagree, (2) whether the people who disagree are separated into distinct geographical locations, (3) how their faith originated, (4) under what circumstances their faith was personally adopted in the first place, (5) the number and nature of extraordinary miracle claims that are essential to their faith, and (6) the kinds of evidence that can be used to decide between the differing faiths. My claim is that, precisely because of these factors, a high degree of skepticism is warranted about religious faiths when compared to the objective results of science.

Informed skepticism is an attitude expressed as follows: (1) it assumes one's own religious faith has the burden of proof; (2) it adopts the methodological-naturalist viewpoint by which one assumes there is a natural explanation for the origins of a given religion, its holy books, and it's extraordinary claims of miracles; (3) it demands sufficient evidence before concluding a religion is true; and most importantly, (4) it disallows any faith in the religion under investigation, since the informed skeptic cannot leap over the lack of evidence by punting to faith.

I'm expressing these things with believers in mind because nonbelievers are, after all, already outsiders. Nonetheless, nonbelievers should also want to know which religion is true, if there is one, especially those who were raised as nonbelievers. So they should likewise treat all religions the same, with the same kind of informed skepticism required of believers, a skepticism born of science. These nonbelievers should know that the burden of proof is on believers. They should examine all religions from a methodological-naturalist viewpoint. And they should require sufficient evidence before accepting a religion without punting to faith in the one under examination.

Believers should begin by asking themselves how they first adopted their religious faith. Ask yourself who or what influenced you to believe? Under what circumstances did you adopt your faith? Did you seriously investigate your faith before adopting it? Did you consider other religious and nonreligious options? Or, like most believers, did you just adopt the beliefs given to you by your parents? If you merely adopted your faith for this reason, then it doesn't matter if your faith originated with people who had sufficient evidence to justify the beliefs they passed on to you. You don't know if they did until you examine the evidence for yourself with the OTF. It also doesn't matter if you feel certain that your religious faith is true. Most all believers feel this way. Neurologist Robert Burton explains this misplaced sense of certainty in this way: "Despite how certainty feels, it is neither a conscious choice nor even a thought process. Certainty and similar states of knowing what we know arise out of involuntary brain mechanisms that, like love or anger, function independently of reason."[8] Burton says that the "feeling of knowing," or certainty of conviction, should be thought of as one of our emotions, just like anger, pleasure, or fear. This feeling is unrelated to the strength of the evidence for what we believe. The feeling of "knowing" can be extremely powerful—so much so that our feeling of certainty wins despite contrary evidence that should mitigate it. Not only this, but our brain prefers to make up reasons to justify this feeling of certainty rather than follow the evidence to its reasonable conclusion.

Believers may object that if they assume the skeptical attitude it will automatically cause them to reject their religious faith, since doing so unfairly presumes its own conclusion. But I think not. So long as there is sufficient, objective evidence for one's religious faith, even an informed skeptic should come to accept it. Many people are convinced every day of the truth of claims when the evidence suggests otherwise. If God created us as reasonable people, then the correct religious faith should have sufficient evidence for it, since that's what reasonable people require. Otherwise, if sufficient evidence does not exist, then God counterproductively created us as reasonable people who would subsequently reject the correct faith. It also means that people born as outsiders to the correct faith (perhaps because they were born in remote geographical locations or during a time before the correct faith was revealed) will be condemned by God merely because of where or when they were born. This doesn't bode well for an omniscient, omnibenelovent, but wrathful kind of god. Even apart from such a god-concept, the only way to settle which religious faith is true is to rely on sufficient evidence.

When Christians examine the claim that Muhammad rode on a flying horse, they should do so by way of a reasonable and informed skepticism, just as they should when considering claims such as levitating Buddhists or the magical properties of Mormon holy underwear or the existence of the Scientologists' evil Thetans that supposedly infest our bodies. Christian believers should examine the specific extraordinary claims of Christianity using the same kind of skepticism. The OTF calls on people to do unto their own religious faith as they do unto the faiths they reject. It is a Golden Rule for testing religious faiths: "Do unto your own faith what you do unto other faiths." It calls on believers to subject their own faith to the same level of reasonable skepticism they use when rejecting other faiths, which is the skepticism of an outsider, a nonbeliever.

FIVE QUESTIONS FOR BELIEVERS

To believers who demur, they need to answer five questions:

1. Do you agree that a consistent standard invoking fairness is the best way to objectively come to know the correct religious faith, if there is one? If not, why not?
2. Do you agree that the default attitude of informed skepticism is the fairest way to objectively examine religious faiths? If not, why not? What's the alternative? How can this alternative method solve the problem of religious diversity in our world?

3. Do you agree that if your faith is true then people born into different religious cultures should *reasonably* be able to become insiders to your faith despite their initial skepticism—a skepticism that they were born into?

4. If you object to the OTF, be honest, is it because you think your faith cannot pass this test? If so, would you agree that such an objection is based on emotions rather than logic, that you are afraid to doubt, afraid to know the truth? What are you afraid of?

5. When you examine the truth of the religions you reject, whether they be Christianity, Islam, Orthodox Judaism, Hinduism, Scientology, Mormonism, Shintoism, Jainism, Haitian Voodoo, the John Frum Cargo Cult, Satanism, or the many African and Chinese tribal religions, do you have a reasoned or informed skepticism? If so, do you agree with the OTF that a fairer method, involving a non–double standard, is to assume your own faith should be evaluated with that same type of skepticism?

PRECURSORS TO THE OTF

For the most part, people who have rejected a religious faith have done so from the outside, with skepticism rather than faith. So I didn't invent this test, although I did discover it on my own. Confound the ancients; they've stolen all my ideas! William Lane Craig didn't originate the Kalam Cosmological Argument for the existence of God either. But, like Craig did with the Kalam argument, I've probably developed the OTF more than anyone else.

There have been several important precursors. Socrates is reported to have said, "The unexamined life is not worth living." Descartes wrote, "Several years have now elapsed since I first became aware that I had accepted, even from my youth, many false opinions for true, and that consequently what I afterward based on such principles was highly doubtful; and from that time I was convinced of the necessity of undertaking once in my life to rid myself of all the opinions I had adopted, and of commencing anew the work of building from the foundation."[9]

David Hume's devastating treatise on miracles in chapter 10 of his book *An Enquiry Concerning Human Understanding* is premised to a large extent on "the wise man," the man who is an outsider to faith. Hume, in the *Natural History of Religion* wrote, "The doctrine of one supreme deity, the author of nature, is very ancient, has spread itself over great and populous nations, and among them has been embraced by all ranks and conditions of men. But whoever thinks that it has owed its success to the prevalent force of those invincible reasons, on which it is undoubtedly founded, would show himself little acquainted with the ignorance and stupidity of the people, and their incurable prejudices in favour of their particular superstitions."[10]

Thomas Jefferson, in a letter from Paris to his nephew Peter Carr on August 10, 1787, offered some outsider advice, reminiscent of the OTF, on how to study religion:

> Fix reason firmly in her seat, and call to her tribunal every fact, every opinion. Question with boldness even the existence of a God; because, if there be one, he must more approve of the homage of reason, than that of blindfolded fear. You will naturally examine first, the religion of your own country. Read the Bible, then as you would read Livy or Tacitus. The facts which are within the ordinary course of nature, you will believe on the authority of the writer, as you do those of the same kind in Livy & Tacitus. The testimony of the writer weighs in their favor, in one scale, and their not being against the laws of nature, does not weigh against them. But those facts in the Bible which contradict the laws of nature, must be examined with more care, and under a variety of faces. Here you must recur to the pretensions of the writer to inspiration from God. Examine upon what evidence his pretensions are founded, and whether that evidence is so strong, as that its falsehood would be more improbable than a change in the laws of nature, in the case he relates.

For example, in the book of Joshua, we are told, the sun stood still several hours. Were we to read that fact in Livy or Tacitus, we should class it with their showers of blood, speaking of statues, beasts, &c. But it is said, that the writer of that book was inspired. . . . In fine, I repeat, you must lay aside all prejudice on both sides, and neither believe nor reject anything, because any other persons, or description of persons, have rejected or believed it.[11]

The eloquent Robert Ingersoll, in his 1872 lecture "The Gods," said:

All that is necessary, as it seems to me, to convince any reasonable person that the Bible is simply and purely of human invention—of barbarian invention—is to read it. Read it as you would any other book; think of it as you would of any other; get the bandage of reverence from your eyes; drive from your heart the phantom of fear; push from the throne of your brain the coiled form of superstition—then read the Holy Bible, and you will be amazed that you ever, for one moment, supposed a being of infinite wisdom, goodness and purity, to be the author of such ignorance and of such atrocity.[12]

Thomas Huxley said, "Sit down before fact as a little child, be prepared to give up every preconceived notion, follow humbly wherever and to whatever abysses nature leads, or you shall learn nothing. I have only begun to learn content and peace of mind since I have resolved at all risks to do this."[13] Huxley coined the word *agnosticism*, which he described as being not a creed, "but a method, the essence of which lies in the vigorous application of a single principle. . . . Positively the principle may be expressed: In matters of intellect, follow your reason as far as it will take you, without regard to any other consideration. And negatively: In matters of the intellect, do not pretend that conclusions are certain that are not demonstrated or demonstrable."[14]

If anyone thinks only skeptics propose such things, G. K.

Chesterton expressed a similar sentiment in his book *The Everlasting Man*.[15] In his introduction he wrote, "The point of this book . . . is that the next best thing to being really inside Christendom is to be really outside it. . . . It is the contention of these pages that while the best judge of Christianity is a Christian, the next best judge would be something more like a Confucian." He recommended "the imaginative effort of conceiving the Twelve Apostles as Chinamen." In fact, he goes on to say, "it would be better to see the whole thing as something belonging to another continent, or to another planet." So it would seem as if he's arguing for an *Alien Test for Faith*. "There are two ways of getting home," he began. "One of them is to stay there. The other is to walk round the whole world till we come back to the same place." His book is addressed to people who have not gotten home in the first way, inviting them to come home in the second way.

Keep in mind that, according to Chesterton, to approach Christianity from the outside "is the *next* best thing," not the *best* thing, and the best "judge of Christianity is a Christian," not a Confucian. I don't think anyone who seriously wants to test one's own religion would say such a thing as this. Just imagine a Mormon or Muslim or Scientologist saying the same thing. So it seems clear he's arguing *from* his faith not *to* it. It's an exercise in apologetics, not an exercise in examining his faith. Still, he tried to make a case from the outside for his faith. For Chesterton goes on to argue

> that when we do make this imaginative effort to see the whole thing from the outside, we find that it really looks like what is traditionally said about it inside. It is exactly when the boy gets far enough off to see the giant that he sees that he really is a giant. It is exactly when we do at last see the Christian Church afar under those clear and level eastern skies that we see that it is really the Church of Christ. To put it shortly, the moment we are really impartial about it, we know why people are partial to it.

The late Antony Flew, before his cognitive faculties ceased to function properly, argued that believers in God have the burden of proof, similar to the burden placed on prosecutors due to the pre-sumption of innocence found in our court systems. Given the extra-ordinary claims of religion and the fact of religious diversity, the burden of proof is on the believer, who must demonstrate his or her case. Flew called this "the presumption of atheism."[16] Because Flew was noncommittal about whether believers can even have a workable concept of God, he argued for the presumption of "negative atheism." According to him, "positive atheism" is the view of the person who positively asserts that God doesn't exist whereas "negative atheism" is merely the view of a nonbeliever who uses reason and science to judge the case presented by religious believers based on the burden of proof. I see no reason to think Flew's type of negative atheism is not basically the same as Huxley's type of agnosticism. It's probably a difference that makes no difference, for an agnostic, in Huxley's sense, could also be noncommittal about the question of whether there can be a workable concept of God.[17] Even Christian apologists J. P. Moreland and William Lane Craig acknowledge this could be a defensible view. For although they falsely claim that "the assertion 'God does not exist' is just as much a claim to knowledge as the assertion 'God exists,' and therefore the former requires justification just as the latter does," they admit, "If anything, then, one should speak at most of a presumption of agnosticism."[18]

In any case, Flew's presumption places the burden of proof squarely in the lap of religious believers. So it is the same presump-tion that is represented by the OTF. And just like the OTF, Flew's negative atheism is based on the same kinds of facts—religious diver-sity and the extraordinary claims of religion. These facts demand that religious believers should shoulder the burden of proof by demon-strating that their religious faith is true based on reason and science.

What then is the difference between Flew's argument and the OTF? He acknowledges the fact of religious diversity. But I stress how religions are geographically situated around the globe. I argue that this diversity is overwhelmingly dependent upon cultural factors. I argue that brain biology leads us to believe in agents behind random natural events. And I argue that psychological studies overwhelmingly show us that human beings are infected with numerous cognitive biases. These biases lead us to believe and defend what we prefer to believe. They lead us to prefer to believe and defend what was taught to us on Mama's knees. Then I make a move he failed to make. *The OTF calls upon believers to examine their own religious faith from the perspective of an outsider with the same level of reasonable skepticism they already use to examine the other religious faiths they reject.* It's this that makes the OTF more helpful than merely arguing that believers have the burden of proof. Why? Because one typical response to Flew is to rhetorically retort, "Who has the burden of proof to show that the other person has the burden of proof?" With the OTF such a debate isn't necessary, since believers already examine other religions with a reasonable skepticism. So the question becomes why they have a double standard, one for the other religious faiths they reject and a different one for their own inherited faith? This is the force of the OTF that keeps believers honest regarding their own faith. It denies the double standard that believers use, thus circumventing the "who has the burden of proof" burden.[19]

CONSISTENCY THOU ART A JEWEL

Mark Twain said: "The easy confidence with which I know another man's religion is folly teaches me to suspect that my own is also."[20] Full stop. Think about it. How do you know your own faith is true, given the facts of the RDVT and the RDPT? Keep in mind the quote widely attributed to Stephen Roberts: "I contend we are both atheists, I just believe in one fewer god than you do. When you understand why you dismiss all the other possible gods, you will understand why I dismiss yours."[21] That last sentence of his is the key. Christian believers are atheists (i.e., nonbelievers) with regard to all other gods but their own. Christians are therefore *narrow atheists* in that they don't believe in the existence of one or more different gods. By contrast, people who don't believe in any god at all are *wide atheists*.[22] The only difference is that wide atheists don't believe in the particular god that narrow atheists believe in. So to some extent we're all atheists. The fascinating thing is that narrow atheists and wide atheists disbelieve in most gods (and the associated religions) based on the same basic reasons. We disbelieve in them because they're based on faith rather than on sufficient evidence. When it comes to these religions, narrow atheists and wide atheists agree that faith is the fundamental problem. For when faith is the foundation, anything can be believed. It's just that narrow atheists are simply not consistent. The OTF asks believers to abandon the double standard they have about religious faiths, nothing more. The process should be fair; no one should place a thumb on the scales.

Liberal believers will bristle at this. They don't reject other religious faiths altogether. Rather, they incorporate the best elements of other faiths by embracing a commonly shared understanding in an ecumenical dialogue. Liberal believers include the most enlightened Jews, Muslims, Catholics, and Protestants, who all share the common understanding stemming from Paul Tillich's notion of "ultimate concern." To liberals I say that the rejection of faith-based reasoning can be seen on a continuum. Faith is much more prominent in some religious sects, most notably the conservative ones that, for instance, reject outright the overwhelming evidence for evolution in favor of a straightforward literal reading of the Genesis texts, and who embrace a literal understanding of hell as eternal conscious torment in an everlasting fire. So the OTF will be more helpful and more important to members of these conservative kinds of faith. The more conservative, exclusivist, and pseudoscientific the religious faith is, the more helpful the OTF will be. The more liberal, inclusivist, and accepting of scientifically based reasoning the religious faith is, the less important the OTF will be. But it is important for all types of religious faiths, to various degrees.

If nothing else, what I argue in the third stage is that liberals are not off the hook. For faith-based reasoning should be rejected by all scientifically informed people. At best, if liberal believers con-clude that a god does exist, then, based on their ecumenical beliefs, it follows that such a god doesn't care which religion we accept. They end up believing in a nebulous god with no definable characteristics, perhaps a deistic god or the "god of the philosophers." This god is quite different from the God of full-blown Christianity or any specific revealed religion though, and can safely be ignored. For a distant god is no different than no god at all.

2
THE FACT OF
RELIGIOUS DIVERSITY

This chapter supports my first contention—that people who are located in distinct geographical areas around the globe overwhelmingly adopt and justify a wide diversity of mutually exclusive religious faiths due to their particular upbringing and shared cultural heritage. This is the Religious Diversity Thesis (RDVT), and it is a well-established fact in today's world. The problem of religious diversity cries out for reasonable explanation, something that faith has not provided so far. Attempts to mitigate it or explain it, as we'll see, either fail to take it seriously or explain religion itself away.

There has been a wide diversity of religions since the dawn of human civilization. According to the sociological (or demographical) facts, this is easy enough to see with regard to some of the major religions in today's world (listed below with the number of worldwide adherents).[1]

Christianity:	2.1 billion
Islam:	1.5 billion
Secular/Nonreligious/Agnostic/Atheist:	1.1 billion
Hinduism:	900 million
Chinese traditional religion:	394 million
Buddhism:	376 million
Primal-Indigenous:	300 million
African Traditional and Diasporic:	100 million
Sikhism:	23 million
Juche:	19 million

Spiritism:	15 million
Judaism:	14 million
Baha'i:	7 million
Jainism:	4.2 million
Shinto:	4 million
Cao Dai:	4 million
Zoroastrianism:	2.6 million
Tenrikyo:	2 million
Neo-Paganism:	1 million
Unitarian-Universalism:	800,000
Rastafarianism:	600,000
Scientology:	500,000

Disregard for the moment that the "Secular/Nonreligious/Agnostic/Atheist" group is ranked as the third largest "religion" in the world, although this ranking is indeed noteworthy. Members of this group do not believe in supernatural forces (like animism or reincarnation) and/or supernatural beings (like gods, goddesses, and demons), so they do not represent a religion in any meaningful sense. They are nonreligious people by definition. If believers think atheism is a religion, then they need to provide a definition of religion that applies both to supernaturalism and to its denial. Any definition of religion that includes atheism will either deny the inherent supernaturalism of religion or end up describing religion as a social grouping of some kind. Nonetheless, we'll return to this demographic later in this chapter.

Within each of the major religions there are a plethora of sects with a wide diversity of beliefs and rituals. And the major religions are just the tip of the iceberg. There are probably somewhere around forty-five thousand religious sects, depending on our definitions and calculations. Professor of anthropology David Eller tells us that "there are many religions in the world, and they are different from each other in multiple and profound ways. Not all religions refer to gods, nor do all make morality a central issue, etc. No religion

is 'normal' or 'typical' of all religions; the truth is in the diversity."[2]
When it comes to belief in god(s), Eller writes,

> Many or most religions have functioned quite well without any
> notions of god(s) at all, and others have mixed god(s) with other
> beliefs such that god-beliefs are not the critical parts of the reli-
> gion. . . . Some religions that refer to or focus on gods believe them
> to be all-powerful, but others do not. Some consider them to be
> moral agents, and some do not; more than a few gods are down-
> right immoral. Some think they are remote, while others think they
> are close (or both simultaneously). Some believe that the gods are
> immortal and eternal, but others include stories of gods dying and
> being born . . . not all gods are creators, nor is creation a central
> feature or concern of all religions. . . . Finally, there is not even
> always a firm boundary between humans and gods; humans can
> become gods, and the gods may be former humans.[3]

Eller tells us: "Ordinarily we think of a religion as a single homo-
geneous set of beliefs and practices. The reality is quite otherwise:
Within any religion there is a variety of beliefs and practices—
and interpretations of those beliefs and practices—distributed
throughout space and time. Within the so-called world religions this
variety can be extensive and contentious, one or more variations
regarded as 'orthodox.'"[4] Among theists, for instance, there are
Reformed Jews, Orthodox Jews, and Hasidic Jews. There are Shi'a
Muslims, Sufi Muslims, and Sunni Muslims. In fact, polytheism is a
form of theism, and as Eller informs us, "the vast majority of theisms
have been polytheistic."[5] Historically there was a Mesopotamian
pantheon of gods, an Egyptian pantheon of gods, a Greek pantheon
of gods, a Roman pantheon of gods, a Norse pantheon of gods, and
a Hindu pantheon of gods, to name just a few.

Eller concludes that

> religion is much more diverse than most people conceive. . . .
> "Religion" does not equal "theism" and certainly not "Christianity,"

let alone any particular sect of Christianity. Indeed, there is no specific religion or type of religion that is *really* religion, the very essence or nature of religion. . . . Not only that, there is no central or essential or uniquely authentic theism but rather an array of theisms. . . . "Christianity" consists of a collection of Christianities including Catholic, Orthodox, and Protestant. And there is no central or essential Protestantism: it is a type of Christianity/mono-theism/theism/religion with many branches. No one Protestant sect is more Protestant or more religious than any other. . . . In fact, there is no "real" Christianity at all, only a range of Christianities.[6]

Not only is there religious diversity, it's also clear that religions are situated around the globe in mostly distinct geographical locations. The reader can see this in the Modern Distribution of World Religions map included in the appendix of this book. Muslims are concentrated in the Middle East, North Africa, the Indian subcontinent, and the islands of the Indian Ocean. Christians are predominantly concentrated in Europe, North and South America, and regions that experienced European colonialism. Hindus are concentrated in the Indian subcontinent. Buddhists are concentrated in India and Asia. While Jews are spread all over the world, Israel is the only nation with a majority Jewish population.[7]

If we contrast this diversity to the conclusions of scientifically literate people seen in the World Distribution of Modern Science map included in the appendix of this book, there is a very stark contrast. We don't find scientists in one part of the world agreeing about the existence of a geocentric (or earth-centered) solar system while scientists in another part agree about the existence of a heliocentric (or sun-centered) one. We don't find scientists in one country agreeing that astrology can predict the future while scientists in the country right next to it reject astrology altogether. We don't find scientists arguing for bloodletting in one nation and scientists arguing against it in a different one. That's because science is not culturally specific to one region of the earth, as is religion. Science isn't forced upon people through the threat of violence either. It proceeds by convincing other scientists of the evidence. It progresses *because* of the evidence. Astronomy replaced astrology; chemistry replaced alchemy; and the germ theory replaced the theory that evil spirits cause disease. Science is based on the idea that scientists in one part of the globe should get the same results from an experiment as scientists in another part of it. But the religious map shows that what religionists believe *depends on where they were born and raised.* If you live in Tibet or Thailand, you are most likely to be raised as a practitioner of Buddhism, which teaches that we are to suppress our desires in order to cease our sufferings and reach nirvana. If you live in Yemen or Saudi Arabia you're more likely to be a Muslim who believes we are here to submit to Allah.

WHAT DOES RELIGIOUS DIVERSITY SHOW US?

The main problem religious diversity presents us with is that not every religious faith can be true. In fact, given the number of mutually exclusive religious faiths in the world, it's highly likely that the one that you inherited in your respective culture is false (given the odds alone). Like the prince in the Cinderella story who must question forty-five thousand people to see which girl lost the glass slipper at the ball, the believer must therefore be skeptical of his or her culturally inherited faith. After all, each of the forty-five thousand girls questioned by the prince claimed that she was the one who lost the slipper. Therefore, an initial skepticism until shown otherwise would be warranted whenever the prince arrived at yet another girl's doorstep. This problem is intensified because, unlike the Cinderella story, where an empirical foot match could solve the issue, religious faith has no method apart from the OTF to solve it. At best there can only be one religious faith that is true. At worst they are all likely to be false.

Robert McKim tells us that it "is clear, therefore, that large numbers of people have held, and now hold, false beliefs in the area of religion . . . at most one of them can be true. . . . And since so many people hold false beliefs in the area of religion, it would seem, therefore, that all groups need to consider the possibility that their beliefs in this area may be mistaken."[8] McKim concludes, "To fail to examine your beliefs when you ought to examine them is to fail to be rational in an important respect."[9] For "when there is disagreement, it is parochial and unsatisfactory to fail to take other perspectives seriously."[10] To believers who are sure they have the correct religious faith, McKim cautions that this is "simply a poor guarantee that you are right, at least in the area in which there is disagreement, including the area of religious belief."[11]

It has been argued that the mere existence of disagreement between rational people does not automatically lead us to be skeptical about that which we think is true. On the contrary, I think it can and it does. As I said, the amount of skepticism warranted depends not only on (1) the number of people who disagree, but also on (2) whether the people who disagree are separated into distinct geographical locations, (3) how their faith originated, (4) under what circumstances their faith was personally adopted in the first place, (5) the number and nature of extraordinary miracle claims being made that are essential to their faith, and (6) the kinds of evidence that can be used to decide between the differing faiths. My claim is that a high degree of skepticism is warranted about religious faiths when compared to the objective results of science precisely because of these factors.

Richard Feldman, professor of philosophy at the University of Rochester, New York, argues that when there are two "epistemic peers" who have a "genuine disagreement" about "shared evidence," the reasonable thing to do is to "suspend judgment" about the issue. Under these conditions, "one should give up one's beliefs in the light of the sort of disagreement under discussion." If, however, "one's conviction survives the 'confrontation with the other' . . . this seems more a sign of tenacity and stubbornness than anything else."[12] By contrast, the more that rational people agree on an issue, the more probable it is that their shared opinion is true. Even though we know that everyone can be wrong, this is still the best we can do. The presence of rational disagreement between epistemic peers should be a red-light warning requiring skepticism.

Disagreement, a book edited by Feldman and colleague Ted Warfield, deals with these issues. When considering the debate between internalists and externalists about epistemic justification, Hilary Kornblith is an externalist. While this particular debate need not concern us, what Kornblith says about the debate is important: "That my epistemic peers disagree with me on this question is surely relevant evidence that I ought to take into account. It is indirect evidence . . . but it is important evidence nonetheless. And it surely seems that the proper way to respond to evidence of this sort is to suspend judgment, to suspend belief about the proper resolution of the debate."[13] Then she says, "I am thus forced to conclude, very reluctantly, that the opinions I hold on most philosophical matters— and I have a great many of them—are not epistemologically justified. Given the current state of the field, no one's opinions on these matters, it now seems to me, are epistemologically justified."[14] In this same book Catholic philosopher and apologist Peter van Inwagen says he is unable to accept the conclusion that because he maintains his faith despite peer disagreements he is not rational about his own beliefs. However, he admits that he is "unable to answer" the type of arguments Feldman has put forth.[15]

CHRISTIAN ATTEMPTS TO MITIGATE RELIGIOUS DIVERSITY

In the book *True Reason: Christian Responses to the Challenge of Atheism*, Christian apologist David Marshall has a chapter on the Outsider Test for Faith. Marshall claims that the diversity of religious faiths "is genuine, but deeply ambiguous." And he notes that G. K. Chesterton has said that religions around the world commonly include four beliefs: God, the gods, philosophy, and demons. Then Marshall comments, "In years of studying world religions, I have found his observation to be largely true. Peel away labels, and many beliefs seem to be universal or at least very widespread. This could be called the 'lack of religious diversity thesis,' and should be kept in balance with its alter ego."[16] I'm not sure what philosophy has to do with this, but since a necessary component of a religion is the belief in supernatural forces and/or beings, this agreement among religions cannot be considered in any meaningful sense to be a "lack of religious diversity." Even if there are a few other similar beliefs among several religions, there is just too wide a gap in what they believe to think the similarities are God-given. They are culturally given and were mostly created by males in an ancient, superstitious, barbaric age. Just consider that almost all ancient cultures sacrificed human beings—mostly children and virgins—to their deities. If Marshall were living in that day, he would be pointing to this similarity as evidence of the "lack of religious diversity," too. So even the similarities don't show us anything positive about the truth of religious faiths.

Some similarities show nothing except that concepts about god have gravitated toward monotheism because such a concept is a simpler one. This is how religions evolve. They either evolve or die. For no religion in our world community could hope to have a big enough god unless that god is the only God. As people became more aware of other city-states, they realized that their god(s) had to encompass those religions. So god-concepts grew bigger as the world got bigger. There is nothing problematic about this at all because religions evolve.

In any case, Marshall is dead wrong, as we previously learned from David Eller. Robert McKim concurs, saying, "There is not a single claim that is distinctive of any religious group that is not rejected by other such groups, with the exception of vague claims to the effect that there is something important and worthwhile about religion, or to the effect that there is a religious dimension to reality and that however the sciences proceed certain matters will be beyond their scope. Obviously even claims as vague as these are rejected by non-religious groups."[17]

Marshall goes on to say that "the first premise of Christianity is that Judaism is true. After all, the Bible has two halves, and the first half is longer. . . . That makes at least two true religions. This principle can be extended, to some extent, to the deepest truths in other spiritual traditions as well." He claims: "Either God is one, many, or not at all. But one doesn't need to choose between Yahweh, Elohim, theos, Allah, and Shang Di: the one only-existing Creator God is recognizable under many aliases." Christian philosopher Victor Reppert made this same claim about Allah. He said, "I believe that Allah exists. Allah is the Arabic word for God, just as Dios is Spanish for God, and Dieu is French for God, and Gott is German for God. I am a theist, therefore, I believe that Allah exists. No problem."[18] Christian philosopher Thomas Talbott agrees. To say otherwise, he opines, is "sheer nonsense," since "more than a few Muslims, I presume, would be the first to insist that 'Allah,' 'Yahweh,' and 'God' are merely different names for the very same individual."[19]

But all this is simply empty rhetoric with no substance at all. None of these writers believe in Allah, for instance, because Allah revealed himself in the Koran. If Allah is the same deity as the one worshipped by Christians then that deity duplicitously revealed two different religions. This means God, by whatever name is used, helped to instigate the wanton slaughter of Muslims by Christians and Christians by Muslims because of his conflicting revelations. It also means God duplicitously promised salvation to believers in one of them who will end up being condemned to hell for not believing according to the other one's creed(s). These are two different gods, each of whom denies doing some of the things the other one claims to have done, especially with regard to the resurrection of Jesus. What Marshall, Reppert, and Talbott should say instead is that they agree with Muslims about the existence of an omnipotent creator god, and so forth, not that they believe in the same deity.

Marshall finally argues that some religious diversity may not actually reflect the true beliefs of people around the world. He writes, "Of course most people in Saudi Arabia are Muslim, because converts from Islam are killed. Even non-Saudi Christians, such as workers from the Philippines, are sometimes imprisoned and tortured."[20] This is very unfortunate. Under these regimes it can be hard to determine what people would believe if they were not forced to believe. But it's clear that in democratic countries Islam is growing very rapidly, so surely many Muslims would still believe if they did not live under an Islamic theocracy. It's also clear that in democratic countries there is much more religious diversity. When people from former communist countries, like the Soviet Union and its satellites, were granted religious freedom, a great deal of religious diversity developed within them. Democratic freedom simply produces more religious diversity, which is the problem that the OTF is trying to solve.

CHRISTIAN ATTEMPTS AT EXPLAINING RELIGIOUS DIVERSITY

Christians try to reasonably explain geographically situated religious diversity by incorporating this fact into their faith. William Lane Craig's explanation for religious diversity basically tries to explain it away. He represented what many evangelical Christians believe when he argued, "It is *possible* that God has created a world having an optimal balance between saved and lost and that God has so providentially ordered the world that those who fail to hear the gospel and be saved would not have freely responded affirmatively to it even if they had heard it."[21] Craig argues that if this scenario is even *possible*, "it proves that it is entirely consistent to affirm that God is all-powerful and all-loving and yet that some people never hear the gospel and are lost."[22] However, there are many things that might be possible, and apologists like Craig seem to resort to that standard far too often. This is an example of what I mean when I say Christians demand that I prove their faith is impossible before they will consider it to be improbable, which is an unreasonable reverse standard. The probability that not one of the billions of people who have never heard the gospel would respond if they did hear it can probably be calculated, if missionaries kept such detailed records of their efforts. To claim what he does against the overwhelming evidence of missionary efforts belies the facts. When we look at the billions of people who have never been given a chance to be "saved" because of "when and where they were born," Craig's scenario seems extremely implausible, to say the least, and it depends not only upon God having foreknowledge of future free-willed contingent human actions, but also upon his knowing what the future would've been like if every single free choice had been different throughout history.[23] No wonder Craig only wants to talk about what is possible. He argues that God has "Middle Knowledge" such that he knows "what every possible creature would do under any possible circumstances . . . prior to any determination of the divine will."[24] So, despite his protests to the contrary, isn't it obvious that if Craig's God has this kind of foreknowledge he could simply foreknow who would not accept his offered salvation before they were even created? He could then have avoided the trouble of creating them in the first place. If he had done that, "hotel hell" would never have had even one occupant.

Christians try to offer other reasons why there is such a geographically situated religious diversity. They will argue that those who don't accept their particular religion are ignorant of the truth (or willfully ignorant), unenlightened, irrational, or deceived by Satan. Or they'll argue that God has unknown good reasons for permitting this state of affairs. But the adherents of the various other religions all have their explanations for religious diversity, too. And their explanations are similar in kind, if not exactly the same.

When religious believers actually do grapple with the cultural basis of religious faith, they will respond in the same manner against what I have been arguing for here. Whether they are Buddhist, Muslim, Hindu, Orthodox Jew, or Christian, they will argue against the sociological data that clearly show that people overwhelmingly believe based upon when and where they were born. William Lane Craig responds, just as most every defender of a different religion might do, when he asks, "Why could not the Christian worldview be objectively true? How does the mere presence of religious world-views incompatible with Christianity show that distinctively Christian claims are not true? Logically, the existence of multiple, incompatible truth claims only implies that all of them cannot be (objectively) true; but it would be obviously fallacious to infer that not one of them is (objectively) true."[25] Craig is correct about this, even if it's a mere possibility when probability is all that matters. But defenders of every other religion could argue the same exact thing, just by echoing Craig's words in defense of their own particular religion. Then, after making such a statement, other believers could proceed all over again to argue that they have the true faith, just like Craig does. Whether or not people accept these arguments will depend upon whether or not they are *insiders* to that particular faith in the first place. Is this not viciously circular? The bottom line is that there is a huge difference between having the evidence of religious diversity separated into geographical locations on one side and trying to explain away the evidence, which is what Dr. Craig is forced to do. When Christians, or any other believers, have to explain away the evidence, they are admitting that the evidence is not on their side. They're arguing that it's merely possible their faith is true and can be known to be so rationally. Again, probability is what matters.

EXCLUSIVISM, INCLUSIVISM, UNIVERSALISM, AND PLURALISM

If we take a look at Christian explanations for religious diversity we find that they actually highlight the amount of diversity we find in the Christian tradition itself. Since Christian responses are religiously diverse, they are responding to diversity with diversity. The explanations run the gamut from exclusivism to inclusivism and from universalism to pluralism. The fascinating thing about these Christian disagreements is watching them debate the relevant biblical texts. Some of them even deny these texts in favor of reason and science. The fact of religious diversity is probably highlighted no better than when people within the same religious tradition cannot come to an agreement about how to understand the Bible.[26] Lost on these Christians is the fact that there are representatives of exclusivism, inclusivism, universalism, and pluralism in other religious traditions as well. How do we decide between them? These explanations all presuppose that one's own religious faith is the true one, something that religious diversity calls into question.

Christian exclusivism, for instance, is the view that there is only one true religion and only one way of salvation (through faith in the atoning sacrifice of Jesus), which means that people outside the Christian faith cannot be saved (except perhaps babes and the mentally challenged). Christianity is the superior religion, the locus of true religion. Only through Jesus can someone be saved. All others will be condemned for not believing. Many evangelicals are exclusivist to a large degree. But this view simply cannot be maintained in the light of the amount of religious diversity in the world along with the subsequent rational disagreement about religious faiths among peers. If there is a God who wants us to believe in him, there would not be so much religious diversity around the globe. The probability that the Christian God exists is inversely proportional to the amount of religious diversity that exists (that is, the more religious diversity there is, the less probable it is that he exists), and there is way too much religious diversity to suppose that he does.

Alvin Plantinga defends exclusivism by arguing that it "need not involve either epistemic or moral failure, and that furthermore something like it is wholly unavoidable, given our human condition." He tells us there are three potential responses to religious diversity: (1) to continue believing, (2) to withhold belief, or (3) to deny one's belief. He argues for (1) by arguing against (2) and (3). Against (2), withholding belief, he argues that "there is no safe haven here, no way to avoid risk. In particular, you won't reach safe haven by trying to take the same attitude towards all the historically available patterns of belief and withholding: for in so doing you adopt a particular pattern of belief and withholding, one incompatible with some adopted by others. You pays your money and you takes your choice, realizing that you, like anyone else, can be desperately wrong. But what else can you do? You don't really have an alternative." Against (3), denying one's belief, he argues that this "is not a way out," for "if I do this I will then be in the very same condition as I am now." Why? He would be denying propositions that others accept and will no more be able to convince them that they are wrong than otherwise. So he opines that the charge of intellectual arrogance "against exclusivism is hoist with his own petard," for it is "self-referentially inconsistent."[27]

I disagree. Given religious diversity, the proper attitude—the adult attitude—is doubt. At minimum it means (2) to withhold belief. At most it means (3) to deny one's belief. I'll argue in the last chapter of this book that there is no reason to believe at all. For now, I'll simply say that Plantinga fails to understand the huge difference between assenting to a belief and *doubting* it or *denying* it. There is no epistemic parity at all between accepting a belief and doubting (or rejecting) it. Doubting (or rejecting) a belief is easy. We all do it all the time. The hard part is to set forth a positive case on behalf of any one particular truth out of the choices available. For Plantinga to say doubt (or denial) is "self-referentially inconsistent" is grossly, monumentally, massively wrong. The person doing the doubting (or denying) simply says there isn't enough evidence to positively assent to the belief in question. And people all over the world, including Plantinga, do this with respect to the other faiths they reject. How is that "self-referentially inconsistent"? People cannot have a "self-referentially inconsistent" belief until they believe something. The way he argues is akin to claiming that historians who conclude they don't know what happened at Custer's Last Stand know what happened after all, even though this is the very thing they deny. Claiming not to know what happened is the exact reverse of claiming to know what happened. If anything, Plantinga's view is self-referentially inconsistent.

More-informed Christians take a more or less inclusivist view about religious diversity, that although theirs is the one true religion, people outside of their faith can be saved because of what Jesus did for the whole world on the cross. God can apply the results of Jesus' sacrifice on the cross to people as he wills, even people who never acknowledge Jesus as their lord and savior. For inclusivists, God knows who would have believed if presented with the Gospel, or he might see that they have sought him earnestly and are therefore *de facto* "godfearers," people with whom God is pleased because they responded to him given the knowledge they had of him. Representative Christian inclusivists are John Wesley (a "hopeful inclusivist"), C. S. Lewis, Clark Pinnock, Karl Rahner, and John E. Sanders.

But the inclusivist view is merely a concession to the fact of religious diversity in order to make the Christian faith seem more reasonable to a religiously diverse world. It would have never entered the mind of a Catholic Christian during the French Wars of Religion or the Thirty Years' War, in which an estimated eight million believers slaughtered each other largely for their faith, that a Protestant was a Christian. Those were the good old days before Christians were faced with the fact of religious diversity, right? Nonetheless, if people can be saved without acknowledging Jesus as lord and savior, why bother evangelizing them? Why not just encourage them to continue living good lives? Many of these inclusivists believe that if someone is presented the Gospel and subsequently rejects it, then he or she cannot be saved at that point. So why take such a risk by trying to convert them at all? Inclusivists have their reasons, of course, since accepting the Christian faith would lead to a more sanctified or clean life, along with a more robust faith. But again, what about the risk involved if they reject the Gospel? Would it be worth it? An inclusivist might respond that if a person rejects the Gospel then he or she would never have been saved by God in the first place, because their rejection only reveals what God would already have known about them. But then again, why bother presenting these people with the Gospel in the first place, since God already knows their hearts?

The bottom line is that if God can know people's hearts like this then the only thing required is that we do good works by helping the poor, doing what's just, and showing kindness to everyone. Works, not faith, will save us, and if that's the case, then atheists should have no fear of God's wrath if they are good, kind people. Inclusivist Christianity should put an end to the Christian faith. After all, many atheists have sought God earnestly, too. I know I have.

Some Christians simply argue that everyone in the world will be saved in the end, and so religious diversity presents no serious problem. This viewpoint is known as *universalism*. There are a growing number of evangelical Christian universalists as a result of religious diversity. Among them are Gregory MacDonald, Thomas Talbott, and Robin Parry. They believe that ultimately everyone who ever lived will be saved through Jesus. They don't believe that all roads lead to God. And they don't deny the existence of hell. They just believe Jesus redeemed everyone through his atoning sacrifice, based upon their exegesis of the relevant "inspired" biblical texts. According to them, everyone will be brought to faith either in this life or in the next, if needed, by being cast into hell for a time. Such a view is a profound concession to the fact of religious diversity in order to make the Christian faith seem more reasonable to a religiously diverse world. And it undermines any need for people to accept the Christian faith in the first place.

The late John Hick argued for an acceptance of religious pluralism in light of the fact of religious diversity. According to him, "The universe is religiously ambiguous in that it is possible to interpret it, intellectually and experientially, both religiously and naturalistically. The theistic and anti-theistic arguments are all inconclusive, for the special evidences to which they appeal are also capable of being understood in terms of the contrary worldview. Further, the opposing sets of evidences cannot be given objectively quantifiable values." That is, "our environment is capable of being construed—in sense perception as well as ethically and religiously—in a range of ways." Thus, "all conscious experiencing is experiencing-as."[28] Even though Hick believed that the universe is religiously ambiguous, he still chose the tradition of liberal Christianity—the religion he inherited—to interpret it. But if he was correct about the ambiguous nature of it all, then it is also rational for someone to be a nonbeliever or an atheist, and he admits this.

Huston Smith, the internationally revered authority on world religions, stated it this way:

> The world is ambiguous. It does not come tagged "This is my Father's world" or "Life is a tale told by an idiot." It comes to us as a giant Rorschach inkblot. Psychologists use such blots to fish in the subterranean waters of their patients' minds. The blots approach the patient as invitations: Come. What do you see here? What do you make of these contours? The sweep of philosophy supports this inkblot theory of the world conclusively. People have never agreed on the world's meaning, and (it seems safe to say) never will.[29]

Such a view is a radical concession to the fact of religious diversity. It concedes the game and throws in the towel of faith. For if the universe is religiously ambiguous then how can Hick or Huston say anything about ultimate reality at all, since they think all attempts to describe it are inadequate? What would prevent a pluralist from becoming an atheist except for the particular tradition he or she was raised in? If the pluralist should seek a disambiguation of such an ambiguous world then what good reason can be given to do so within one's own culturally inherited religious tradition? After all, the reason why one exists in one's religious tradition is because of the "accidents of history," that is, when and where one was born. Why then should the accidents of history constrain one to stay within one's inherited religious tradition? I see no good reason for this. What prevents pluralists from simply saying that religion is a human invention? They should.

WHAT ABOUT ATHEIST DIVERSITY?

Christians have responded by asking about atheist diversity. Nonbelievers represent the fact of diversity as well as any religious grouping, and they seem to be geographically located in various regions around the globe. Phil Zuckerman has conducted research into where these nonbelievers are located,[30] and here is a list of the top thirty countries, ranked by the estimated percentage of citizens who are agnostics/nonbelievers (using the highest possible estimated percentage of nonbelievers to rank them [estimates vary due to differences in the polls and questions used]):

1. Sweden 46–85%
2. Vietnam 81%
3. Denmark 43–80%
4. Norway 31–72%
5. Japan 64–65%
6. Czech Republic 54–61%
7. Finland 28–60%
8. France 43–54%
9. South Korea 30–52%
10. Estonia 49%
11. Germany 41–49%
12. Russia 24–48%
13. Hungary 32–46%
14. Netherlands 39–44%
15. Britain 31–44%
16. Belgium 42–43%
17. Bulgaria 34–40%
18. Slovenia 35–38%
19. Israel 15–37%
20. Canada 19–30%
21. Latvia 20–29%
22. Slovakia 10–28%

23. Switzerland 17–27%
24. Austria 18–26%
25. Australia 24–25%
26. Taiwan 24%
27. Spain 15–24%
28. Iceland 16–23%
29. New Zealand 20–22%
30. Ukraine 20%

Why are the number of atheists higher in some countries than in others? In some countries it could be because of the ravages of war in the past century, most notably World War II. And in other countries it could be due to higher levels of scientific literacy.[31] Zuckerman, however, advances the idea that it's because of societal health and security. "High levels of organic atheism are strongly correlated with high levels of societal health."[32] Atheist countries have higher life expectancy, lower infant mortality, less crime, fewer suicides, fewer homicides, higher literacy, less poverty, greater gender equality, better healthcare, and so forth. "Most nations characterized by high degrees of individual and societal security have the highest rates of organic atheism, and, conversely, nations characterized by low degrees of individual and societal security have the lowest rates of organic atheism."[33]

This is corroborated by a May 2011 study by Cross-Cultural Research called "A Cross-National Test of the Uncertainty Hypothesis of Religious Belief," an abstract of which reads:

According to the uncertainty hypothesis, religion helps people cope psychologically with dangerous or unpredictable situations. Conversely, with greater control over the external environment due to economic development and technological advances, religious belief is predicted to decline (the existential security hypothesis). The author predicts that religious belief would decline in economically developed countries where there is greater existential security, including income security (income equality and redistribution via welfare states) and improved health. These predictions are tested in regression analyses of 137 countries that partialed out the effects of Communism and Islamic religion both of which affect the incidence of reported nonbelief. Findings show that disbelief in God increased with economic development (measured by lower agricultural employment and third-level enrollment). Findings further show that disbelief also increased with income security (low Gini coefficient, high personal taxation tapping the welfare state) and with health security (low pathogen prevalence). Results show that religious belief declines as existential security increases, consistent with the uncertainty hypothesis.[34]

If a healthy society can lead people to doubt the certainties of religion then this is very problematic for religious faith. It means religious faith is best sustained in societies where there is little individual and societal health. Christians will say this reveals the human tendency to throw off God when we don't need him. But a much better explanation is that a God who can thrive only where there is little societal health must therefore desire for us to have little of it. If that's so, he does not want the best for us. So at the very least this provides disconfirming evidence that such a God cares for us.

Diversity exists among human beings. This is a fact. None of us should be surprised by this in the least. This is what we would expect to find if there is no truth to religion. The difference that makes all the difference is that religious diversity exists among believers who are certain they are right in what they affirm to be the case. This should mitigate their certainties at the very minimum. And at the most it should cause them to look for a reasonable explanation for it, along with an objective test to know which religion is true, if any of them are. People of faith don't have any way of critically evaluating their own adopted religion so long as they have faith in that religion. As I have said, when faith is the foundation, anything can be believed.

3
THE FACT OF
RELIGIOUS DEPENDENCY

This chapter supports my contention that the best explanation for the Religious Diversity Thesis (RDVT) is that adopting and justifying one's religious faith is not a matter of independent rational judgment. Rather, to an overwhelming degree, one's religious faith is causally dependent on brain processes, cultural conditions, and irrational thinking patterns. This is the Religious Dependency Thesis (RDPT), which is based upon the noncontroversial findings of science, notably neurology, anthropology, and psychology. Given the fact of the RDPT, it is *highly* likely that any given religious faith is false and quite possible that they could all be false. At best there can only be one religious faith that is true. At worst they could all be false. It's because of the RDPT that we should embrace the informed skepticism of the outsider when examining the truth of our respective religious faiths.

Brain biology, anthropological data, and psychological findings individually support the RDPT. Taken together, they overwhelmingly support the RDPT by offering the best explanation of this religious diversity. So I turn now to the biology of belief, the cultures of belief, and the psychology of belief.

THE BIOLOGY OF BELIEF

Recent scientific studies on the brain strongly suggest, as Michael Shermer writes, that the brain is a belief engine. From sensory data flowing in through the senses the brain naturally begins to look for and find patterns, and then infuses those patterns with meaning. The first process I call *patternicity: the tendency to find meaningful patterns in both meaningful and meaningless data.* The second process I call *agenticity: the tendency to infuse patterns with meaning, intention, and agency.* We can't help it. Our brains evolved to connect the dots of our world into meaningful patterns that explain why things happen. These meaningful patterns become beliefs, and these beliefs shape our understanding of reality.[1]

The most obvious example of patternicity is that our brains see faces where there aren't any. Shermer cites such cases as those of people who recognize a face in the random shadows on Mars and people who see faces in random patterns in photographs. My personal favorites are the many Catholics who have seen an image of the Virgin Mary in a potato chip and on a bank in Clearwater, Florida. Based on our ability to recognize patterns as faces, human beings also have the strong tendency to detect agenticity where there isn't any. "Examples of agenticity abound," Shemer writes. "Subjects watching relative dots move about in a darkened room, especially if the dots take on the shape of two legs and two arms, infer that they represent a person or an intentional agent. Children believe that the sun can think and follows them around. When asked to draw a picture of the sun they often add a smiley face to give agency to it. Genital-shaped foods such as bananas and oysters are often believed to enhance sexual potency. A third of transplant patients believe that the donor's personality or essence is transplanted with the organs."[2]

As agency detectors, human beings detect personal agents in random natural events, and there is a reason why. This tendency stems from our animal predecessors. Recognizing faces as agents helped them to survive, for even though it produced many false positives, they were able to recognize predators among the patterns of stimuli they encountered in the wild they inhabited. They detected agency everywhere. In the tall, swaying grasses of the savannah they saw stalking lions, even if the movement was caused only by the wind. When they stooped to drink from the watering hole, they came to attention, ready for flight at the slightest sound of ripples, lest the crocodile lurking just beneath the water's surface catch them unaware, even if the ripples were only the result of the first rain-drops of an approaching shower. Doing so helped them escape from predators whenever they were correct. Not to flee could mean they could be eaten. We humans have this same strong tendency to ascribe divine agency to natural events or "acts of God" such as "punishing" thunderstorms that to the prescientific mind were inexplicable without some theory of divine agency.

From this we developed our religions.[3] Shermer argues that patternicity leading to agenticity forms

> the cognitive basis of shamanism, paganism, animism, polytheism, monotheism, and all modes of Old and New Age spiritualisms. And much more. The intelligent designer is said to be an invisible agent who created life from the top down. Extraterrestrial intelligences are often portrayed as powerful beings coming down from on high to warn us of our impending self-destruction. Conspiracy theories predictably include hidden agents at work behind the scenes, puppet masters pulling political and economic strings.[4]

Our human propensity for detecting supernatural agency behind random events produced as many gods and religions as the human imagination around the globe would allow.

THE CULTURES OF BELIEF

Given this strong biological propensity of ours, it stands to reason that our ancestors created various gods, or super agents, who lived in the clouds and doled out blessings and curses upon human beings for our supposed obedience or lack thereof. And it stands to reason that the ones who created these religions also created the moral rules that would please these gods and goddesses. There is power in dictating the rules, you see. And it also stands to reason that as their worlds got bigger, these gods and goddesses got bigger too, until people could only conceive of one God ruling over the whole world. When people discovered there were many other mountains and large swaths of people who lived beyond them, who would want to worship the pantheon of gods and/or goddess of just one mountaintop? The concept of monotheism seems inevitable because of the tendency of our brain toward agenticity coupled with the discovery of a bigger world. Not all religions have followed suit though, and one reason might be because they have not taken seriously how big our world has become.

Christian professor Randal Rauser demurs by asking me, "What makes the level of a religion's causal dependence on culture 'overwhelming'? How would one judge that? You need to defend that premise. You can't just *assume* it, because I find no reason to accept it. So tell me, *why* do you think cultural influence is 'overwhelming'?"[5] Let me explain.

Xenophanes, in the fifth century BCE, was among the first to notice religious diversity in other cultures:

> Ethiopians have gods with snub noses and black hair, Thracians have gods with gray eyes and red hair. If oxen or lions had hands which enabled them to draw and paint pictures as men do, they would portray their gods as having bodies like their own; horses would portray them as horses, and oxen as oxen.[6]

I was first alerted to the force of this problem by philosopher of religion John Hick, who wrote that "it is evident that in some ninety-nine percent of the cases the religion which an individual professes and to which he or she adheres depends upon the accidents of birth. Someone born to Buddhist parents in Thailand is very likely to be a Buddhist, someone born to Muslim parents in Saudi Arabia to be a Muslim, someone born to Christian parents in Mexico to be a Christian, and so on."[7]

Richard Dawkins said the same thing:

Out of all of the sects in the world, we notice an uncanny coincidence: the overwhelming majority just happens to choose the one that their parents belong to. Not the sect that has the best evidence in its favour, the best miracles, the best moral code, the best cathedral, the best stained glass, the best music: when it comes to choosing from the smorgasbord of available religions, their potential virtues seem to count for nothing, compared to the matter of heredity. This is an unmistakable fact; nobody could seriously deny it. Yet people with full knowledge of the arbitrary nature of this heredity, somehow manage to go on believing in their religion, often with such fanaticism that they are prepared to murder people who follow a different one. . . . The religion we adopt is a matter of an accident of geography.[8]

If you were born in Saudi Arabia, you would be a Sunni Muslim right now. This is an almost undeniable cold, hard sociological fact. In today's world, if you were born in Iran, you'd be a Shi'a Muslim. If you were born in India, you'd most probably be a Hindu right now. If you were born in Japan, you'd probably be a Shintoist, and if you lived in Mongolia, you'd most probably be a Buddhist. If you were born in the first century BCE in Palestine, you'd adhere to the Jewish faith, and if you were born in Europe in 1200 CE, you'd be a Roman Catholic. These things are as close to being undeniable facts as we can get in the sociological world.

But there's more. Had we lived in ancient Egypt or Babylon, we would have been very superstitious and polytheistic to the core. We would have sought divine guidance through divination and sought to alter our circumstances through magic. If we'd been first-century Christians, we would probably have believed that God sent illnesses and disasters to discipline and punish people for their sins, and we would have believed in what has come to be called the ransom theory of Jesus' atonement. Had we been Christians in Europe during the Middle Ages, we would probably have seen nothing wrong with killing witches, torturing heretics, and ruthlessly conquering Jerusalem in the Crusades. In short, we are overwhelmingly products of our times. Our country of origin and era of our birth, our parents, our extended families, and the year of our birth within each country all have a significant role to play in the formation of the kind of religion we think is true. According to Voltaire (*Essai sur les Moeurs et l'Esprit des Nations*, 1756), "Every man is a creature of the age in which he lives, and few are able to raise themselves above the ideas of the time."

What is the reasonable conclusion we can draw from this? The religious faith believers adopt is overwhelmingly caused by when and where they were born. Their faith is causally dependent on the biology of our brains and the accidents of our births. It also has to do with our DNA and such things as our IQ, race, gender, age, and sexuality—things that are not mutually exclusive of course. This all seems undeniable to me.

One of the best ways to understand this, short of extensively traveling the world ourselves, is to listen to what anthropologists have discovered among the peoples of the world. One of the best anthropologists to learn from is David Eller, who wrote the book *Introducing Anthropology of Religion*, a standard college textbook hailed as "one of the most engaging, comprehensive, and compelling overviews of the anthropology of religion ever published," according to Stephen D. Glazier, graduate professor of anthropology and geography at the University of Nebraska–Lincoln. Eller has written about these topics in the first chapters of both *The Christian Delusion* and *The End of Christianity*, which show exactly what I'm arguing for here. Eller succinctly tells us the lessons from anthropology:

> All reality is social reality—experienced through the filters or visors of some culture system—and all social reality is virtual reality . . . all of us live in a virtual reality all the time. . . . Cultural reality seems so real to us, of course, because it is there before any of us is individually and because everyone else is doing it. It is difficult to question—sometimes even to see—culture because we enter the cultural world at the second of our birth. . . . When we first open our eyes, and every time after that, culture is there. Culture is just

what everyone around you does. That is how it is shared and how
it is learned. For some people it takes a monumental effort even to
discover that it is there, let alone escape it.[9]

Eller continues,

Like a pair of glasses, humans see with culture, but they do not
usually see culture. Computers do not know they are running a
program; they simply follow the instructions. Seeing your glasses,
recognizing your program, is a rare thing, achieved by few individuals in even fewer societies. . . . And these glasses are not pro-
phylactic—they do not help the person to see "better." They make
seeing at all possible. Maybe an ultimate analogy for culture in
general and religion in particular is not glasses but the very eyes
themselves. You could not expect to pull someone's eyes out and
have them see better, any more than you could expect to take away
someone's culture and have them understand and act better.[10]

After describing the colonization process that Christian missionaries foisted upon Latin America and Africa, which involved Chris-
tianizing the language, rituals, habits, institutions, sacred spaces, and
dates of these native cultures, Eller says of people in the Western
industrial world, "We are surrounded, occupied, permeated, literally
colonized by religion just as surely as the natives of Latin America or
Africa were. If anything, we are more colonized, since it all seems so
normal and self-evident to us. So, whether or not we *believe* religion,
we *experience* religion constantly and everywhere, in every facet of our
existence."[11]

Eller says that as anthropologists come to grips with what cultures do to us, at some point along the line "comes the epiphanal
moment, when the realization strikes that if the Other could be so,
then potentially we ourselves could be so. If they have a culture, then
we have a culture. And if culture is manmade, then my culture is
manmade too. Certainty evaporates, skepticism pervades . . . when
you are forced to face and accept the Other as real, unavoidable,

and ultimately valuable, you cannot help but see yourself and your 'truths' in a new—and troubling—way."[12] Speaking of this enculturation process in the Christian Western world, Eller contends that "Christians are not easily argued out of their religion because, since it is culture, they are not ordinarily argued into it in the first place."[13] He tells us why: "Christians like other religionists, are not so much convinced by arguments and proofs as colonized by assumptions and premises. As a form of culture, it seems self-evident to them."[14]

Christian apologists have questioned Eller's conclusion, of course, asking how he knows the Christian faith is only cultural rather than additionally produced by the hand of God down through the centuries through culture. Well, the answer, of course, is that it's possible the Christian God of one's own particular sect has done this. But possibilities don't count. Probabilities do. If God revealed the true religion through one particular culture in the same way that other religions developed in other cultures, then God revealed this in a way that is indistinguishable from how other false religions developed. Not only does this seem unlike something a divine being who wants us to believe would do, since it leads to doubt, but it would equally be reasonable for other believers in different religions to claim their own god has done this. That's how religions solve these problems without a method. Hint: they don't.

In any case, such an answer means that most everyone in the past, the present, and the future has been or will be wrong, except those few believers out of countless religious sects who get lucky to have the correct faith. This raises important questions, such as: Why did it take such a god or gods so long to help believers get it right in our day? And how can believers of today know that they have the correct revealed faith, once they admit the evolutionary process through which their god has revealed the truth? How can they? Perhaps their god will eventually lead believers in the future to deism or even to the secular Christianity that came to the fore during the '60s in America, which was also known as the death-of-God theology? Acknowledging the evolutionary process by which religions develop leads to a theological relativism, since there is no point in the history of the church where any theologian could say that a final unchanging theology has been attained. If God supposedly reveals the truth to each generation then the theology of yesterday was true for past generations, just as the present-day theology is true for others and the theology of tomorrow will be true for future generations. So don't talk to me about an unchanging theological truth. Don't talk to me about an absolute standard for theological truth either. It doesn't exist. Never has. Never will.

On my blog, Dr. Eller responded to this type of criticism as follows:

> No one rejects the suggestion that religion, including Christianity, is cultural. If we accept, then, that Christianity is cultural too, the only real question is, *Is Christianity cultural ONLY?* If theists accept the idea that their religion is cultural, then it is their burden to prove that it is something MORE than culture. Beyond a doubt, Christianity emerged in the first place as a historically and socially contingent movement in the context of late ancient Judaism and the Roman occupation. Over the years and around the globe, Christianity has changed to fit its local circumstances; that's why there is no such thing as "real" Christianity but rather many (and often incompatible) Christianities. If the "periphery" of Christianity—all the little flourishes and details—is cultural, and it indisputably is, then what is to convince us that the "core" of Christianity is not just cultural too? In other words, I hold that Christianity (and every other religion) is cultural through and through—that it holds no "truth" but merely cultural thinking. Like the anecdote about the religion that believes the world stands on a turtle, and that turtle on another turtle, with "turtles all the way down," so I assert, and see no argument to disprove, that Christianity is "cultural all the way down."[15]

The bottom line is that if it looks like culture, smells like culture, acts like culture, and evolves like culture, then it is culture, all the way down.

THE PSYCHOLOGY OF BELIEF

Now let's turn to our irrational thinking patterns. Cultural and biological conditions provide us with the control biases we use to incorporate all known facts and experiences into our inherited religious belief systems. Control biases are like blinders. From the moment you put them on, you see only what your blinders will let you see because reason is mostly used to serve these biases. Given that our brains are belief engines, and given the influence of our cultures, is there any reason to suppose believers are capable of rationally examining their inherited religious faiths without the Outsider Test for Faith? I think not. I know not.

Let's take our start again from Michael Shermer, who said, "Once beliefs are formed, the brain begins to look for and find confirmatory evidence in support of those beliefs, which adds an emotional boost of further confidence in the beliefs and thereby accelerates the process of reinforcing them, and round and round the process goes in a positive feedback loop of belief confirmation."[16] Full stop. Think about the implications of this. Again: "Once beliefs are formed, the brain begins to look for and find confirmatory evidence in support of those beliefs." And where do people get religious beliefs from? From our biology and cultural influences. Shermer goes on to explain in another place that smart people, "because they are more intelligent and better educated, are better able to give intellectual reasons justifying their beliefs that they arrived at for nonintelligent reasons," even though "smart people, like everyone else, recognize that emotional needs and being raised to believe something are how most of us most of the time come to our beliefs."[17]

According to Robert McKim, "We seem to have a remarkable capacity to find arguments that support positions which we antecedently hold. Reason is, to a great extent, the slave of prior commitments."[18] Hence the whole notion of "an independent rational judgment" is suspect, especially when there are no mutually agreed-upon reliable scientific tests to decide what to conclude, even if

Christian apologists continue to defend their religious faith with reasons. These apologists, if they're good at what they do, will be smart people. But, again, according to Michael Shermer, "Smart people, because they are more intelligent and better educated, are able to give intellectual reasons justifying . . . beliefs that they arrived at for non-intelligent reasons."[19] Because it takes a great deal of intelligence to defend a religious faith I would describe as a delusion, smart people, because they are smart and educated in their faith, can actually be more deluded than others, not less. Hence, it is more difficult to convince them to see what they are defending as the delusion it is.

Psychiatrist Valerie Tarico describes the process of defending unintelligent ideas by smart people. She claims that "it doesn't take very many false assumptions to send us on a long goose chase." To illustrate this she tells us about the mental world of a paranoid schizophrenic convinced that he's being persecuted by the CIA. "You can sit, as a psychiatrist, with a diagnostic manual next to you, and think: as bizarre as it sounds, the CIA really is bugging this guy. The arguments are tight, the logic persuasive, the evidence organized into neat files. All that is needed to build such an impressive house of illusion is a clear, well-organized mind and a few false assumptions. Paranoid individuals can be very credible."[20] Tarico argued from the findings of psychology that "it is easy for us to distort the evidence in our own favor, in part because we aren't so great with evidence in general. One of the strongest built-in mental distortions we have is called confirmation bias." She argues that "once we have a hunch about how things work, we seek information that fits what we already think."[21]

According to conclusive scientific studies in this area of research, we have a very strong tendency to believe what we prefer to believe and to confirm what we believe, depending on how important our beliefs are and how much of a commitment we have in maintaining them. This has been demonstrated time and again by psychological studies.[22] Once our minds are made up it is very hard to change them. We seek to justify our decisions, especially the ones that are costly in terms of commitment, money, effort, time, and inconvenience.

Almost shockingly, these studies have shown us that reading information that goes against our point of view can actually make us convinced we are right. We will even take a lack of evidence as evidence for what we accept as the truth. Social psychologists Carol Tavris and Elliot Aronson document these types of phenomena in their book *Mistakes Were Made (but Not by Me): Why We Justify Foolish Beliefs, Bad Decisions, and Hurtful Acts.* They tell us: "Most people, when directly confronted with proof that they are wrong, do not change their point of view or course of action but justify it even more tenaciously."[23]

This is backed up by the conclusion derived from a series of studies in 2005 and 2006 by researchers at the University of Michigan:

> Facts don't necessarily have the power to change our minds. In fact, quite the opposite . . . when misinformed people, particularly political partisans, were exposed to corrected facts in news stories, they rarely changed their minds. In fact, they often became even more strongly set in their beliefs. Facts . . . were not curing misinformation. Like an underpowered antibiotic, facts could actually make misinformation even stronger.[24]

Gary Marcus, professor of psychology at New York University, wrote a book titled *Kluge: The Haphazard Evolution of the Human Mind.* It shows how the evolution of our brain accounts for why we think so poorly, and in so doing it goes a long way toward showing that religious belief is a product of this poor thinking. Marcus argues that "if mankind were the product of some intelligent, compassionate designer, our thoughts would be rational, our logic impeccable. Our memory would be robust, our recollections reliable."[25] Instead, our brains evolved as a kluge. A kluge "is a clumsy or inelegant—yet surprisingly effective solution—to a problem."[26] Just picture a house constructed in stages by different contractors, with various additions tacked on at later times, and you can get the picture. The structure of our brains is like this, with three brains built on top of one another: the hindbrain (or reptilian brain), the midbrain (the limbic system) and the forebrain (the neocortex). This three-tiered structure has profound implications for our memories, beliefs, choices, language, and pleasure.

Marcus argues that we are not objective machines even though most people think they have arrived at the logical truth with a capital "T." Instead, "our capacity for belief is haphazard, scarred by evolution and contaminated by emotions, moods, desires, goals, and simple self-interest."[27] "Because evolution built belief mainly out of off-the-shelf components that evolved for other purposes, we often lose track of where our beliefs come from—if we ever knew—and even worse, we are often completely unaware of how much we are influenced by irrelevant information."[28] "We feel as if our beliefs are based on cold, hard facts, but often they are shaped by our ancestral system in subtle ways that we are not even aware of."[29] Marcus proceeds to inform us of how we gain and maintain our ideas, many of which are illogical. We accept that which is familiar. We seek to confirm what we have accepted as true on other grounds. We cling to our treasured truths despite evidence to the contrary. More often than not we fail to consider disconfirming evidence. "Once we decide something is true (for whatever reason), we often make up reasons for believing it."[30] We scrutinize ideas more carefully if we don't like them than if we are familiar with them. This is because evolved creatures "were often forced to act rather than think."[31] Marcus's closing warning is that "the truth is that without special training, our species is inherently gullible."[32]

The book by Ori and Rom Brafman called *Sway: The Irresistible Pull of Irrational Behavior* focuses on several hidden forces that cause us to act irrationally. The first is *Value Attrition,* which they illustrate with several good examples before concluding: "Once we attribute a value to a person or thing, it dramatically alters our perceptions of subsequent information,"[33] making it "very difficult" to view that person or thing "in any other light."[34] It is such "a strong force that it has the power to derail our objective and professional judgment."[35] Another hidden irrational force is *Commitment.* The more that a person has a commitment to an idea, the more it's virtually impossible for him or her to take a different path. Independently these two forces have a powerful effect on us, "but when the two forces combine; it becomes that much harder to break free and do something else."[36] The third force is *Diagnosis Bias*, which in their words "causes us to distort or even ignore objective data."[37] As a result, "we often ignore all evidence that contradicts what we want to believe."[38]

This data is undeniable, noncontroversial, and obvious. We must think about the implications of what these undeniable facts tell us about who we are as human beings. Those raised as Christians seek to confirm the tenets of Christian belief because of the demonstrated human bias toward accepting what one was raised to believe. Those raised as Muslims seek to confirm the tenets of Islam because they, too, are influenced by the human bias toward accepting what one was raised to believe. The same is true for Orthodox Jews, Hindus, Scientologists, and all other believers. Get the picture?

To further clarify, let me offer several mundane examples. Just think back to a time when you thought you needed something really badly, but then your hopes were dashed. What did you do? You eventually convinced yourself you didn't need that thing after all, that you were better off not having had your hopes realized. It may take a bit of time, but that's what we human beings will do almost every time. It's our natural tendency. It helps us deal with our pain, loss, and disappointment. It keeps us feeling sane.

Christian author and instructor Jim West has a blog that's popular among the bloggers for the Society of Biblical Literature. In one post, West rants against the "exploitative" nature of college accreditation companies.[39] But guess what? He has a degree from an unaccredited college and teaches for one too. Here we see a person, who should know better, arguing against that which he doesn't have simply because he doesn't have it. Why are we not surprised? I've never heard an educated person from an accredited college ranting against an accredited education. Only people who wish they had accredited degrees do this.

A woman friend of mine took two of her grandchildren to see the movie *How to Train Your Dragon* when it was newly released. The movie was released in 3-D, but this particular theater did not have 3-D technology. One child asked the owner, who was standing in the lobby, if the movie was in 3-D. The owner went off for ten minutes, telling them that watching movies in 3-D is bad for their eyes. Of course he thinks that. Why? Because his movie theater did not have 3-D technology. Get it? Just imagine what he would say if he had that technology. Then he would change his tune. We know this. It happens all the time.

There is a massive amount of documentation for these facts. Scientists have done such a good job of finding out how irrational we human beings are that Dan Ariely, professor of psychology and behavioral economics at Duke University, argues in his book *Predictably Irrational: The Hidden Forces That Shape Our Decisions* that we are not just irrational; we are *predictably* irrational.[40] He shows that salespeople and advertisers who understand this can tap into our irrationality in order to sell us more of their products.

WE'RE ALL IN THE SAME EPISTEMOLOGICAL BOAT

What does this psychological data imply? It implies that we're all in the same epistemological boat. Again for emphasis, *we are all in the same boat.* The sciences conclusively show that, for the most part, we are all susceptible to the same types of errors when it comes to selecting and maintaining beliefs. However, people who understand these findings are in a much better position to look at this whole process more critically. People who are aware of how irrational they are can then apply tools such as the OTF to identify and correct for erroneous biases and presuppositions. This is the difference that makes all the difference. Once we understand what the sciences tell us we become much more likely to question what we think. We become more demanding of sufficient evidence before concluding much of anything. Just as Dan Ariely has shown with regard to predicting our irrational behaviors in order to overcome them, understanding what science teaches us helps us to overcome our irrational thinking patterns. We can therefore learn to better control how we use information to understand the truth. Because I know these things I know that I must demand sufficient evidence before concluding much of anything. Because of these findings I know to reject faith-based reasoning in favor of science-based reasoning. It's that simple, and yet for most people this seems profound.

Plato's cave allegory is useful when applied to the issues that separate believers and nonbelievers. In this allegory prisoners have been chained up facing the wall of a cave their whole lives. They watch the shadows projected on the wall by objects being passing in front of a fire behind them. The shadows are the only reality the prisoners can see. Then one prisoner breaks free from the cave and comes to understand that the shadows on the wall do not represent reality at all. The allegory is in part used to explain that the philosopher, who has been freed of his chains and the cave, knows what's real and can in turn help enlighten the prisoners still chained in the cave.

Because I understand the biological and cultural basis of religious faith, and because I understand how irrational our brains are about justifying beliefs, especially about religious matters, I know enough to know that I should doubt what I don't have sufficient evidence to accept as true. I know I'm in a culturally derived cave. So I can reflect on that which I have been led to accept, since I realize I'm in it, and this makes all the difference in the world. My conclusion is that I can only trust science to tell me what I should accept about the origins, nature, and workings of the universe. Doing so allows me to think outside the cave, to question the reality I was raised to see in front of me, and even to transcend my own given culture. Believers raised in their respective religious cultures are in the cave and in denial. They have accepted and now defend what they were raised to believe.

Some time ago, in that cave, during a dispute between prisoners, one of the prisoners said, "Let's test that idea," and the test solved the issue in dispute. As time went on, human beings learned that this is how to settle disputes, and science was born. The world got bigger, too. People met and interacted with individuals from other cultures who had come to accept different realities with the same level of assuredness. Taken together, when we reflected on both science and a global world we began thinking outside the cave, outside our perceived realities, our culturally inherited ones. We questioned our culturally inherited truths in the face of different religious cultures, and we used science to solve the questions that separated us.

In specific cases, people of faith will sometimes denounce science, saying that science has no method. But that is the height of delusionary thinking, the likes of which I can only shake my head at. There is a big difference between the overwhelming consensus of scientists in a vast number of areas, where the evidence has been gathered and the facts have been settled, and current disagreements between scientists on the cutting edges of science, where hypotheses are new and the experiments and observations to test these hypotheses have only just begun to generate evidence. Science has produced the goods in an overwhelming number of areas. Therefore, there is good reason to think it will produce the goods in a number of areas on the cutting edges of science, too. It has a proven track record. There isn't anything controversial about this.

Christian philosopher Matt Flannagan has misused the argument of philosopher of science Larry Laudan, who states that there is no clear demarcation between science and nonscience. He attempts to use Laudan's position to bring science down to the level of faith.[41] But the problem of defining a correct demarcation of science from nonscience is not a problem for science at all. It's an informal fallacy, like trying to specify which whisker, when plucked, leaves us without a beard. Just because we cannot define that exact point between science and nonscience doesn't mean there isn't a huge difference between them. I call this definitional apologetics, and Flannagan revels in it. There is most emphatically a difference between science and nonscience. *That's* the point! It does nothing to show there may be a small point at which the distinction between them is blurred.

Let me just offer three responses to attempts to level the intellectual playing field between science and faith. The first response is that believers who assert that science has no method have the burden of proof to show us how science advances without one and how faith solves anything. That cannot be done, just try it. One such attempt casts doubt on the basis for the scientific method itself along with all empirical results gained by means of it. I'm speaking of the dreaded problem of induction. In inductive reasoning, scientists make a series of observations and then infer something based on these observations, or they predict that the next observation under the same exact test conditions will produce the same results. It's argued there are two problems with this process. The first problem is that regardless of the number of observations it is never certain the next observation of the same exact phenomena under the same exact test conditions will produce the same exact results. For scientists to inductively infer something from previous results or predict what future observations will be like, it's claimed they must have *faith* that nature operates by a uniform set of laws. Why? Because they cannot know nature is lawful from their observations alone. The second problem is that the observations of scientists in and of themselves cannot establish with certainty the validity of inductive reasoning.

There is a great deal of literature on the problem of induction, and I cannot solve it here.[42] This problem is not unique to science though, for theologians must also "induce" how God acts based on past statements about him found in the Bible. But if all we ever do is think exclusively in terms of the probabilities, as I'll argue later (in chapters 7 and 10), then this problem is pretty much solved. We're not looking for certainty. We only need to think in terms of the probabilities. To someone who objects that we cannot know enough to determine what the actual probabilities are, I simply respond by looking at the overwhelming evidence. The daily evidence from scientists around the globe is that when they replicate the same exact tests of the same exact phenomena under the same exact conditions they receive the same exact results. Could there be on a rare occasion a scientific test like this where different results obtain? Yes, this is possible. So what? Possibilities that rare, that as far as we know have never occurred in the laboratory, simply do not matter. They change nothing about how scientists should proceed, or what they should infer, or what they should predict from their observations, even if someday on some extremely rare occasion they end up being wrong. Is it relevant to us that the process of induction may not work at the subatomic/quantum level or into the far reaches of the universe (or multiverse)? No. Scientific induction works extremely well in our plane of existence, and it is worth noting, too, that quantum physics is still in many ways in its infancy.

My second response is that if believers demand we prove with certainty that science has a method by poking a tiny pinprick of doubt about it, then this emphatically does not mean there is any parity at all between science and faith. It is simply amazing to me how believers claim to have certainties based on little or no evidence, things a child could easily deny, and then invoke a double standard upon people of science to prove with certainty what they have come to conclude.

My third response is that science is a human endeavor, and like any human endeavor, there is a human element to it. So if science proceeds with a certain degree of theory-laden data, probabilities rather than certainties, and is not done by completely objective scientists, that is not the problem of the scientific method itself. Science proceeds because the evidence has a way of eventually changing people's minds. Science progresses because the evidence has a way of breaking through. It is self-correcting by nature.

By contrast, people of faith reinvent what they believe in every generation because of the need to continue believing despite contrary scientific evidence and the harsh social realities. As human beings live longer it will become more and more obvious that that's what believers do. I've seen it in my lifetime. Science continues to advance while faith continues to retreat.

People who refuse to doubt are almost always fearful of looking at the evidence squarely in the face. They are like the prisoners in Plato's cave. Fear and ignorance result when faith reigns. Faith imprisons people within their cultural realities, so to speak. Believers are fearful of leaving the comfort of their perceived social realities. They are also fearful of displeasing their perceived divine realities. So they are forced to deny what is clearly obvious. They must even deny science. It's time to wake up and think. It's time to grow up and become adults. It's time to throw off fear and superstition.

Given the facts presented in this chapter, what should you do? Be skeptical. Demand sufficient evidence based on scientific reasoning before coming to any firm conclusions about religion. There should be no controversy about this. The only reason controversy exists is because people prefer to remain ignorant in order to protect their fear-based faith. There might be other reasons, but that seems to be the major one, the one we can help to correct by simply pointing out what is obvious.

4
THE PERSPECTIVE
OF THE OUTSIDER

So far I have given good, solid reasons based on the RDVT and the RDPT to support my contention that it is highly likely that any given religious faith is false, and since that's true it's quite possible that they could all be false. At best there can be only one religious faith that is true. At worst, they could all be false. Therefore, believers need a test—an objective non-double-standard, self-diagnostic test—to help determine if their particular culturally inherited religious faith is true. So I've proposed the Outsider Test for Faith (OTF). The only way to rationally test one's culturally adopted religious faith is from the perspective of an outsider, a nonbeliever, with the same level of reasonable skepticism believers already use when examining the other religious faiths they reject.

In this chapter I'll describe in greater detail what the OTF requires of believers who want to honestly examine their own inherited faith, and I'll argue that there isn't a better alternative. As I said, I want people to see the OTF as a solution to the problem of an incredible amount of religious diversity. Taken together with what we've found about how our brains create beliefs, and how we adopt them within our respective cultures and then seek to justify them, this is a problem that needs a reasonable solution. No other methods have worked. The goal is to offer a fair test to find out which religion is true, if there is one, and that means such a test should include the nonreligious option (the possibility that no religion is true). If someone disagrees, he or she will need to find fault with the OTF and also propose a better test. So what's the alternative? I'll examine several proposed alternatives and show that the OTF is the only way to know which religion is true, if there is one.

Given the facts of the RDVT and the RDPT we cannot have a Milquetoast test when it comes to the truth about religion. We cannot merely say to believers that they should be skeptical without offering a standard of skepticism. Why? Because if we ask believers who are certain of their faith to test it with doubt, almost all of them will say they have done so and that their faith is sure. Just imagine asking the nineteen militant Muslims who hijacked planes as part of their suicide mission on 9/11 whether they had critically examined their faith. Just imagine asking them if they were really sure that their faith was true. Ask the Inquisitors. Ask the witch hunters. Ask the Christians who slaughtered each other during the years following the Protestant Reformation. But ask them instead to test their faith with the same level of reasonable skepticism they already use when examining the other religious faiths they reject, and that will get their attention like nothing else can. Once you think about this you'll understand the need for the OTF, which does more than merely ask believers to critically examine their faith. It gives believers a single, consistent, nonbiased, non–double standard to test their inherited faith.

HOW DO BELIEVERS ARGUE AGAINST OTHER FAITHS?

But wait, haven't I jumped the gun? If the OTF asks believers to test their faith with the same skepticism they use to test other faiths, then shouldn't we examine how they do this? This is a fair question.

Evangelical Christian philosopher Thomas Talbott, a universalist, objects to the outsider's perspective, saying, "The problem . . . is that not all Christians adopt the same dismissive attitude towards other religions."[1] Talbott claims he is not that skeptical of other religions and wants to learn from them. But I'm sure he knows what it's like to be skeptical of snake handlers, six-day creationists, hellfire-and-brimstone preaching, Scientology, Cargo Cults, militant Islam, and

Mormonism, so why the disingenuousness? He either knows what it's like to be skeptical of other religions or he doesn't. Which is it? Even if he doesn't know what it's like to be skeptical (and who is he trying to kid anyway?), the OTF targets the faiths of an overwhelming number of believers with a force they have probably never considered before, and that's a good thing if we want to solve the problem of religious diversity. But he is correct to some small degree.

Some believers, mostly liberals, and some moderates, will approach other religious faiths from the perspective of a learner. In more extreme forms they take an eclectic approach to the study of religions, trying to find common ground as much as possible so as to adopt the best aspects that each religion has to offer. This approach is definitely admirable. But how they decide which parts of religions to adopt is based upon reason and/or scientific thinking, or it should be. If they adopt parts of other religions for any other reasons then such a method is bogus from the start. Their method is doubly bogus if they fail to seriously consider the nonreligious option. Otherwise they are not considering the whole range of choices available.

Randal Rauser, associate professor of historical theology at Taylor Seminary in Edmonton, Canada, is willing to consider the nonreligious option in his book *You're Not as Crazy as I Think: Dialogue in a World of Loud Voices and Hardened Opinions.* He writes: "Time and again we [evangelicals] have revealed ourselves to be more interested in defending and perpetuating our beliefs on a given issue than in discerning where the truth really lies. Often we have preferred to secure our present beliefs against challenges rather than to embrace the open risk of real dialogue."[2] "The real person of truth," he argues, "is one who expresses a genuine willingness to listen to the other as an equal conversation partner."[3] So he endorses a resolution "to engage with the other—the liberal, the Darwinist, the animal rights activist, and the atheist—as an equal partner in dialogue and so to treat each one as a person we can learn from and need to listen to."[4] He acknowledges that "whenever we engage with another person honestly in such a way that we present our own opinions as well as listening to the opinions of others, we are placing ourselves at the risk of the unknown. It could lead to us converting the other, but, for all we know, it could just as well result in the other converting us. That is the final unsettling consequence of a character formed by truth. We just never know which conversation could ultimately change our lives."[5] We must risk this conversation if we are truly interested in the truth, he rightly argues. So I am very happy to have cowritten a book with him titled *God or Godless?* since he has been willing to risk a discussion with me, "the other," in pursuit of the truth. This doesn't mean his conclusions after our dialogue are right. And it doesn't mean he is not obtusely stubborn in his faith, because he is. So dialogue has its limits. He still objects to the OTF.

Most believers argue that other religious faiths are false simply because they take it for granted that theirs is the one true faith. They'll argue that other religious faiths don't deal with the right issues or that, when they do deal with the right issues, they come to the wrong conclusions. Christians argue that Orthodox Jews and Muslims lack an atoning sacrifice for the forgiveness of sins along with the necessary proof of redemption in the resurrection of Jesus. They do this based upon their faith. Given that they believe the tenets of their faith are true, these other religions must therefore be false. Orthodox Jews and Muslims reject the whole idea of an atoning sacrifice as incoherent and don't think there is sufficient reason to believe Jesus was raised from the dead because their faith tells them otherwise. But this method is faulty to the core. It's begging the question. It first presumes what they believe based on what they were raised to believe. When they argue in this fashion it is nothing short of special pleading on behalf of their own culturally adopted religious faith. What they need to show is that their own faith can be justified.

A much better method is the one that believers already use, the OTF. The outsider's attitude when it comes to examining other religions is one of informed skepticism: (1) It assumes one's own religious faith has the burden of proof. (2) It adopts the methodological-naturalist viewpoint whereby one assumes there is a natural explanation for the origins of one's religion, its holy books, and its extraordinary claims of miracles. (3) It demands sufficient evidence, scientific evidence, before concluding a religion is true. And most importantly, (4) it disallows any faith in the religion under investigation, since the informed skeptic cannot leap over the lack of evidence by punting to faith.

THE CHALLENGE OF THE OTF

The OTF is simply a challenge to examine one's adopted religious faith as an outsider, a nonbeliever, with the same level of reasonable skepticism believers already use when examining the other religious faiths they reject. Outsiders must assume for the purpose of investigation that their own culturally inherited religious faith is probably false, since doing so is consistent with how they approach the other religious faiths they reject. To take the outsider test is to assume that one's adopted faith has the burden of proof. Assume human rather than divine authors of your holy book(s) and see what you get. If there is a divine author behind the texts who wants you to believe, then it should be knowable even with that initial skeptical assumption. Outsiders begin their journeys as informed skeptics who do not think the religious faith in question is likely true because there are so many different religious faiths that are believed and defended by intelligent people. Outsiders are people who are truly interested in the question of which religious faith is correct, if there is one. They do not have an intellectual affiliation with any one religion. They must eschew faith answers to intractable questions and only go with the probabilities because the probabilities are all that matter. In other words, no punting to faith. They must consider natural explanations for the phenomena under consideration. They must be fully aware of the cognitive biases inherent in how they think through these issues by seeking evidence that disconfirms their faith rather than merely looking for evidence that confirms what they already believe.

Surely believers will object that this is quite draconian in scope. Why take such a skeptical position? It's because that's how believers correctly approach all other religious faiths, so why not use the same approach with one's own religious faith? Why is there this discrepancy in how believers evaluate religious faiths? For any individual who objects that what I'm asking is unfair, he or she will have the burden of proof to show why his or her inconsistent approach to religious faith is justified in the first place. Why the double standard? The outsider test presents us with a consistent standard that helps us see the proper presumption we should take when evaluating the faith we were born into. I'm arguing in favor of the presumption of skepticism, based on what believers already do.

In a way, adopting the OTF is like following the Golden Rule, or so argues Dr. James McGrath, associate professor of religion at Butler University. He claims this is the way to assess the likelihood of Christian miracles in history:

> One doesn't have to be committed in advance to history's inability to deal with miracles in order to begin to realize that one cannot claim Christianity is grounded purely in history while other traditions are at best shrouded in myth. One simply has to apply the most basic Christian principle to one's investigation of the competing claims: *The Golden Rule.* And so what does it mean to do history from a Christian perspective? It means doing to the claims of others what you would want done to your claims. And perhaps also the reverse: doing to your own claims, views and presuppositions that which you have been willing to do to the claims, views and presuppositions of others. Once one begins to attempt to examine the evidence not in an unbiased way, but simply *fairly*, one cannot but acknowledge that there are elements of the Christian tradition which, if they were in your opponent's tradition, you would reject, debunk, discount, and otherwise find unpersuasive or at least not decisive or compelling.[6]

No doubt many Christians will further object that no one can approach any area of learning without some presuppositions, assumptions, or control biases, and this seems especially true when it comes to religious faiths. Thus, I'm arguing that the facts strongly suggest that adherents of a particular religious faith should switch their presuppositions. I'm arguing that they should adopt the presumption (or presupposition) of skepticism. If they simply cannot do this, then they should do what René Descartes did with a methodological (or hypothetical) doubt, although I'm not suggesting his type of extreme doubt. Hypothetically consider your faith from the skepticism of an outsider, a nonbeliever. I'll grant that what I'm asking is a tough thing to do. But believers must attempt this if they truly want to examine that which they were taught to believe. Only the honest, the consistent, and the brave will ever do this. But it is possible. Consider that you believe mainly for emotional and not intellectual reasons, just as people who have a fear of heights are afraid to stand at the edge of a precipice for emotional, not intellectual reasons. They intellectually know people go up to the top of skyscrapers and come down safely. So they must face their fears. They must go up to the second floor and look around. When comfortable they must continue up to the third floor, and so on until they get to the top.[7] This may take some time. Julia Sweeney, a former *Saturday Night Live* comedian, faced her fears when she put on her "No God Glasses" for a moment to look around at the world as if God did not exist. Then she put them on for an hour a day. Try this. As she faced her fears, she "began to see the world completely differently." Eventually she was "able to say good-bye to God."[8]

Remember, *brainwashed people do not know that they have been brainwashed.* We know that billions of people have been brainwashed to believe, if you grant that they have been misled by their parents and their culture. So you must take seriously the real possibility that you are one of them. If you really want to know if you've been brainwashed to believe by your particular religious culture, then taking the OTF is the only way to know the truth, since there seems to be no reasonable alternative, as we'll see shortly.

At the very minimum, believers should be willing to subject their faith to rigorous scrutiny by reading many of the best-recognized critiques of it. Christians should be willing to read this book of mine and others like it. What's more, church groups and Christian colleges should be willing to host study groups to discuss, chapter by chapter, books that take a skeptical position regarding the Christian faith. After all, wouldn't Christians want to know whether what they have been led to believe is true? If they want to be reasonable, they should.

For the Christian theist the challenge of the OTF means there can be no more quoting of the Bible to defend the claim that Jesus' death on the cross saves us from sins. The Christian theist must now try to rationally explain why such an atoning sacrifice for sins is not incoherent. There can be no more quoting the Bible to show how it's possible for Jesus to simultaneously be 100 percent God and 100 percent man. The Christian theist must now try to make sense of this claim that originated in an ancient, superstitious culture that didn't have trouble believing this could happen (Acts 14:11, 28:6). Christian theists must not assume there is an answer to the problem of evil before approaching the evidence of suffering in our world. And they must be skeptical of believing in any of the miracles in the Bible, just as they would be skeptical of any contemporary claims of miracles that support other religious faiths. Why? Because they can no longer start out by believing that the Bible is true. Nor can they trust the people close to them to know the truth, because those people adopted their faith the same way. Nor can they trust their own anecdotal religious experiences, since such experiences are had by people of all religious faiths. Christian theists who accept the challenge of the OTF should not be satisfied by anything less than sufficient evidence for what they believe.

The OTF challenges believers to examine the social and cultural conditions that influenced the adoption of their particular religious faith in the first place. In other words, it encourages believers to ask themselves who or what influenced them and what the actual reasons were for adopting their faith in its earliest stages. What were those reasons? Do those reasons hold up to the evidence that was initially presented, if any was presented at all? Usually what produces a conversion to faith is the Gospel story itself and the divine hope and love it promises. Nearly all believers simply end up believing what they were taught to believe by their parents or the people they consider to be trustworthy, sometimes peers or authority figures. The reasons they adopted their faith in the first place can almost always be traced to social and cultural conditions.

Take for example Dr. William Lane Craig's conversion testimony, as presented on his website Reasonable Faith.[9] Craig is considered the leading Christian apologist in our generation by many people today. Craig tells us he felt "empty" inside with no purpose, and he didn't see anyone as "genuine," even himself. Yet he really did want meaning in his life. And he wanted to love and to be loved by others.

One day he met a girl who "was always so happy it just makes you sick!" She told him she was happy because Jesus saved her and that Jesus loved him, too. This hit him "like a ton of bricks." That "thought just staggered me," he wrote. "To think that the God of the universe should love me, Bill Craig, that worm down there on that speck of dust called planet Earth! I just couldn't take it in." So he began reading the New Testament from cover to cover and was "absolutely captivated by the person Jesus of Nazareth." And he began worshipping with other people who were happy just like this girl. In that group he found the meaning and love that he craved. So he cried out to God in prayer and found what he was looking for. He looked up at the Milky Way and thought, "God! I've come to know God!"

I'm not convinced, based on his story, that Craig had good initial reasons to believe, just as I didn't. His personal story stresses his need for happiness, love, significance, and meaning. And he found these things simply as a result of a wonderful story that was told to him by a happy person during a vulnerable time in his life. He initially read the Bible uncritically along with some other Christian books. But how does someone properly investigate whether or not a claim is true? He or she doesn't do it by only reading the literature of the people who advocate it. He or she does it by also reading the best critiques of the people who disagree with it, and Dr. Craig knows this. By now he also knows there is a lot of hypocrisy and unhappiness among church people. He has had problems with church people, and he surely suffers like most of us do from unhappiness and bouts of anger toward others.

Does this subsequent experience cause him to doubt the initial youthful rush of friends and the happiness he felt at the time? I suspect so, or it should. By now he also knows that the need for significance and meaning isn't a good reason for accepting a religious story, since there are many religious stories to choose from. I'll bet he can also pick up those very same Christian books he first read and find several holes in their arguments. So would Craig have believed in the first place if he knew then what he does now? Remember, back then he didn't believe. He was an "outsider." I dare say that if he knew what he does now and hadn't already chosen to adopt his faith, he would not have believed in the first place.

Christian, just ask yourself if your initial reasons for your faith were strong ones. Do what I did in chapter 1 of my previous book, *Why I Became an Atheist.* I really didn't have good initial reasons to believe. Very few of us do, as a matter of fact. We just ended up believing what we were taught to believe.

Consider also what you would think of your faith if you heard it for the very first time. The fact that it's familiar to you is probably the reason you don't consider it to be bizarre. This is something I wrote about elsewhere.[10] It's also something that the Brafman brothers tell us to do in order to overcome *diagnosis bias,* our propensity to pigeon-hole people and things based on our initial impressions of them and our corresponding difficulty in reconsidering those value judgments once they have been made. The Brafman brothers, in *Sway: The Irresistible Pull of Irrational Behavior,* describe business leaders who continued pursuing a failed project rather than pursuing a more promising one because they were committed to what they had always done in the past. To overcome such behavior, the Brafman brothers propose answering this question: "If I were just arriving on the scene and were given the choice to either jump into this project as it stands now or pass on it, would I choose to jump in?"[11] Christians should adopt this same question when considering their own religious faith.

To the outsider the sciences are the paragon of knowledge. Scientific knowledge has so decisively passed an outsider test that we must examine all religious faiths in light of it. Show me the math, and we'll agree. Show me the experiment, and the argument will be over. Show me the scientific poll, and the case will be closed. The sciences, then, provide the only way to keep us from deluding ourselves.

WHAT'S A BETTER ALTERNATIVE?

One way to see the value of the OTF is to consider the alternatives, none of which can help believers, given the force of the RDVT and the RDPT.

1. The Gamaliel Test for Faith

Christian apologist David Marshall presents what I call the *Gamaliel Test for Faith*. Marshall argues that based upon its success Christianity has been passing the OTF ever since it began. He says, "Christianity is one of just a few belief systems that can be said to have passed the OTF, and to have done so most spectacularly. . . . The real intellectual challenge is, how do skeptics explain the unique empirical success of the Gospel?"[12] Tom Gilson defends Marshall by saying, "The core of David's argument is that Christianity has passed the OTF millions of times: every time someone converts to Christianity, especially when they do so from within a predominantly non-Christian culture."[13]

This test is the same one offered by Gamaliel in Acts 5, when he advises the Jewish Sanhedrin what to do about the budding Christian sect, reportedly saying, "Leave these men alone! Let them go! For if their purpose or activity is of human origin, it will fail. But if it is from God, you will not be able to stop these men; you will only find yourselves fighting against God." Gamaliel's propaganda used in defense of the spread of Christianity is ignorant superstition. If a religion succeeds in getting a sizable following it doesn't mean anyone should conclude that it must be true or that it was reasonably accepted based on sufficient evidence. Just think about Buddhism, Islam, Mormonism, or even Scientology. But that's exactly what Marshall argues for. So how do skeptics explain the success of the Gospel? Two words: *superstitious people.* The question is whether any faith can *reasonably* pass the OTF. The fact that a religious faith has succeeded in a society says nothing about whether it has *reasonably* passed the OTF, otherwise Scientology, Islam, and Mormonism are all passing the test in today's world.

2. Stone's Test of Neutral Evidence (STONE)

In a 2010 self-published book called *The Loftus Delusion,* David Reuben Stone, who has degrees from UCLA, criticizes my Outsider Test for Faith and proposes an alternative one called *Stone's Test of Neutral Evidence* (STONE). I reviewed his book online and consider it to be an epic failure.[14] Stone makes a distinction between *neutral agnosticism,* which he defines by the statement, "I don't know whether any faith is likely or unlikely," and *skeptical agnosticism,* which he defines by the statement, "I don't know any faith is likely, and I know all faiths are probably false."[15] Then he criticizes the OTF for arguing on behalf of skeptical agnosticism rather than for neutral agnosticism. He thinks we should all be neutral agnostics rather than skeptical agnostics, even though he inconsistently admits that "utterly pure and complete neutrality may be impossible to attain with respect to all belief systems."[16] This is high-sounding rhetoric, but rhetoric it is. It's the democratization of extraordinary miracle claims that Robert Price criticizes so effectively in the essay "Jesus: Myth and Method."[17]

Stone wants us to take seriously all claims no matter how bizarre or outlandish, which allows Christians to smuggle in their own extraordinary miracle claims. This position of theirs is a strange land to stand on. They never started on this piece of ground in the first place. No, they were born into Christianland and accepted what they were taught to believe. So there is no neutral position. Even if such a land exists, we cannot be so gullible as to treat every bizarre claim seriously. If we actually attempt to do so we will not be able to conclude much of anything until we examine them all, which is practically impossible. Reasonable people make generalizations about extraordinary supernatural claims; otherwise each one of them would have to be considered in isolation from all others. Neutrally assessing each one with no bias one way or another is simply not a good way to reason. We must make generalizations about such claims, and the best one to make is that we should be skeptical about any particular one of them under examination, no matter which one it is, because many other similar ones have been found out to be false. The question the OTF asks us is how we can properly test these claims. Given the fact that we are born into faith, and given the sociological facts that one's faith is probably false, and given how poorly we justify our beliefs, we should test our handed-down faith with skepticism, just as believers do to the faiths they reject.

3. Talbott's Test of Suspended Belief

Akin to the STONE test above, Thomas Talbott questions whether I have a clear definition of the kind of skepticism that forms the basis for the OTF. According to him there are three "different kinds of skepticism." There is "the skepticism of disbelief," which "*sometimes* [my emphasis] requires a kind of dogmatic certainty." This is my kind of skepticism he opines, and he implicitly suggests I come across as a "closed-minded dogmatist." The second kind of skepticism is that of "suspended belief," which is a kind of skepticism whereby someone will proceed with caution by examining with care "all of the relevant evidence he can find, and . . . will not jump to conclusions. . . . It implies, on the one hand, being on the alert for fallacious arguments, vague and meaningless utterances, hasty generalizations, and the oversimplification of complicated issues, and it implies, on the other hand, making a serious effort to purge one's own thinking of the same." This type of skepticism is "incompatible with dogmatic certainty and sometimes arises when one has the humility to recognize the limits of one's own knowledge." Since he thinks this describes his approach, he says of himself, "I am a true skeptic."[18] But don't Christian apologists all say this nowadays? Sure, they are skeptics in an unreasonable sense. As I argue, theirs is a faith-based skepticism that is skeptical of anything that disconfirms their faith. *This is not an informed, reasonable, science-based skepticism.* The third kind of skepticism is "merely the opposite of being overly gullible," which is a "healthy skepticism" that everyone should have. We're agreed on this.

My answer is that for the most part I deal with concrete examples rather than definitions. All we have to do is listen to the various religious stories out there from around the world to see what is required. As we hear believers one by one we would surely begin scoffing to ourselves about how bizarre one story after another sounds. This is why I liked Bill Maher's movie *Religulous.*[19] It's obvious from watching the many different (and even bizarre) religious opinions expressed in it that any given one of them is false. And Maher didn't even deal with the vast array of Eastern religious options, which would sound even more bizarre to Westerners than the ones he dealt with. I have seen them though. I have seen videos of people bathing in the Ganges River in hopes of being healed, of people who claim they are a god or a goddess, and of people who claim that incantations and voodoo dolls can bring healing or sicknesses. I have seen interviews of people who claim to be someone reincarnated from the past, and so on. Roger Nygard's documentary *The Nature of Existence* (2010) does an excellent job of showing this, and it is much more thorough than *Religulous,* covering all kinds of bizarre religions all over the world. By putting them on an equal playing field they all appear to be false, which is what the OTF is meant to force us to consider. The OTF is an evenhanded and informed approach to religions that I think is warranted given the RDVT and the RDPT. So I say that the kind of skepticism called for is the first kind, the "skepticism of disbelief," although Talbott mischaracterizes it as sometimes involving "a kind of dogmatic certainty." That's what I argue for anyway. If Talbott or anyone else wants to show how his so-called suspended belief can help a believer to truly evaluate the various religious *and* nonreligious options out there, then I'm all ears. Given what we know, the skepticism of disbelief is how reasonable people should examine all religious faiths, including their own, since that's already how they do it. Part of what needs to be done is to inform believers of these other religious options so they can develop that kind of informed skepticism, the skepticism of disbelief toward them.

This is why Talbott is misguided when asking me which outsider perspective "is the most relevant" one: "(a) someone who has never encountered the Christian religion and therefore has no beliefs about it at all or (b) someone who has indeed encountered the Christian religion but has not yet acquired any settled beliefs about it or (c) someone who has considered the Christian religion and chooses, for whatever reason, not to be identified with this religion."[20] While they all represent outsiders by degree, I'm arguing for an informed skepticism regardless of whether people fall into one of these three groupings of people, one that understands the massive and ubiquitous religious diversity in the world, on the one hand, and the science that offers the best explanation of it, on the other hand. That there are outsiders, as he describes them, is irrelevant to my argument. I'm arguing that upon examining any religion, including their own, people should adopt the OTF as the gold standard.

Talbott further asks, "Just how might one go about adopting an outsider perspective, or the skepticism of an outsider? Should Christians merely pretend that they have never encountered the Christian faith, or pretend that they do not believe it, or pretend that they have considered it and then rejected it? If so, how are they to manage such a feat? . . . I have no idea how to manufacture in myself, however heroically I might try, skepticism concerning a host of common sense beliefs."[21] First, religious faiths are not "common sense beliefs," given the RDVT. Nonetheless, I've already suggested earlier in this chapter ways believers can do this. It's required, given the force of the RDVT and the RDPT, even if it's tough to do. Ex-Christians are doing this on a daily basis.

Since this seems beyond him, Talbott says, "You can, of course, re-examine your beliefs as often as you want; that is, you can examine the logical relations between them, consider the position of a given belief in the complex web of your beliefs, and evaluate different kinds of belief and the kind of justification that may (or may not) be relevant to each of them. . . . But if the OTF represents nothing more than an exhortation for people to examine their own beliefs critically and carefully, then it contributes nothing new and nothing substantial to any dispute that might arise between theists, atheists, and agnostics."[22] Really? So with this we're back to where we started from, with a diversity of believers whose religious faiths are overwhelmingly causally dependent on the biology of their brains, the influences of their cultures, and the tendency toward irrational thinking patterns common to all human beings. This has repeatedly shown itself to be a failure, and Talbott wants more of the same? If you do more of the same you will get the same results. I am sure most believers would say the same kinds of things and remain in their faiths, too. Talbott simply refuses to step outside his cultural cave and see it for what it is, and he must continually find reasons not to. This is a prime example of the inherent irrational thinking patterns so amply documented by psychological studies.

4. Rauser's Intellectual Virtues Test

I'm sure Randal Rauser would agree with Talbott, so his test isn't that much different. Rauser commented on the OTF by agreeing "that we ought to think about our beliefs from an outsider's perspective" and "that the OTF aims for at least one specific intellectual virtue: objectivity." Good, that's the most important agreement. But Rauser's disagreement is threefold: "1) There are a range of intellectual virtues to strive to exemplify. 2) We do not achieve them through one test but in an ongoing way every day. 3) The challenge for exemplifying intellectual virtue is one that extends to all people."[23] For the record, I don't have any disagreement with 1–3 at all, except that with (2), once believers conclude their faith is false there isn't much left to do unless new information surfaces that challenges the result. Regarding (3), I wouldn't have it any other way. Atheists should also seek out which religion is true, if any of them are, by utilizing the full range of intellectual virtues available. I've met lots of atheists online who are not trying to debunk religion so much as they are trying to test to see if their unbelief is warranted.

With regard to (1), Rauser claims that objectivity is merely one of the intellectual virtues. Others include fairness and open-mindedness, and he opines that the OTF does not include these other virtues in the quest for truth. But I see no reason why the OTF does not include all these intellectual virtues. When it comes to fairness, if a judge has a conflict of interest he is not likely to be fair. That's why judges must take seriously an attorney's charge that they recuse themselves from a case because of a conflict of interest, and why not doing so (if true) is considered an ethics violation by the American Bar Association. The OTF requires fairness in how people examine not only the religious faiths they reject, but also their own religious faith. Contrary to Rauser, fairness is its hallmark! No one should judge religions based on double standards. The scales of justice should be fair. No one should place a thumb on the scales in favor of one's particular culturally adopted religious faith.[24]

That leaves us with the virtue of open-mindedness, an interesting word. I suspect Rauser easily rejects Scientology, Mormonism, militant Islam, Orthodox Judaism, Hinduism, Buddhism, Jainism, and the many other religious faiths around the globe, including all the dead religions and gods and goddesses without much thought at all. Most of them he simply dismisses out of hand even though he has never given them serious consideration. Is that being open-minded? Is he really open-minded about astrology, tarot-card readings, weeping statues of the Virgin Mary, werewolves, vampires, or alien abductions? Whether or not he realizes it, he's arguing for an uncritical kind of open-mindedness that he himself does not share. This is *emphatically not* an intellectual virtue if it means being open to every claim no matter how bizarre it is, as I've said, or relaxing the standards of evidence or proof needed before accepting a claim.

Being open-minded is indeed an intellectual virtue associated with humility though, since we must be humble enough to realize we all accept some things that are probably not true. We know we do it, all of us. It's surmised that we accept most of what we think based upon authority, perhaps 95 percent of the time. So yes, we all must have the humility to admit that there are things we accept that are not true, which requires us to be open-minded to different conclusions than our own. But we cannot, nor should we be, open-minded to any and every claim. It wouldn't be rational to do so. There must be an objective method that helps us to determine what we should accept and what we can't, and an uncritical open-mindedness is not it.

So it's one thing to say we should embrace the intellectual virtue of open-mindedness. It's another thing to propose how we should go about doing that. I'm arguing that the *only* way to be truly open-minded is to adopt the intellectual virtues of fairness and objectivity represented in the OTF. From what I've seen, people of faith are close-minded. The OTF should open their minds. Their culturally adopted faith makes most of them impervious to reason, like Rauser himself, for they are not open to fairly and objectively testing their faith. They would rather hold on to double standards. When it comes to one's religious faith anything short of objectivity is being gullible rather than truly open-minded. *Rauser should therefore be open-minded enough to look at his culturally inherited faith objectively*, but he's not, despite any protestations of his to the contrary.

Should I be open-minded about the possibility that the OTF is not actually a fair test for faith? Yes, I should be, and I am. But I have not seen anything that calls it into question. In order for me to change my mind about the OTF someone must offer good objections to it and propose a better alternative method to solve the problem of religious diversity. As I'm arguing, this has not been done.

5. The Critical-Stance Alternative

Robert McKim argues on behalf of "tentative belief," what he calls the *Critical Stance.* Based on the obvious rational disagreement between peers, especially concerning religion, it requires both that believers "examine" their beliefs more closely and that they hold them "to be tentative."[25] For McKim, tentative belief involves awareness that one's beliefs "need revision, and may be false, and that there may be viable alternatives."[26] "The tentative believer" though "is not an agnostic: he believes that God exists, albeit in a way that involves recognition that he may be wrong."[27] Such a stance "suggests that the beliefs of each side may be incomplete; it may be that there is some way to combine the best of each of them."[28]

McKim's Critical Stance is welcome. If nothing else, it creates an atmosphere of tolerance between people of faith, a virtue for which he argues. If his arguments succeed, they could take believers down a path that leads to the OTF. But most believers are psychologically incapable of holding their beliefs in such a tentative manner, just as no sports fan can sit in the stands and not root for his or her favorite team. To think of a tentative sports fan is not to think of a fan at all. Likewise, to think of a tentative believer is not to think of a believer at all. By adopting the Critical Stance believers could by definition never be passionately committed to their faith, and yet faith for most people demands passion. For that reason the Critical Stance is unsatisfactory from a religious point of view. To such an objection McKim responds by rhetorically asking that "if a strong case can be made for the Critical Stance, why should we be concerned about the fact that it will be found unsatisfactory from many religious points of view?"[29] Good for McKim.

McKim's Critical Stance could be embraced fairly easily by liberals, but it just doesn't offer a method for deciding which religious faith is true, if there is one. It's one thing to say we should hold religious beliefs tentatively. That should be clear. It's another thing entirely to offer a method that can help us settle which religious faith is true, if any are. That's why he calls it the *Critical Stance* rather than the *Critical Method*. His exposition of the Critical Stance is done from the perspective of the religious believer. So his Critical Stance fails because it doesn't even include the possibility of atheism, the nonreligious alternative. This means he's not being fair with all the options. Any fair method should leave room for all options. The Critical Stance does not do this. As I'll argue in the last chapter, faith is the problem. That's the reason why there is so much religious diversity. McKim apparently doesn't realize this problem for what it really is. The OTF, however, offers a self-diagnostic method to decide which tentatively held religious faith is true, if there is one. All options are on the table. None are excluded.

6. Yandell's Axioms of Appraisal

The late Christian professor Keith Yandell offered seven axioms for the rational appraisal of experience, religious or otherwise. They are as follows: (1) If a conceptual system contains as an essential element a set of propositions that are logically inconsistent, it is false. (2) If a conceptual system is such that it being true is incompatible with it being *known* to be true, then this fact provides a good (though perhaps not conclusive) reason for supposing that it is false. (3) If a conceptual system is such that it being true is incompatible with its truth-conditions then it is false. (4) If the only rationale for offering a conceptual system is that it supposedly provides a solution for a particular problem, and the problem remains, there is no reason to accept it. (5) If an essential element in a conceptual system is contradicted by well-established data then it is probably false. (6) A conceptual system that incorporates ad hoc hypotheses in order to escape counterevidence is less plausible than one that contains no ad hoc hypotheses. (7) A conceptual system that cannot explain or assimilate phenomena that lie within its relevance range is false or incomplete.[30]

Yandell doesn't go into much detail about these axioms, even though we would have wanted him to. The problem is that I can think of reasons why the Christian conceptual system fails every single one of them, whereas, since Yandell was a Christian, he thought otherwise. And I'm sure other people of different faiths would agree with me that Yandell's faith fails some or all of them, whereas Easterners would probably disagree with some of the axioms themselves. This is what rational disagreement between peers entails. So while they are helpful, I don't see how Yandell's axioms can settle the disputes of faith. As far as I know Mormons and Scientologists can agree with the axioms and still maintain their faith. That's how bad our reasoning abilities are that seek to justify what we believe. So these axioms are not a good alternative to the OTF.

To sum up, given these six other alternative "tests" for faith, I see no reason at all to think they are better than the OTF. Some of them are bad, really bad. My claim is that if we keep on doing the same things we will get the same results. To date, all proposed alternative "tests" to solve the problem of religious diversity have not worked. So why keep on doing the same things? I see no reason why we should. As I said, we cannot have a Milquetoast test when it comes to the truth of religion. Believers already think that their faith is justified and that they are objective in examining their own religious faith. And almost all of them are certain their religious faith is true.

I realize most believers will continue to object to the OTF, just as Christians have always done in order to keep their certainties, as we shall see in the next few chapters. Even if believers learn to embrace it as a fair test they will most likely go on to argue that their faith passes it, just as G. K. Chesterton and David Marshall have claimed, and just as Christian philosophers Steve Lovell and Victor Reppert have likewise claimed, even though they object to some aspects of the test. I argue for the OTF, since, if nothing else, it provides the basis for all future debates about which religion is true, if there is one. Once it's accepted by all parties the debate can really begin. If it does nothing else, the OTF is a good thing. It is the only way to settle our disagreements, if they can be settled at all.

5

OBJECTING TO THE FACTS

In the following four chapters I want to answer some relevant objections to the outsider test, in no particular order. I'll confess from the start that I think all the objections are weak at best. I think the facts represented in my defense of the RDVT and the RDPT are uncontestable. In this chapter I'll look at objections to the facts that should cause believers to become informed skeptics. The crucial fact that is either disputed outright or watered down significantly by believers concerns the RDPT. I'll focus on this, since, as David Reuben Stone has noticed, the RDPT "is critical to Loftus' case for the Outsider Test."[1]

I would think most reasonable Christians will admit the RDPT. Pastor and apologist Fred DeRuvo, who has a Doctor of Divinity degree from Cambridge Theological Seminary, is at least reasonable enough to admit both the RDVT and the RDPT. In his self-published book *The Anti-Christian Bias of Ex-Christians and Other Important Topics*, he wrote: "It would be difficult to argue against [Loftus's] idea that the religion an individual embraces is built largely upon that individual's sociology and culture."[2] DeRuvo says, "It is obvious that people gravitate toward one particular faith as opposed to another largely because of family, and in the absence of family, it would be because of friends. Christians have no difficulty with this."[3] However, he goes on to argue, "This means absolutely nothing since it is clear from Scripture that God calls people out of their sociological culture into the kingdom of heaven. John's argument is cannon fodder. Light it up and watch it blow up."[4] He's answering this intractable difficulty with a dance I call *The Delusional Sidestep* (TDS). After recognizing the data, he then asserts his faith is true, which is representative of that very data. He's responding to diversity with diversity, his own. He's special pleading his case. He makes a quick sidestep to avoid the consequences of the data by claiming his faith is true despite the odds. Wait just a minute! What about the odds? Ahhh, just ignore them.

1. Is Culture an Overwhelming Influence?

David Marshall asserts that the RDPT is not as obvious as I make it sound, since there are still a lot of non-Christian influences in a Christian culture, especially in today's world. As he did with religious diversity, he again attempts to mitigate the fact of dependency. He argues that "in most of the world, serious Christian faith is not the default position; even most American Christians go to secular schools, listen to secular music, watch secular movies, and (in extreme cases) read the blogs of John Loftus or PZ Myers. So cultural dependency is real, but not 'overwhelming.' None of us is purely an insider to 'Christian culture.'"[5]

This depends on what we consider to be a culture. For a boy who is homeschooled by snake handlers or a girl raised by KKK parents, those are the only cultures they know. This is the smallest level of culture, one's immediate family and relatives. And although Marshall says the Internet allows different perspectives to be heard, some countries limit what the people in their countries can access. There are many Christians who don't have any non-Christian friends or relatives. But the fact is that the culture we are a part of greatly influences what we think. Just take four babies and raise one in China, another in Saudi Arabia, the third in Kentucky, and the fourth in Russia and you will see clearly how cultures influence us all. And it's never more pronounced than when it comes to religion. This sociological fact is indeed obvious: our respective cultures have an overwhelming influence on us. This is undeniable.

What Marshall is getting at is that there are small minorities of people who choose to be Christian theists despite having been born and raised in countries dominated by Islam or other religions, which demonstrates that people can escape their culturally adopted faith. But these are the exceptions. Christian theists respond by asking me to explain the exceptions. I am asking them to explain the rule. Why do religious beliefs dominate in specific geographical areas? Why is that?

Then, too, there are several social reasons for leaving the faith that one was born into. If believers had some bad experiences at the hands of someone who taught them what to believe (for instance, Catholics who have been molested by priests), they may leave that faith for another. These kinds of bad experiences cause people to do what they should have been doing all along: critically examining the faith they were taught. If believers think through their faith and just cannot reconcile it with everything they've learned and experienced in life, then they may leave their faith. When believers do decide to leave their faith and choose another one, most times that different faith (or sect) will be one they were already exposed to in their culture. By contrast, former believers can become nonbelievers without ever having been exposed to atheism, since it's simply the denial of one more god in addition to all the other gods they have already denied.

Recent polls are showing that many Americans are leaving the faith of their parents. If correct, this is supposed to undermine the sociological basis for the OTF somehow. A 2008 Pew poll tells us that "28 percent of American adults have left the faith of their childhood for another one. When we include people who switched from one Protestant denomination to another the number would jump to 44 percent."[6] But this poll data does not undermine the sociological data at all. Americans are embracing syncretism, pluralism, and pragmatism when it comes to religion. American culture is changing, so it should not surprise us in the least that Americans are also changing their religious faiths. If someone lives and breathes in a pluralistic culture then he or she will be a pluralist, you see, even if raised otherwise by his or her parents. More and more believers are treating religion like they do diet and sex. Variety is the spice of life when it comes to these things. So it is with religion. Many Americans think that there is little difference between many of the sects within Christianity, and some think that way about religions in general. So it stands to reason that believers will switch church affiliations to attend where their friends do, in churches that have more to offer them and programs that meet their practical needs. They'll switch churches for a warmer pew, a better church building, or to hear better music and a better sermon. After all, the moral message still seems to be the same, and that's what more and more Americans think the value of religion provides anyway.[7] In any case, the fact is that these newly chosen faiths, if they are chosen reasonably, must still pass the OTF. So all this poll data shows us is that their choices could very well be emotional ones based on psychological needs.

It's objected that there are lots of people raised in parts of Asia and the Southern Hemisphere, where Christianity is growing phenomenally, who choose to be Christian theists.[8] These people are represented as outsiders who escape their culturally adopted faith. The question is whether or not they do so based on the same standards they reasonably use to reject other religions. Is reason and science rather than faith their guide? Are people accepting a religious faith by initially assuming that it has the burden of proof? Are these potential converts assuming a human rather than a divine author of your holy book(s)? I think not, not by a long shot, not even close. A religion may grow due to many factors unrelated to how it should be reasonably accepted, if one can be reasonably accepted at all. Most of the converted do not objectively weigh the evidence when making their initial religious commitments. They mainly change their minds due to the influence and believability of the evangelist and/or the wondrous nature of the religious story itself. In these parts of the globe, people already share many of the same social, economic, political, and superstitious viewpoints that were characteristic of ancient biblical people, so it should be no surprise that the Gospel is being accepted there. Philip Jenkins, in his book *The New Faces of Christianity: Believing the Bible in the Global South*, documents this quite well.[9]

These new converts have no initial way of truly investigating the proffered faith. Which evangelist will objectively explain the ugly sides of the Bible and the church while preaching the good news? None that I know of. Which evangelist will tell a prospective convert about the innumerable problems Christian scholars must solve? None that I know of. Which evangelist will give potential converts a copy of a book like this one to read alongside a copy of a Christian apologetics book? Again, none that I know of. Only if they do will I sit up and take notice. Until then I am not impressed.

2. Causation Is Not Shown by Merely Showing Correlation

David Reuben Stone questions how the inference from religious diversity leads me to posit dependency as the best explanation. He argues that I have not developed "anything close to a justified interpretation of the concept of 'causation.'" He says that I merely appeal "to the strong influence (i.e. correlation) between religious faith and the correlated social/cultural/geographical/psychological conditions, as if that's all we need to prove the causal RDPT thesis. In response, correlation does not imply causation. . . . The point, here, is that something is missing in Loftus' inference from 'A is correlated with B' to 'A is caused by B.'" Continuing, Stone writes, "I do not claim religious faith does not strongly depend on, for example, social and geographical conditions. The mere acknowledgement of a dependence relation, however, is not synonymous with the acknowledgment of a causal relation. It is clear that 'A depends on B' need not entail 'A is causally related to B'. . . . The mere identification of a relationship is an insufficient condition of identifying that that relationship is causal."[10]

I'll grant that it can be problematic to determine what causes something in some cases. Does eating an apple a day keep the doctor away, or is it that people who don't need a doctor are the kind of people who eat apples? But given that we already know on other grounds that eating fruit is good for us we can make a generalization that eating apples can help people be healthy. What then are these other grounds that lead me to argue for religious dependency? Science, the kind of science I've already argued for: neurology, anthropology, and psychology. I don't need to rehearse them again. Together they provide more than enough evidence for the RDPT.

Keep in mind that I have not argued that one's social/cultural/ geographical/psychological factors cause one's faith, only that they overwhelmingly do so. It may well be that they do cause one's faith, but that's not my argument. Stone says this isn't good enough though, for if these factors are merely overwhelming then I have not established a casual relationship, which is necessary for my case. According to Stone, if I don't establish a causal relationship "the door is opened wide to reject the RDPT, since a multitude of other causal factors may be at play."[11] But what are these other causal factors? I didn't speak much about such factors as DNA, IQ, gender, race, age, or sexuality. I could look into them in more detail as factors that give rise to our beliefs. But if I did, these other factors would more than sufficiently reinforce the dependency thesis. Religious faiths would not only be based on cultural conditions but also on a wider level of biological conditions other than just brain biology. It would reinforce dependency just the same. What other factors are there? One such factor Stone mentions is free will, that people have the free will to supposedly overcome these influences. I have argued instead that even given free will we do not have as much of it as is needed:

> It does absolutely no good at all to have free will and not also have the ability to exercise it . . . some people don't have the rational capacity needed to spot a con artist. Gender, race, age, brain matter, where we're born, and how we're raised all limit the free choices available to each of us, even granting that we have it. Our genes and our environment both restrict what choices are available for us to make.
>
> I dare say that if God exists and created a different "soul" inside my mother's womb at the precise moment I was conceived, and if that organism experienced everything I did and learned the exact same lessons throughout life in the same order that I did at the

same intensity, then the resulting person would be me, even given free will. And if you won't go that far, the limits of our choices are still set by our genetic material and our environment. We don't have as much free will as we think. All of us have a very limited range of free choices, if we have any at all.[12]

Another factor Stone doesn't mention but probably implies is religious experience. However, Stone needs to take seriously the fact that people of diverse faiths all claim to have religious experiences. They are private, subjective experiences though, which can be explained as natural phenomena based on the biology of belief that Michael Shermer and others have shown us. And they are interpreted within one's own religious culture to come from one's own particular god and religious faith. So even if we grant them, the fact is that they do not establish any given religion, and that includes Stone's self-described "Messianic Israelism."

Stone's whole case reminds me of David Hume, who pointed out that he never sees one billiard ball "causing" another one to move. In this same sense Stone thinks there is no direct causal relationship between the RDVT and the RDPT. Is it possible that despite the separation of religious faiths into distinct geographical locations on our planet, the influence of local and regional cultures, and the reinforcement of irrational thinking patterns, these factors have little to do with what people of faith believe? My answer is that this is possible, but it is an exceedingly small possibility. Do Christians really want to hang their faith on such a slender reed as this? Any believer who argues for this is a prime example of what I mean when I say that Christians demand that I prove their faith is nearly impossible before they will consider it to be improbable.

3. The Genetic Fallacy

The genetic fallacy is committed whenever it's argued that an idea is false because of its origination or source rather than based on its merits. Even unreliable sources can produce ideas that are true. So just showing that an idea originates from an unreliable source does not necessarily make the idea false. David Marshall argues that I commit this fallacy: "If we adopt certain beliefs because we have been taught them, does that really mean they are probably false? Obviously not. The general form of Loftus' argument is: 1) Ideas about X vary among cultures; 2) The beliefs one adopts about X originate in one's culture, and in that sense depend on it; 3) Therefore one's beliefs are probably wrong. This seems to commit the genetic fallacy."[13]

This charge of his is false. I allow that a religion could still pass the OTF even despite its unreliable origins in our respective diverse cultures, so I'm committing no fallacy by arguing correctly that those origins are demonstrably unreliable. At best there can be only one true religion in what we observe to be a sea of hundreds of false ones, which entails a very high rate of error for how believers first adopt a religion. Hence, believers need some further test to be sure their faith is the correct one. That conclusion is not fallacious, nor is the skepticism that it entails. I'm not arguing that religious faiths are necessarily false because of how believers originally adopt them. I'm merely arguing that believers should be skeptical of their culturally adopted religious faith because of it.

Acknowledging these disclaimers of mine, retired Christian professor of philosophy Mark M. Hanna let's me off the hook on this; otherwise, he says, "the genetic fallacy charge would stick."[14] But he also alleges that my disclaimers contradict other assertions of mine in which I state that no religion can pass the OTF.[15] The problem here is that Hanna has failed to distinguish between the three stages of the arguments for the OTF in this book. My disclaimers are real. It's just that statements in which I argue that no revealed religion can pass the test represent the third stage of argumentation. The third stage, as I said, is where people can use the OTF as a basis for debates about religious faith.

Hanna claims, however, that any conclusions based on the anthropological data argued for by David Eller "fall into the genetic fallacy." Anthropology is a merely descriptive science, Hanna argues, and so any conclusions based on it "fall outside the scientific parameters of anthropology."[16] Eller knows that anthropology is merely a descriptive science, but there is no reason why he cannot state his conclusions based on all that he knows. He is someone we ought to listen to, since anthropology is his field of expertise. He's studied world religions, their origins, their pervasiveness, their cultural impact, and their evolution. And he concludes that if there is a correct religion, it looks indistinguishable from how the others originated, took root in a culture, and evolved down through the centuries. They all look like human inventions to meet the perceived needs of the people of their times. So he says that at some point along the line "comes the epiphanal moment," whereby, just "like the anecdote about the religion that believes the world stands on a turtle," it dawned on him that "Christianity is cultural all the way down."[17] Is this a conclusion derived from deductive logic from certain premises that come from anthropology itself? No. It's an inductive conclusion from all that he knows. Can we dismiss it then like Hanna does? No. We cannot dismiss it, especially since so many other anthropologists say the same thing. Cultural and religious relativism are widely accepted by anthropologists.

Let me state for the record that I have probably never met anyone who has committed the genetic fallacy. Instead, people use their background knowledge about the general reliability of an idea's source to determine the likelihood that an idea originating from that source is true. Almost no one says, for instance, that we can *never* trust a particular tabloid news story because of the tabloid's past reputation for dishonesty. What people might say instead, or intend to say, is that we *probably* cannot trust a particular tabloid news story because of the tabloid's past reputation for dishonesty. People can reasonably judge the odds of an idea being true based on their background knowledge about the general reliability of the source of that idea. If an idea originates from a known unreliable source then it's entirely reasonable to doubt any idea coming from that same source, even though we have not yet shown that idea to be false in any other way.

Take for example a person who has the paranoid belief that the CIA is spying on him, and let's say we find that it originated from his taking a hallucinogenic drug like LSD. Since we have linked his belief to a drug that creates many other false beliefs, we have some really good evidence to be skeptical of it, even though we have not actually shown it to be false in any other way. Likewise, when many false beliefs like these are produced at a very high rate by the same source, we have a good reason to doubt any beliefs arising out of that same source.

Hanna objects by arguing that the cultural origin of one's religious faith is irrelevant to whether it is true. But the origination of one's faith within a particular culture is indeed relevant to the probability that one's faith is the correct one, for we know that cultures produce a wide diversity of religious faiths. Given that many of them are mutually exclusive, we also know that many of them are false. So we have very good reasons to think that cultures are an unreliable source for producing one true religion, since they have produced so many false ones. I'm arguing that the source of most people's religious faith is an unreliable one, coming, as it does, from the geographical accidents of birth. Differing cultures produce many different and irreconcilable religious faiths that cannot all be true. Sure, it's possible there are people born into the correct religion, if we grant there is one. But possibility doesn't count. Probability is all that matters.

For all I know, even if religious faiths were 100 percent correlated with the "accidents of birth" it could still be possible that there is one true religion. After all, someone can be right for no other reason than simple luck. However, one cannot punt to a mere possibility when probability is all that matters. The question is how a believer can rationally justify such luck? This is why I'm arguing for the OTF in the first place, to test religious faiths against such luck. If the test between religious faiths is based entirely on luck, then what are the chances, based on luck alone, that the particular sect within Christian theism that one adheres to is correct?

At this point the objections to the fact of religious dependency basically drop off. Believers do not, nor can they, object to the facts that support the RDPT. Believers are reduced to saying that, even though their religious faith originated inside a particular religious culture that looks indistinguishable from the origination of other faiths, and even though we have a strong built-in propensity in our brains for seeing patternicity and agenticity, and even though psychology conclusively shows us that, as human beings, we tend to seek confirming evidence for what we believe and ignore disconfirming evidence, their particular God is nonetheless somehow behind these influences, leading them to believe in the one correct religious sect. Wow! Just wow! But guess what? Every believer in a different religion who encounters these same facts could say the same thing. Is it not crystal clear by now that faith has no method and cannot settle any differences between religions?

4. Objecting to Science Itself

Given that the OTF is based on science, the only thing left for believers to do is to bring science down to the level of faith. This is what David Marshall does: "Faith involves a continuum of four levels of trust"—trust in our own minds, trust in our senses, trust in the testimony of people, and trust in God. The first three levels of trust are

> as true in science as anywhere. . . . In fact, scientific evidence is based on faith—exactly the same sort of faith as informed Christians have in God. Science is always based on at least three kinds of reasonable but fallible faith; trust in the mind, in the sense, and in other people. None of these can be proven—to use mind to prove mind is to argue in a circle. And the senses might be wrong. And there is no scientific test to prove our colleagues honest, reliable, and competent—only social tests. Yet without reliance on all three, good science cannot be done.[18]

I am sure all scientists, except for perhaps pseudoscientists within Marshall's own evangelical tradition, would absolutely scoff at this comparison between faith and science. He's negating the trustworthiness of science by placing it on an equal plane with faith. They are basically the same you see. The method of science is the same as the method of faith. They both require trusting the conclusions of our *brains*, our senses, and other people, none of which "can be proven," since there is always an element of doubt, no matter how small. How much doubt Marshall doesn't say, but he should, because there really isn't any doubt about gravity, for instance, or the overwhelming consensus of scientists around the world on things like the Big Bang, evolution, continental drift, or the heliocentric solar system. Scientific results like these, and many others, are accepted by all scientists as being *virtually certain*. Is there room for doubt? Yes, because they are not *certain* conclusions, only virtually certain ones. By contrast, however, there is a great amount of doubt when it comes to world religions, since not all of them can be true. When we compare the assured results of science to the assured faiths of believers in extraordinary supernatural miracle claims that are *virtually impossible* within the natural world (for example, virgin births, fulfilled prophecies, resurrections, and miraculous healings), if science is based on faith there is a gigantic difference between scientific "faith" and religious faith. At their very best, miracle claims are extremely improbable, as they concern rare, nonrepeatable, and nontestable events. At their very worst, scientific claims are extremely probable, regular, repeatable, and testable. There is simply no epistemic parity here at all.

Marshall opines, "Those who make wild claims about the scientific method often base their arguments not on good human evidence, but rumor, wild guesses, and extrapolations that would embarrass a shaman."[19] This sentence expresses such a low view of science that I mention it only to embarrass him. On my blog, Marshall even defended what he said: "Actually, John, I would say that almost all scientific evidence comes to us as historical evidence. Science," he continued, "is, in effect, almost a branch of history, as it transmits knowable and systematically collected and interpreted facts to our brains."[20] There is so much wrong about this response and so little space. The only reason he wants to bring science down to the level of the historian's very difficult but honorable craft is because he needs to believe his faith history is on an equal par with scientific results, only he places history above science because, he says, science is a branch of history. People of faith must denigrate science in at least some areas, simply because science is the major threat to their faith. That's the nature of faith.

Marshall goes on to ask, "Why believe that only truths grounded in scientific evidence are worth believing?" According to him, "That idea cannot be proven scientifically!"[21] Mark Hanna said similar kinds of things:

> If the only thing we should trust is the sciences, then we should not trust the claim that the only thing we should trust is the sciences. The assertion itself is not a scientific one nor is it discovered or justified by any of the sciences. It is a non-scientific, mistaken *philosophical* judgment about knowledge and the sciences, and yet he [Loftus] trusts it. So the sciences are not the only thing he trusts. . . . It is beyond dispute that the empirical sciences neither contain all knowledge nor are they the only means for gaining knowledge.[22]

It's very hard to convince people of faith like this that science is extremely trustworthy, which is my point, not that the empirical sciences contain all knowledge. My claim is context dependent, and the context is religious faith and how to settle the vast amount of religious diversity in the world. Believers themselves admit that science is trustworthy because they trust science in an overwhelming number of areas except for the rare ones that threaten what some ancient, prescientific, superstitious people wrote down in their holy books. Why should reasonable people ever trust the words of superstitious ancients over the repeatable results of science? Believers also trust scientific findings when examining the other religious faiths they reject. This, too, is my point. Why the double standard? My contention is that since people of faith use scientific reasoning to examine the religious faiths they reject, they should also use it to examine the truth of their own faith.

Science is trustworthy because it has a trustworthy method, whereas faith does not. Science is trustworthy because it's based upon objective evidence, whereas faith doesn't need objective evidence. Science is trustworthy because it's self-correcting due to the evidence itself, whereas people of faith don't have the evidence to convince other believers. Science is trustworthy because the evidence is the final arbiter between scientists, whereas with people of faith almost anything can be believed. Science is trustworthy because it progresses and has produced impressive results that have led to our world of microchips, cruise ships, and video clips, whereas people of faith are still debating endless questions without coming to any consensus. Scientists eventually come to a consensus, whereas religionists can only agree about what they've always agreed to, that supernatural beings and/or forces exist.

Apart from science, what else should we trust? Religious experience? Philosophy? Faith? What's the alternative? Do people like Marshall and Hanna know how science even works? Over the years I have found that one bastion for Christian apologists has been philosophy, especially the philosophy of religion, but also in some part the philosophy of science. The scholars have honed their definitional apologetics (as I call them) in such a fine-tuned manner that engaging them in this discipline is like trying to chase them down the rabbit's hole in an endless and ultimately fruitless quest for definitions. What's an *extraordinary claim*? What's the definition of *supernatural*? What's the *scientific method*? What's a *miracle*? What's a *basic belief*? What's a *veridical religious experience*? What's *evil*? They do this just like others have done over questions like, "What is the definition of *pornography*?" And then they gerrymander around the plain and simple, concrete facts of experience. Don't get me wrong. I value philosophy. In fact, I use it, and it certainty helped me to think critically. It's just that I no longer value any philosophy that is not scientifically informed. Marshall and Hanna are clearly uninformed about science.

Hanna demands that I chase him down a rabbit's hole of definitions. He claims that I have not defined the scientific method or provided a theory of science, a theory of truth, a theory of arguments (deductive, inductive, probability, improbability, plausibility, implausibility, etc.), and a theory of evidence. He argues, "Without an adequate analysis of these fundamental issues and a cogent case for his own theories about them, his [Loftus's] assertions are superficial pontifications that are problematic at best and opaque at worst."[23] Do I really need to chase him down this rabbit's hole of definitions? Could I really convince him afterward? I've tried chasing Christians down that rabbit's hole without any success. Why does he think such an effort would change anything? Plenty of atheist philosophers are doing these things. I prefer to deal in concrete examples, like virgin births, resurrections, magic Mormon underwear, supposed Golden Plates, miracles in the Ganges River, people claiming to be a god, voodoo dolls, and the like, comparing these miracle claims to the monumental results of science. Science works. Faith does not work. What's not to understand about this?

Believers love to mention that postmodern philosophers of science like Paul Feyerabend, have argued that there is no scientific method.[24] So, in a like manner, Christian apologists J. P. Moreland and William Lane Craig claim that "there is no such thing as *the* scientific method." If they really think that, I'm all ears to hear them explain why science continues to advance without one. And if science has no method, then what method does faith have by comparison? In Moreland and Craig's words, the hypothetico-deductive method advocated by Carl Hempel "sees scientists as, in one way or another, forming and putting forth a hypothesis, deriving test implications from it, then seeing if observations corroborate with the hypothesis. . . . We can then make observations to see if this is supported by the data we gather." They go on to claim that this "does not capture everything that a scientist does."[25] But Hempel's view is a more-than-adequate description of the scientific method, even if it's not a complete one. If a total description and justification of the scientific method is elusive, Paul Kurtz reminded us that such a requirement is inappropriate anyway, "for science is implicit in our ordinary ways of thinking. . . . The vindication of scientific methodology is based to a large extent upon an analysis and reflection of what we already do."[26]

The best antidote to the pseudoscientific thinking among apologists is a book written by Victor J. Stenger, a former professor of physics and astronomy. His *God and the Folly of Faith: The Incompatibility of Science and Religion* is the only book they will need to read on this topic.[27] There are others, of course, but if Stenger's book doesn't help them then they cannot be helped. He takes the reader through the history of science and faith, showing repeatedly what science has solved and what faith hasn't. "Science," he writes, "has earned our trust by its proven success. Religion has destroyed our trust by its repeated failures. Using the empirical method, science has eliminated smallpox, flown men to the moon, and discovered DNA. If science did not work, we wouldn't do it. Relying on faith, religion has brought us inquisitions, holy wars, and intolerance."[28]

Stenger writes in the hope that he can stem the tide of the growing distrust of science, especially in America, where believers do not trust science in areas that conflict with their holy books. If we want to compare the trustworthiness of science with the Bible, the Bible loses miserably over and over and over again. Stenger writes, "Science and religion are fundamentally incompatible because of their unequivocally opposed epistemologies—the separate assumptions they make concerning what we can know about the world."[29] It's a massive refutation of the claim that science is a religion or that science is based on faith.

Jerry Coyne, a biologist who teaches at the University of Chicago and wrote the book *Why Evolution Is True*,[30] tells us how science is justified:

We justify science rather than faith as a way of finding out stuff not on the basis of first principles, but on the basis of which method actually gives us reliable information about the universe. And by "reliable," I mean, methods that help us make verified predictions that advance our understanding of the world and produce practical consequences that aren't possible with other methods. Take a disease like smallpox. It was once regarded as manifestations of God's will or displeasure; indeed, inoculation was opposed on religious grounds—that to immunize people was to thwart God's will. You can't cure smallpox with such an attitude, or by praying for its disappearance. It was cured by scientific methods: the invention of inoculations, followed by the use of epidemiological methods to eradicate it completely. Scientific understanding advances with time; religious "ways of knowing," even by the admission of theologians, don't bring us any closer to the "truth" about God. We know not one iota more about the nature or character of God than we did in 1300, nor are we any closer to proving that a god exists![31]

But Hanna isn't finished with me yet. He opines, "Loftus . . . should recognize that only a relatively small number of scientific 'conclusions' are unrevisable. Not only have there been monumental shifts in scientific paradigms but there are continual revisions in numerous subparadigmatic theories. One must be exceedingly cautious about hanging his hat on a theory, for it may later be shown to be inadequate or false."[32] Is this cause for a little doubt? Yes, I suppose, in some extremely small way it could be. Despite his claims, though, new paradigms of science do not completely overthrow the previous ones, and there are countless scientific conclusions that seem impervious to revision. Should we doubt the present scientific consensus merely because science continues to advance? How can we? Does this cause him to doubt continental drift, the germ theory of disease, or the heliocentric view of our solar system, as but a few concrete examples among many? I don't see how it can unless Hanna can produce evidence that the results of science are wrong. He cannot punt to faith until such time as science overthrows its own conclusions with more evidence, and that's it. That some scientific results could be overthrown in the future is always a possibility. But probabilities are all that matter, and the science of the day sets the standard for what is probable.

Let me put this another way. There is a possibility that his God did a plethora of miracles in the past, as recorded in the pages of the Bible, and that his God will do a plethora of them again. After all, every claim, no matter how bizarre, has a nonzero probability to it. But in our present-day experience we don't see anything like the miracles recorded in the Bible. Should I therefore believe in a mere possibility even though my present-day experience tells me otherwise? I don't think so. While his God may have done a plethora of miracles and will do them again I have no other way to judge such a claim except from the probabilities of my own experience. It's all I have to go on. The evidence required to overturn my own daily experience must be massive. All Hanna has is the weak evidence of the distant past, which by comparison is no evidence at all, something I'll argue in a later chapter when it comes to the resurrection of Jesus.

Hanna also disputes my contention that the OTF is based upon science, especially the sciences of anthropology, neurology, and psychology. He says they offer "nothing more than banal generalizations."[33] This is an extremely low view of the science. Banal generalizations? I showed how science applied specifically to testing his Christian faith. I see nothing banal or trite about its conclusions. He argued:

> The OTF cannot be trusted if the only thing we should trust is the sciences, because the OTF itself is neither a scientific finding nor justifiable by any of the sciences. It includes more (e.g., logic, value judgments, and philosophical theories) than an appeal to the sciences, and it is based on an "ought" that cannot be derived from any of the sciences.[34]

I find this all to be reflective of a science denier, which is typical of people of faith. I have justified the OTF more than amply from science. Is he asking that I prove the science that supports the OTF before he can accept it? I think he just might be. So let me get this straight, if I cannot prove beyond a shadow of doubt that the sciences I utilized support the OTF then he can reject it? It's not good enough for me to say that science overwhelmingly supports the OTF? Why? Certainty is hard to come by in almost any area. Why does he require certainty here before he will doubt his own possibilities? No wonder I repeatedly say that believers must be shown that their faith is impossible before they will ever consider it to be improbable. Furthermore, to comment on his last claim, believers *ought* to take the OTF if they really want to know whether their faith is true, since no other method has worked before. If they don't want to know if their religious faith is true then they ought not to take it. It's as simple as that. The "ought" is a practical or pragmatic one.

From all I can tell, when it comes to science, apologists like Marshall and Hanna are impervious to reason. Their faith has blinded them from reasoning clearly about science. Unfortunately, they are not alone. But that's the nature of faith.

6

IS THE TEST SELF-DEFEATING?

Whereas I think I have already basically proven my case such that the next three chapters are unnecessary for most people, for many believers they are still needed. For people who are already sufficiently convinced, they will reveal the kind of gerrymandering required for continuing to object to the Outsider Test for Faith despite some really strong arguments and overwhelming evidence to the contrary.[1]

Believers who object that the OTF is *faulty* charge that there is an inherent self-defeating nature to it, or to how I argue for it. Believers who object that the OTF is *unfair* charge that it sneaks faith assumptions in the back door and/or unfairly targets religion. These objections overlap a bit, but they are both misguided and misinformed. Beginning in this chapter, and continuing through chapter 8, I will deal with these objections, none of which have any merit at all.

Many believers have objected that the skepticism required of the OTF is self-defeating. A self-defeating argument is one that is internally inconsistent and, therefore, by definition false. Christian professor Norman Geisler has written over sixty books in defense of the evangelical Christian faith, and he thinks this is the case with the OTF. In a review of the OTF he offers four objections that support his contention. The first three are based on the "You Too," or the *Tu quoque*, informal fallacy. It's difficult for me to conceive that Norman Geisler doesn't recognize this, since he cowrote a textbook on logic with Ronald M. Brooks.[2] For some reason he thinks that if he can turn the tables back on my arguments he won't have to think about what the RDVT and the RDPT have to do with his evangelical faith. He's skirting the whole issue to avoid what the facts force him to consider. Does Geisler agree with the facts or not? If so, he needs to provide some kind of reasonable response to them. He cannot merely say the OTF is self-defeating and leave it at that. He needs to deal with the facts and come up with a reasonable alternative to the OTF.

We'll see this momentarily, but for now let's just say why the "You Too" fallacy is a fallacy. It's because there are too many yous to too. One must "you too" everyone except the people who agree with you on the particular issue at hand. Geisler is saying that atheists have the exact same problems as he does, given the RDVT and the RDPT. But if we keep in mind the distinction between narrow atheists (who reject all other religions but their own) and wide atheists (who reject all religions) then all narrow atheists, who believe in other religions but reject Geisler's evangelical faith as outsiders, would be charged with this crime. He cannot just single out wide atheists (who reject all religions) for prosecution. He must charge all nonbelievers in his particular evangelical sect with this crime. What he would end up saying is that it is self-defeating for anyone to reject his particular sectarian religious faith. He would be saying that the informed skepticism of an outsider is self-defeating except when he does it. I don't know about you, but that's a very large claim to make, a claim of faith. I'm dealing with the facts as honestly as I can. Geisler is not. Geisler is special pleading his case, just like every other narrow atheist would in the face of the facts.

To be sure, the OTF does not even need to have been noticed and argued by me, an atheist. G. K. Chesterton used a version of the OTF to argue *for* his faith. Any theist could have used this test. So to turn this back on me, a wide atheist, is utterly misguided. We must *all* deal with the facts of religious diversity and dependency, all of us. Not to do so is to fail to argue as intellectually honest people. Nonetheless, let's look at his four objections.

1. Are Atheist Views Also Dependent on Culture?

Geisler argues: "If 'most of us most of the time come to our beliefs for a variety of reasons having little to do with empirical evidence and logical reasoning,' then can we not assume that Loftus came to his atheistic views the same way?"[3] This echoes what Christian philosopher Alvin Plantinga rhetorically asked: "If the pluralist had been born in Madagascar, or medieval France he probably wouldn't have been a pluralist. Does it follow that he shouldn't be a pluralist or that his pluralist beliefs are produced in him by an unreliable belief-producing process?"[4] He doubts it. In the same manner, Christian philosopher Victor Reppert says: "Imagine growing up on atheism in the Soviet Union. Couldn't I start thinking 'You know, if I hadn't grown up an atheist here in Moscow, if I had instead been born in Birmingham, Alabama, I would probably be a Southern Baptist instead of an atheist. How did I get to be so lucky as to realize that religion is the opiate of the masses, as I have been taught since childhood? I could have been born in Mexico as a Catholic or St. Paul as a Lutheran. Or in Mumbai as a Hindu.' On the other hand, he might think, 'somebody has to grow up believing the truth. Why couldn't it be me?'"[5]

There are several things wrong with these rhetorical questions. Like most people, I was raised to believe. I had to think my way out of it, and it took a personal crisis to force me to do what I should have been doing all along; that is, critically examining my culturally inherited faith. That's why I say doubt is the adult attitude. There are just too many ways to be brought up wrong, too many sociological factors that produce too many false ideas that are in turn justified by irrational thinking patterns. Because of this we must doubt what we were raised to accept as true when our accepted truths cannot be corroborated with sufficient evidence.

Utilizing Plato's allegory, I've already argued that we are all in a cultural cave. The difference that makes all the difference is that I know I'm in a cultural cave, and the only way out of it is to recognize the facts of the RDVT and the RDPT and then use the findings of science to guide us in assessing what is true. I think that it's extremely difficult to transcend our respective cultures because they provide us with the very eyes we use to see, as Eller argued. But precisely because we know from science that this is what cultures do to us, it's possible for us to transcend the culture we were raised in. *What we've learned is that we should be skeptical about that which we were led to believe even though we can't actually see anything about our beliefs to be skeptical about.*

Take for instance the case made by neurologist Sam Harris. He asserts that we don't have metaphysical free will. His conclusion comes directly as a result of science itself. Based on several scientific experiments, he argues that "free will is an illusion."[6] In one experiment, brain activity was observed in the motor cortex area of the brain 300 milliseconds before a person decided to move. In another one, where subjects were asked to press one of two buttons while watching a "clock" of randomized letters, it was observed that the brain regions containing information about which button would be pressed were active "a full 7–10 seconds before the decision was consciously made." Harris concludes, "One fact now seems indisputable: Some moments before you are aware of what you will do next—a time in which you subjectively appear to have complete freedom to behave however you please—your brain has already determined what you will do. You then become conscious of this 'decision' and believe that you are in the process of making it. . . . I, as the conscious witness of my experience, no more initiate events in my prefrontal cortex than I cause my heart to beat."[7]

I'm sure more testing needs to done, since these results are contested. I have no settled opinion on these experiments, since this isn't my focus or specialty. But let's grant for the moment Harris's case based upon the science. Can you hear Geisler opining that if Harris doesn't have free will then he cannot trust his own conclusion that he doesn't have free will? The obvious answer would be that there is evidence for what Harris argues. Why wouldn't others come to the same conclusion? It would be because they haven't seen the evidence yet. Their inputs would be different. Would that mean Harris has better inputs? Yes. Why? Because science is the only game in town. It works. It produces the goods. There isn't a better alternative. And I'm saying that science is the basis for the OTF. If we do not have metaphysical freedom and are essentially bound by the inputs of our births and cultures then the only way out of our cultural cave is to make use of the results of science. My claim is that this is exactly what I have done. My conclusions are not merely the result of my upbringing, even if I have no free will. They are based upon the better inputs of science.

Nonetheless, for the sake of argument, let's say I have become a nonbeliever of religion because of my own "accidents of birth," which includes everything I have experienced and learned. Then that's a sociological fact everyone must wrestle with when thinking about such matters. I am much more willing to accept the consequences of this than a great majority of religious believers, who are dogmatic about their faith. If this is the case, then we agree that what people think and believe is based upon when and where they're born. And so we should all be skeptics, people who demand sufficient evidence for what we will accept as true. And science offers us the only reasonable method for conducting this fact checking.

Do I then consider myself "lucky" to have been born in an era and in a place in which the rise of modern science and rational inquiry has progressed to the point where I have the necessary critical-thinking tools to argue for the OTF? Can I offer a "rational justification" for this luck? If not, why am I justified in advocating the OTF based upon this privileged position in time? In answer I would have to say yes, I was indeed lucky to have been born when and where I was born in order to offer the OTF as a critique of religious faith. We have experienced an explosive growth in scientific knowledge, which has in turn produced the modern world. Without the vast scientific knowledge bequeathed to us by Galileo, Isaac Newton, Charles Darwin, and Albert Einstein, along with a long list of others, I wouldn't know any differently than those who lived before the rise of modern science. So the rational justification for this luck is to be found in the solid advancement of science itself.

Science alone produces consistently excellent results that cannot be denied, and these results are continually retested for validity. My claim is that religious beliefs learned on our mama's knees are in a different category than the results of repeatable scientific experiments. This claim is both obvious and noncontroversial. We can personally do the experiments ourselves, and if we cannot do them all we can do enough of them to establish the consistency of the scientific method, which provides good evidence that where scientists have come to a consensus, those conclusions are established as facts. When it comes to religious faiths, there are no mutually agreed upon reliable tests to decide between them, and this also makes all the difference in the world. Even believers are not opposed to modern science anyway, as David Eller has argued.[8] They adopt its methods and conclusions in most areas, except in a few limited ones concerning their faith. So the question is why they adopt such a double standard with regard to science. Why do they accept the results of science the vast majority of the time but subsequently reject them with regard to their faith?

Besides, I'm only arguing that cultural conditions strongly influence us to believe what we were taught to believe. Such an admission doesn't undercut the reason for the OTF and the skeptical attitude that goes with it. If cultural factors overwhelmingly cause us to believe what we believe, then we should all become skeptics, which is something I can be quite comfortable with. And informed skepticism, or agnosticism, becomes the default attitude.

2. Should Skeptics Be Skeptical of Skepticism, Too?

Geisler argues next: "Further, if one should have the presumption of skepticism toward any belief system, especially his own, then why should Loftus not have the presumption of skepticism toward his own atheistic beliefs? The truth is that the outsider test is self-defeating since by it every agnostic should be agnostic about his own agnosticism and every skeptic would be skeptical of his own skepticism."[9]

I'll take issue with his statement that atheism is a belief system later. What Geisler fails to realize is that skepticism is a reasonable approach to truth claims. Skepticism is the hallmark of adults who thinks for themselves. I see nothing self-defeating about this at all. If after approaching a truth claim with skepticism it passes intellectual muster, then the skeptic has good reasons to accept it. And so the reasonable skeptic does indeed accept many claims to be true. No one can be skeptical of everything. It's just that we should be skeptical to some degree about everything we were taught to accept unless we can confirm it for ourselves. That confirmation process is not Cartesian though, and we cannot confirm everything we accept as true.

This is especially the case with extraordinary supernatural miracles claims, since they cannot all be true. Claims of miracles are used to support mutually exclusive religions in many cases, and each religion denies the essential miracle claims of different religions or sects. Evangelicals will dispute the miracle claims concerning the Virgin Mary at Lourdes, France. Catholics will dispute the various miracle claims by evangelical Pentecostals. Members of most Christian sects dispute the miracle claims of snake handlers in the Appalachian Mountains.

As an atheist, believers ask me if I am equally skeptical of my skepticism, whether I have subjected my nonbelief to nonbelief or my disbelief to disbelief. These questions express double negatives. When retranslated, they are asking me to abandon skepticism in favor of the faith of the gullible. The bottom line is that *skepticism* is a word used to describe doubt or disbelief. It doesn't by itself represent any ideas we've arrived at. It's merely a filter we use to strain out the bad ideas, leaving us with the good ones. We cannot be skeptical of that filter because there is no alternative except gullibly accepting anything and everything.

Skepticism is best expressed on a continuum, anyway. Some claims will warrant more skepticism than others. There are some claims about which we should be extremely skeptical ("I saw a pink elephant," "the

CIA is dogging my steps"), while others, on the opposite side, will not require much skepticism at all ("there is a material world," "if you drop a book it will fall to the ground," "George Washington was the first president of the United States of America").

I'm arguing that religious faiths warrant the same level of skepticism that other similar beliefs require, like beliefs in the elves of Iceland, the trolls of Norway, and the power of witches in Africa. They must all be subjected to the same levels of skepticism, given both the extraordinary nature of these claims and how some of these beliefs were adopted in the first place.

Consider some odd sort of phenomenon, and let's say there are only seven known theories to explain it, some more probable than others. Skeptics may deny outright three of them and weigh the others in the balance. Then they might conclude that one theory is the best explanation for the phenomenon. But they also acknowledge that they could be wrong, and even that there might appear an eighth theory to explain it that no one has thought of yet. Believers may only consider one particular theory, the one they were taught to believe, and they may pronounce it to be true beyond what the evidence calls for, even though there are other theories that have some degree of probability to them as well. True believers have an unusually high degree of confidence that they are correct, as Valerie Tarico has argued.[10] They may not even consider other theories at all, or, if they do, they do so to refute them. That's the difference. There is a huge difference between affirming a truth claim and denying one. The hard part, as someone quipped, isn't in smelling a rotten egg, it's in laying a good one. The OTF calls us to be egg smellers with the same level of critical olfactory senses that we use to detect other rotten religious eggs. The denial is the easy part, since there are many possible theories to explain a phenomenon. The hard part is to affirm which one of the theories is the correct one.

The skeptic has the more reasonable position, by far, and it simply is not self-defeating at all. There are just too many ways to be wrong. Simply trusting in what you were taught about religion is a method we know to be unreliable, especially since so many sincere people in the world believe differently. Let me make this personal. *Since you came to accept your faith in the same way that believers in other faith communities did, you should be skeptical that you've made the right choice, precisely because you are skeptical that they did.*

Professor Geisler is skeptical of evolution, which is based on so much well-founded evidence that it has convinced all the traditional mainline Protestant denominations to support or accept theistic evolution, including many Methodist, Lutheran, Episcopalian, Presbyterian, Unitarian, Congregationalist, United Church of Christ, American Baptist, and community churches. There is a growing number of people who might be considered evangelical in their thinking (or considered former evangelicals) who have embraced evolution, like Bruce Waltke, a former president of the Evangelical Theological Society; Dennis Venema, a biologist at Trinity Western University; Kenneth R. Miller, professor of biology at Brown University; Denis Lamoureux of St. Joseph's College, University of Alberta; N. T. Wright, Anglican Bishop of Durham; Francis Collins, director of the National Institutes of Health and director of the Human Genome Project; microbiologist Richard G. Colling of Olivet Nazarene University; Alister McGrath, professor of historical theology at the University of Oxford; and Timothy Keller, founding pastor of Redeemer Presbyterian Church in New York City. Then there are Ted Peters, Kenton Sparks, Conrad Hyers, Mark A. Noll, Keith B. Miller, Howard J. Van Till, Peter Enns, Darrel Falk, Randal Rauser, Victor Reppert, and a growing list of others.

The reason why these evangelical-inclined people are embracing the evidence is because of the evidence. As biologist Jerry Coyne says,

Every day, hundreds of observations and experiments pour into the hopper of the scientific literature. Many of them don't have much to do with evolution—they're observations about the details of physiology, biochemistry, development, and so on—but many of them do. And every fact that has something to do with evolution confirms its truth. Every fossil that we find, every DNA molecule that, we sequence, every organ system that we dissect, supports the idea that species evolved from common ancestors. Despite innumerable possible observations that could prove evolution untrue, we don't have a single one. We don't find mammals in Precambrian rocks, humans in the same layers as dinosaurs, or any other fossils out of evolutionary order. DNA sequencing supports the evolutionary relationships of species originally deduced from the fossil record. And, as natural selection predicts, we find no species with adaptations that only benefit a different species. We do find dead genes and vestigial organs, incomprehensible under the idea of special creation. Despite a million chances to be wrong, evolution always comes up right. That is as close as we can get to a scientific truth.[11]

My question to Geisler is, what is the basis for his type of skepticism? He's skeptical of evolution as well as the OTF and other things many people find compelling, but why? The basis for his skepticism needs to be justified. If we were to look at a faith-based skepticism we would find a history of errors. As John Shook explains:

Every generation of theologians who made careers predicting that science could never explain something had impressive stances right up until the time when science did explain it. Examples over the last ten centuries are assertions that science would never explain non-linear motion, the nature of the stars, magnetism, light, how organisms use air, the age of the earth, the diversity of life, and the transmission of life in reproduction. Upon these mysteries and many more, believers constructed elaborate philosophical and theological systems to do what they thought science could never do. But in time, physics, astronomy, chemistry, geology, biology, and genetics have satisfactorily explained all these things. The history of such metaphysical speculations trying to outmatch science is littered with exploded and abandoned systems of thought. . . . It has always been a bad bet to bet against science.[12]

But there is more. Edward Babinski has developed a list of things that believing Christians have been skeptical about. They have been skeptical of the innocence of cats and described them as "emissaries of the devil." Believers have been skeptical of forks, musical instruments in church, of the intelligence of women to vote, child labor laws, birth control including condoms, masturbating, anesthesia, inoculations and vaccinations, striped clothes, split breeches, short dresses, long hair (on men), short hair (on women), dancing, rock and roll music, playing cards, billiards or pool, going to the movies, watching TV, drinking, dishwashing, democracy, and working or playing on Sunday. Evangelicals in America for a long time were even skeptical of Christmas.[13] This type of skepticism based on religious faith should be rejected outright. The progress of modern society and science requires it. Only a skepticism based on scientific reasoning can be justified.

Furthermore, since his type of skepticism is based in his religious faith, let's ask Geisler if he's skeptical of his skepticism of Scientology or his skepticism of Islam or his skepticism of animism. And let's ask believers in these different faiths if they have the same type of skepticism toward other faiths; it will become crystal clear that they do. As I said, faith has no method. If faith is the foundation for truth then anything can be believed, and consequently anything can be doubted whenever necessary to maintain one's faith, even science itself.

Claiming to be skeptical of skepticism may make apologists like Geisler feel like they've made an important point, but this is nothing short of empty rhetoric. A skepticism based in scientific reasoning works. It works because it has the explanatory power to make sense of the relevant data with the fewest ad hoc hypotheses. Science solves problems, produces fruitful discussions, and can predict the future. Faith-based skepticism can do none of this.

3. Should Atheists Take the Outsider Test for Atheism, Too?

Geisler next argues: "One form of the outsider argument leads Loftus to claim 'believers are truly atheists with regard to all other religions but their own. Atheists just reject one more religion.' But can't theists use the same basic argument and reject atheism. In brief, atheists are unbelievers with regard to all beliefs other than their own. Why don't they just become unbelievers with regard to one more belief (namely, their atheism)?"[14] This reflects what several others have said when claiming that atheists should take something they call the "Outsider Test for Atheism."

But Geisler's argument is simply skirting the issue. Even if it's true that an atheist should take the OTF for atheism, this doesn't give believers any excuse to avoid taking the OTF themselves. The truth, however, is that atheism is not a set of beliefs. If atheism were such a beast then why do atheists disagree about most everything else except that no religious set of beliefs have made their case? The fact is that no one can predict in advance what atheists think about politics, economics, environmental issues, or social ethics. In fact, not much can be said about all atheists just because they're atheists. There are Marxists, Freudians, existentialists, and the "New Atheists" of our generation. There are even atheistic religions, like Buddhism, Jainism, Daoism, Confucianism, and yes, even a religionless Christian atheism. An atheist is a nonbeliever, just as Geisler is a nonbeliever with respect to reincarnation, Islam, Mormonism, Scientology, and the many dead gods and dead religions of the past. Everyone can understand this quite easily, since we all know what it's like not to believe something that doesn't have sufficient evidence for it.

Theists have developed a deeply flawed view of these things because they fail to make at least two simple but critical distinctions. The first is that no matter how you define religion it must include the belief in one or more supernatural forces or beings, and atheists don't have them. Atheism can probably best be defined as the view that there isn't sufficient evidence to believe in any one or more proposed gods, such as Zeus or Hathor or Odin or Baal or Yahweh. More to the point though is that someone cannot say atheism is a religion simply because it takes a position (or stance) on metaphysical issues. For by the same token, people could be considered Buddhists or Scientologists or Mormons by taking a position on those religions.

The second distinction is that my atheism is not a set of beliefs I hold to. Atheism for me is equivalent to a scientifically based skepticism. It's a filter I use to strain out well-founded beliefs from ill-founded ones. As such, whatever I examine and subsequently accept as true has already passed through my skeptical filter (to the best of my ability) and doesn't need to pass through it again (except as new information emerges). The truth is that atheists are almost always nontheists or nonbelievers because they are, first and foremost, skeptics. Consequently, atheists do not have a "viewpoint" subject to examination by an outsider test. We are already outsiders, nonbelievers. That's all there is to it.

So when Christians ask if I have taken the outsider test for my own "belief system," I simply say, "Yes, I have; that's why I'm a nonbeliever." Atheists do indeed take the OTF. That's why atheists are atheists in the first place. As wide atheists we do not think believers have produced enough evidence for their extraordinary supernatural claims. It's accepted by everyone that extraordinary claims demand extraordinary supporting evidence (that is, a lot of evidence), especially when the evidence should be there and is not. And religious claims are indeed extraordinary, since believers accept at least one thing more than the atheist does: that a god exists in addition to the universe. Such an additional claim requires more by way of justification due to Ockham's razor. By contrast, what extraordinary claims are wide atheists making? None that I know of. Wide atheism is a reasonable conclusion arrived at by the process of elimination due to taking the OTF. By finding the evidence lacking for the extraordinary claims that supernatural entities exist, the atheist simply concludes these claims are false.

Christian thinkers, in a desperate attempt to defend their faith with Orwellian double-speak, will claim that they are more skeptical than I am because they are skeptical of skeptical arguments—a "full-blown skepticism" as Christian scholar Thomas Talbott basically says. Their claim is that a true skeptic is open-minded about the miraculous, which in turn is supposed to leave room for their faith. But if this contorted epistemology is embraced, then "skepticism" becomes an utterly unjustified open-mindedness, leaving us with no way to test what to believe. Then other religionists can use this same epistemology to defend their own faiths, and so every claim that a witch flew through the night to have sex with the devil would be, technically speaking, on the boards. No, I am not open to that extraordinary claim without a lot of evidence to support it. With such an epistemology, we would have no way to determine which faith—or which wildly improbable claim—is true.

On top of this, if nonbelievers are to take the OTF, then Christians need to tell us what an outsider perspective for us would be. Is it the perspective of Catholicism, Greek Orthodoxy, Protestantism, or fundamentalism? Is it the perspective of a young-earth creationist? Is it the perspective of snake handlers, holy rollers, or the obnoxious and racist KKK? Is it that of a Satanist, a Scientologist, a Shintoist, or a Sikh? What about that of a Mormon, a militant Muslim, or a Moonie? How about a Jew, a Jain, or a Jehovah's Witness? Is the outside perspective that of a Wiccan or Haitian witchdoctor? The problem is that there just isn't a worthy religious contender from the countless religions that can be considered an outsider perspective for nonbelievers. This is not a fault with the OTF itself. It's the fault of religion.

In desperation to avoid facing the OTF themselves, Christians have actually asked me if I have ever examined modernism from a nonmodernist point of view. We might as well return to the prescientific, superstitious era of ancient peoples, but we can't. We can only go forward with the sciences. To the outsider, the sciences are the paragon of knowledge. That's why scientific inquiry replaced our former ways of knowing. Scientific knowledge has so decisively passed an outsider test that we must examine all religious faiths in light of it. Show us the math, and we will agree. Show us the experiment, and the argument will be over. Science, then, is the only way to keep us from deluding ourselves. So for a religious faith to pass the OTF the truth of its claims must be detectable by science. Period. If believers want to claim that science cannot detect God, then that means we cannot objectively know God at all.

The only true outsider position is an informed skepticism, or agnosticism, which I've called the default attitude. I see no reason why we shouldn't start by looking at the world as agnostics, for doing so helps us determine fact from fantasy. All metaphysical claims must pass the OTF before we should believe them. Atheists and agnostics share this skeptical common ground. It's just that atheists are willing to conclude that there are no supernatural beings or forces with enough assurance to say so. That's pretty much all there is to it. This isn't a radical doubt. It's the same doubt believers already embrace—just not when it comes to their own "faith." And I'm saying they're using a double standard, and that's wrong.

Does the OTF advocate a double standard, one for religious faiths and another one for atheists? No! Religious people have the double standard. Why do they evaluate other religious faiths with a level of skepticism that they do not apply to their own culturally inherited faith? Why do they use scientific reasoning to evaluate (and reject) other religions but not their own?

Okay then, but what about children raised as atheists in Sweden or Denmark? Were they enculturated by their parents in their cultures, too? Probably. Should these children test what they were taught by being scientifically informed? Of course, yes. Science produces repeatable evidence that convinces people all over the globe. But science also undermines faith-based reasoning.

4. There Is No Outsider Perspective for Insiders

Geisler finally argues: "Loftus' 'outsider test' is contrary to common sense. By it we could eliminate the credibility of any holocaust survivor's testimony because he was an 'insider.' But who better would know what happened than someone who went through it. Likewise, by this odd test one could deny his own self-existence since from an outsider's view his existence could be doubted or denied as an illusion. But what is more obvious and self-evident than one's own existence?"[15]

Geisler's Holocaust-survivor and self-existence analogies, like other ones that have been proposed, simply do not work. First and foremost, they rely on personal experiential testimony about ordinary claims within the bounds of our natural world rather than extraordinary claims of miracles, which are by definition supernaturally caused. When it comes to the natural world there is objective evidence available to confirm that insiders know what they know and have experienced what they have experienced (with rare exceptions). Extraordinary claims, however, need to be justified by a lot of objective supporting evidence.

Second, Geisler is attributing to the skeptical outsider a kind of radical skepticism that no reasonable person should accept. The OTF does not ask anyone to deny his or her personal experience within the natural world. The kind of skepticism required of the OTF is that of an informed skeptic, as I've argued. So Geisler is falsely attributing to the OTF a radical skepticism and then using that as a reason not to be skeptical at all. No wonder, as I have argued, defending the faith makes otherwise intelligent people look, well, stupid.

Third, Geisler's type of analogies concern one's own personal knowledge or experience. People who have personally experienced something are in a privileged position compared to others who didn't have that experience. So they have better evidence for what they think on such matters than others do. But the fact is that these analogies show that evidence, objective evidence, is what we all need before accepting something as true. And some of the things we accept as true have more evidence for them than other things. Even if the evidence of personal experience has greater weight for the person who has had the experience, the evidence of that person's public testimony cannot carry the same weight for others, especially when that testimony concerns an extraordinary, miraculous, nonrepeatable claim that goes against the processes of the natural world.

What Geisler is basically left with is a God who supposedly spoke privately to Moses, to many of the prophets of the Old Testament, and to Paul in various visions (2 Cor. 9, 12). Other believers claim that their God likewise spoke privately to Joseph Smith, or Muhammad, or David Koresh. Why does God always speak to people privately? Why do most people claim to know God in a private way? A private, subjective experience provides no objective evidence. Given that most people are delusional when they make such claims, it's probable that Geisler is delusional, too. The *only* reason evangelicals would buy into Geisler's argument is because they *need* to believe. Evangelicals would never entertain these same claims if Mormons or Muslims or Catholics or Jews made them. At best, a private, subjective experience proves nothing other than that a private, subjective experience took place. But they do not offer us a reason to think they come from any god. By the very nature of these experiences they cannot produce this evidence.

7

DOES THE TEST HAVE HIDDEN FAITH ASSUMPTIONS?

I have found that all the objections to the Outsider Test for Faith are either asking it to be something it is not or are based in a gross lack of understanding. The objection I'll deal with in this chapter is that all of us have a set of presuppositions based on faith that provide a framework for seeing the world as a whole, called a worldview. In other words, there isn't a presuppositionless way of looking at the world from an "outside" perspective. We all have faith commitments, it's claimed, so there cannot be an outsider's perspective.

Pastor and bestselling author Timothy Keller introduces us to this objection by arguing that "skeptics must learn to look for a type of faith hidden within their reasoning." "All doubts," he continues, "however skeptical and cynical they may seem, are really a set of alternative beliefs. You cannot doubt Belief A except from a position of faith in Belief B." Writing to skeptics, he proclaims: "The reason you doubt Christianity's Belief A is because you hold unprovable Belief B. Every doubt, therefore, is based on a leap of faith."[1] Keller's thesis is that "if you come to recognize the beliefs on which your doubts about Christianity are based, and if you seek as much proof for those beliefs as you seek from Christians—you will discover that your doubts are not as solid as they first appeared."[2] Skeptics have faith, he opines, whenever we accept something that is "unprovable," and all of us "have fundamental, unprovable faith commitments that we think are superior to those of others."[3]

While Keller is not writing directly in response to the OTF, what he says does have to do with it. Nonetheless, he agrees that it's "no longer sufficient to hold beliefs just because you inherited them."[4] That agreement is welcome. The problem is how he proposes to test his inherited beliefs.

What can we make of this kind of objection? Surely Keller doesn't mean to say that if we cannot be absolutely certain of something all we have left is blind faith, or that everything that is unprovable has an equal epistemological merit. Christians like him want to claim that skeptics have unproven beliefs, and then they try to drive a whole truckload of Christian assumptions and beliefs through that small crevice. If that's what he's doing, then Mormons and Muslims could write the same things he did and then drive their own truckload of assumptions and beliefs through that small crevice. We would then be in no better position to judge between competing faiths, which is the basic problem the OTF addresses. What I'm proposing with the OTF is a way to distinguish what we should accept from what we should not. I'm arguing that there isn't a better test when it comes to religious beliefs. So again, what better test is there?

THE DEMON, MATRIX, MATERIAL WORLD, AND DREAM POSSIBILITIES

The bottom line is that I do not accept Keller's definition of faith. He manipulates the debate by using a language game in his favor. I reject his game. I know as sure as I can know anything that there is a material world and that I can reasonably trust my senses. I conclude that the scientific method is our only sure way for assessing truth claims. These things I know to be the case.

Christian philosopher Alvin Plantinga argues that there are countless things we have proper warrant to believe without proof or evidence, such as the existence of other minds; the continuous existence of the world, even when we don't perceive it; that we have been alive for more than twenty-four hours; that the past really happened; that we aren't just brains in a mad scientist's vat; that we can trust our minds and our senses about the universe; that cause and effect are laws of nature; that nature is ordered, uniform, and intelligible; and so on. So Plantinga rhetorically asks why the belief in God is in a different category that needs evidence for it.

Apologist and philosopher William Lane Craig uses some conjectures to argue as Plantinga does. Dr. Craig writes:

> Most of our beliefs cannot be evidentially justified. Take, for example, the belief that the world was not created five minutes ago with built-in memory traces, food in our stomachs from meals we never really ate, and other appearances of age. Or the belief that the external world around us is real rather than a computer-generated virtual reality. Anyone who has seen a film like *The Matrix* realizes that the person living in such a virtual reality has no evidence that he is not in such an illusory world. But surely we're rational in believing that the world around us is real and has existed longer than five minutes, even though we have no evidence for this. . . . Many of the things we know are not based on evidence. So why must belief in God be so based?[5]

Randal Rauser does the same thing:

> Our sensory experience leads us very naturally to believe in the external world. So it is for the Christian's experience of God. To believe in God is not some arbitrary, top-down explanation we force onto life. Rather, like our experience of matter, it's a natural, ground-level description of our experience of the world. . . . To put it another way, belief in the external world of matter can be believed rationally without evidence or reasoning. My challenge to you is to explain why belief in the external world is properly basic but belief in God cannot be.[6]

I have come to the conclusion that all these scenarios are not good defeaters of the demand for sufficient evidence. Take for instance the Cartesian demon hypothesis. Descartes conjectured that there could be an evil demon that deceives us about everything we think is true, and consequently there would be no evidence that could lead us to think otherwise. Is the evil demon hypothesis possible? Yes. Is it probable? Not by a long shot. Descartes used his extreme method of hypothetical doubt like a massive sword. The mere possibility that there is such a demon was enough to cast doubt on his knowledge about the material world. But why must we base what we think on a mere possibility? Once again, probability is all that matters. There is no reason and no evidence to suppose that such a being exists. If looking for and not finding such a demon does not constitute grounds for denying his existence, then looking for and not finding the elves of Iceland, the trolls of Norway, the Loch Ness monster, the abominable snowman, bigfoot, the tooth fairy, Santa Claus, satyrs, ghosts, goblins, unicorns, mermaids, or hobbits does not constitute grounds for denying their existence either. Even if such a demon exists I should still conclude what I do because of the lack of evidence.

Michael Martin argues that if there is an evil demon that deceives us, then we would have to say that no belief is rational, and as such "it would seem to entail that we could never be justified in thinking that it was."[7] Such a possibility undercuts any hope of knowing anything at all, and that's a pill no reasonable person should swallow. Martin adds that it's more reasonable to think we can come to correct conclusions based on the evidence than that such an evil demon exists, because it's a much simpler view without adding entities unnecessarily (Ockham's razor), and he argues that there is no reason to accept the demon possibility because it is unfalsifiable. He also argues that the demon hypothesis cannot explain the survival of the human race, since in order to survive in this world human beings have needed to act on correct conclusions derived from the world around us. So this is strong evidence that we are not being deceived by that demon.

Descartes searched for certain knowledge, a goal that was long ago abandoned by most philosophers. But a lack of certainty does little to undercut the need for sufficient evidence before accepting a proposition about the nature of our experience in this world. All we need to do is (1) think inductively rather than deductively, (2) think exclusively in terms of probabilities, and (3) understand that when speaking of sufficient evidence what is meant is evidence plus reasoning based on that evidence. The requirement for sufficient evidence does not come from a deductive argument stemming from the first principles of philosophy. No, it comes by means of an inductive argument based on the results of science. So an inductive argument that leads to a probable conclusion about the need for sufficient evidence cannot be self-defeating. This conclusion might be wrong, as improbable as that is, but it's not self-defeating. If, in addition, we think exclusively in terms of probabilities rather than possibilities, we won't need to achieve certainty with regard to any proposition either. A good argument based on some evidence is good enough. This means that if we understand the requirement for sufficient evidence is based on evidence plus reasoning based on that evidence, there can be no objection to this requirement.

Who in their right mind would not want sufficient evidence for what they accept as true? The evidence for this requirement can be found everywhere, leading us to an exceedingly probable conclusion. Again, probability is all that matters. Christians cannot slip in the mere possibility that there are things they can believe without sufficient evidence when the total weight of evidence is against such a bald-faced assertion. We need only look to the alternative proposition that people are within their epistemic rights to believe without sufficient evidence in any other area. That's a recipe for disaster.

What about the possibility seen in the blockbuster movie *The Matrix*? The possibility that I'm presently living in a virtual, matrix world, rather than in the real world, cannot be taken seriously by any intelligent person. The story is extremely implausible. I see no reason why there would be any knowledge of the matrix by people living in it, since the matrix determines all their experiences. So how could taking a virtual red pill while in the matrix get someone out of it and into the real world in the first place? As far as Neo, the protagonist in *The Matrix*, knows, the red pill could have been nothing more than a hallucinogenic drug. And even if Neo came to believe a real world lies beyond his own virtual, matrix world, how could he know that the so-called real world isn't just another matrix beyond the one he experiences? Neo would have no good reason for concluding that he knows which world is the *really* real world at that point. The *really* real world could be beyond the one he experienced after taking the red pill, or beyond that one, or beyond that one, and so forth. If all we need to be concerned with is what is possible rather than what is probable we couldn't claim to know anything at all. We would end up as epistemological solipsists. So, as David Mitsuo Nixon has argued with respect to the matrix, "The proper response to someone's telling me that my belief *could* be false is, 'So what?' It's not *possibility* that matters, it's *probability*. So until you give me a good reason to think that my belief is not just *possibly* false, but *probably* false, I'm not changing anything about what I believe or what I think I know."[8]

In fact, believing we're in a matrix would be a much closer parallel for believing in God than Craig may realize. Craig is actually giving us a reason to *doubt* an ad hoc, unevidenced assumption like God. For if it's silly to believe in the matrix, it should be silly to believe in God. As I've argued before, Christians repeatedly retreat to the position that what they believe is "possible" or "not impossible." A possibility is not a probability. The inference does not follow. It's a huge non sequitur.

These questions are the stock-in-trade of Western philosophers who want to explore the boundaries of knowledge. But ask them if they seriously entertain them and they will almost to a person say no.

Take as another example the existence of a material world. Christian philosopher Thomas Talbott takes issue with the OTF because he thinks I would have no basis for thinking there is one based on it.[9] I find it amazing that philosophers propose things that they do not accept in order to criticize the OTF. I mean, really, for all of Talbott's verbosity he thinks, like I do, that there is a material world. I taught philosophy. I know what it's like to argue that there isn't a material world. I did it every semester whenever I taught my introduction to philosophy class. It was fun to do. It takes students by surprise as they struggle to find reasons why they think otherwise. It was, to use Talbott's own phrase, "a pedagogical device."[10] Apparently then, Talbott is stuck in a pedagogical mode, which he states as follows:

> As any good teacher knows, a less than fully accurate statement will sometimes reveal more to beginning students, or do more to nudge them in the right direction, than a fully accurate statement will when the latter would be unintelligible to them. As I have elsewhere put it: "Like many teachers, I often find myself saying things to beginning students that I would prefer them to reinterpret (perhaps even to discard) as they mature into more advanced students."[11]

Being pedagogical just won't do here. Either Talbott thinks there is a material world or he does not. If he does, then why bother with this objection at all? Christian philosopher Mark Hanna thinks there is a contradiction in my reasoning: "It is patently contradictory to say, on the one hand, as Loftus does, that the scientific method is our 'only' sure way for assessing truth claims and to say, on the other hand, that we know certain things, such as the existence of a material world and the essential reliability of our senses, which are not the results but the pre-requirements of implanting 'the scientific method.'"[12]

My reasons for thinking there is a material world are similar to Dr. Samuel Johnson's kicking a stone and declaring he had refuted George Berkeley's idealism. They are also similar to G. E. Moore's assertion that he's more assured he has a pencil in his hand than that the skeptical arguments to the contrary are correct.[13] There are plenty of other reasons. One of them is simply that it makes no difference at all if there isn't a physical universe. There ought to be some sort of difference between propositions if we are to make sense of them as different propositions. Ockham's razor does the requisite work after acknowledging this. Another reason is science itself. How can we conceive of it working without a materially existing world?

Why do we need brains, a liver, lungs, and organs of any kind? Why does surgery save us from death if these organs are not real? How does a doctor prescribe a pill to heal us if there is no material body? What then causes us to be healed if the pill doesn't do it? Where's the mechanism for producing a healing effect from a nonphysical cause? To argue there is a spiritual reality that heals us means we do not need to take the prescribed pill at all. Why not just pray instead? Why bother with medicine or surgery at all?

Additionally, why do I have the experience of moving from place to place? Who is moving if I am not the one doing this? How can there be a change of scenery if I do not have a physical body that moves? And who or what guarantees that when I step outside my house day after day the house has the same physical characteristics when I return? Why should our experience be the same every time we look at a given object unless there really is a physical object and a physical world?

The burden of proof is therefore laid squarely on the back of anyone who denies this. But there is no way anyone can deny a material world, since one must presuppose it for the sake of the arguments. After all, these arguments require physical evidence of some kind, so where are we supposed to find this physical evidence if it doesn't exist? Why not just dispense with the physical evidence altogether and simply assert that an external material universe does not exist, since if this is the case, the physical evidence is irrelevant?

Even scientists who argue for a holographic universe, who think our experience is nothing but a hologram, do not deny that a physical universe exists, because they base their conclusions on the physical evidence. How is it possible to argue there is no material world from evidence that cannot exist without a material world? This would be contradictory. There must be some physical evidence for this conclusion. And if there is evidence, then the material world—at least some kind of material world—does exist. It may not be like the one we experience, but it still would exist.

How would such a nonmaterial idealist be able to exclude the possibility that there is a totally different kind of reality beyond the spiritual one, or another reality beyond that one, and so forth? That's why Ockham's razor stops these kinds of questions with the simplest explanation rather than adding on entities endlessly. The simplest explanation is that a physical universe of some kind exists.

Talbott argues that

> with respect to his [Loftus's] belief in an external physical reality, the perspective of an outsider would be that of many Hindus, an idealist, a panpsychist, a panentheist, or perhaps even a philo-sophical skeptic such as David Hume. So if Loftus should subject his own belief in an external physical reality to the Outsider Test, then he would need to examine that belief at least as skeptically as an idealist or some other outsider might examine it. And yet, one searches in vain for the slightest hint of doubt on his part or even for a willingness to examine an outsider argument against physical realism (of which there are many).[14]

I think I have dispelled this criticism. It is utterly without foundation. If he thinks for one moment that, as an outsider, I must take an outsider stance to an informed skepticism based in science and reason, then he needs to show why the science I base my argument on is faulty and then propose an alternative that can solve the problem of religious diversity better than the OTF. The bottom line is that idealism is religious in nature. It seems to me the only people who argue that there is no material world are believers, like George Berkeley, who used this as an argument to God's existence. He used it in an attempt to solve the mind/brain problem, which would otherwise undercut his religious faith, by denying the existence of brains. Only religious people would think this, and only a philosopher would use this to make an argument against the OTF, which is one reason so many people, mostly scientists, eschew philosophy as vacuous.

Talbott also argues that because David Hume was looking for and did not find certainty when it came to a material universe, I should likewise be skeptical that there is a material world. But Talbott should know that the quest for certainty died soon after Hume. Certainty is an unattainable goal. To Talbott or anyone else who may suggest that I might possibility be wrong about a material world, all I can say is, so what? Probability is the only thing that matters. Until he gives me a reason to think I am probably wrong, I'm not changing anything I think. We're always talking about probabilities, not certainties. And we're not in his introduction to philosophy class either. He should own up to what he really thinks on this issue. I have provided my reasons, just as I did about the matrix and demon hypotheses. That there is a material world passes the outsider test of an informed skepticism.

Consider next the reasons to think the world has existed for more than five minutes. We have memories that are usually correct. We know people with whom we can reminisce. We have baby pictures of ourselves and old shoes, clothes, and memorabilia from previous years. There are artifacts from previous eras, too, including archaeo-logical evidence of our ancient past. There are rock formations that show the earth to be a few billion years old. We also have scientific evidence for the Big Bang. That the world has existed longer than five minutes is extremely probable. To someone who claims differ-ently, I merely say again, so what? Possibility does not matter. No wonder I think scientifically uniformed philosophy is of little use. No wonder it has little or no respect among real scientists.

As one last example, when it comes to the question of whether I'm dreaming right now, Norman Malcolm, in his book *Dreaming*, and Bernard Williams, in his book *Descartes*, have made the case that there is a difference between dreams and our waking experience.[15] The fact that we can distinguish between them presupposes that we are aware of both states as well as the differences between them. It's only from the perspective of being awake that we can explain our dreams. Hence we can only make sense of this distinction if we are sometimes awake. And since this is the case, all our experiences throughout our entire lives cannot be made up merely of a sequence of dreams. I still may not know exactly when I'm dreaming, but it's highly probable that I'm awake right now as I type these words and as I read over them. One thing I have personally found is that when it comes to reading a document of any kind I cannot do so in my dreams. I suspect it's because my dreaming mind has to simultaneously write whatever it is I'm reading in a dream, and writing is hard mental work, the kind that doesn't take place on the spur of the moment even when I'm awake. But when I'm awake I can read through a whole book. So I can know I'm awake whenever I'm reading a book.

Furthermore, I can have conversations with people during my waking hours that can be the basis for subsequent conversations the next day, after I've slept and subsequently risen from bed. I don't fall asleep while eating dinner and I don't wake up while running a race. I fall asleep in bed and wake up in the same bed I laid down in, except if I sleepwalk or someone picks me up and carries me to another bed while I'm sleeping. I sometimes wake up from dreams a couple of times per night. But I always wake up in the same bed in which I fell asleep. In my dreams I can have the experience of seeing or doing things that go against the laws of nature, like having the superhuman power of flight or seeing something transformed into something else. The best explanation is that we know when we are awake, even if our dreams can fool us.

I live my life based on short-term memories. If I were to doubt them and habitually fail to arrive for appointments I've made the previous day, I would fail in life, groping without a compass through a haphazard dream world of random choices. I would be an unreliable person. Life demands that I trust my short-term memories, that I know I am not now dreaming, that I arrive at appointments I made the previous day while awake. I should do so even if I am dreaming right now. It doesn't change a thing if I am. My point is that faith has nothing to do with this reasoning process. Probabilities are all that matter.

What Christian apologists are doing with all these bizarre scenarios, besides helping us to think about the limits of knowledge, is leveling the playing field between what they claim to know on faith and what we know based on experiencing the natural world.

So David Eller has rightly argued that "knowing is not believing." He claims that if believers "can drag down real knowledge to their level and erase any distinctions between the true and the false, the known and the merely felt or believed or guessed, they can rest comfortably in their own undeserved self-certainty." According to him, "knowledge is about reason" while "belief is about faith." He says, "The two are logically and psychologically utterly different and even incompatible."[16] He simply refuses to play this religious language game.

WHAT ABOUT WHOLE WORLDVIEWS?

Victor Reppert asks me, "Well, why an outsider test for faith as opposed to an outsider test for world-views."[17] Others have also argued for this, such as Christian blogger Rados Miksa.[18] He reformulates my OTF along the lines of an Outsider Test for Worldviews by substituting the word *worldview(s)* in place of *religious faiths*: "The best and probably only way to rationally test one's culturally adopted *worldview* is from the perspective of an outsider with the same level of reasonable skepticism believers already use to examine the other *worldviews* they reject. This expresses the Outsider Test for *Worldviews* (OTW)." Then he proceeds to argue why worldviews need to be subjected to the skepticism of an outsider for some of the same reasons that religious faiths should. He does this in hopes of showing that there can be no outsider perspective for worldviews, since we all have one and they are all based on faith. He argues that even if there were such an outsider perspective, my own particular worldview would not survive the skepticism of the OTW, since it's too extreme. So if the OTW is impossible therefore so is the OTF.

Miksa, like other apologists, is trying to escape taking the OTF. As I mentioned in chapter 6 with regard to Norman Geisler, apologists attribute to it an extreme form of skepticism that no one can possibly have and then use that misunderstanding as an excuse not to be skeptical at all. Miksa extends the OTF to the OTW with the same goal. Since the OTW is impossible to do, as he claims, so is the OTF. He's asking us to imagine a total outsider, or a super outsider, perhaps a differently evolved alien from another planet, as if "Outsiderness" represents a nonhuman Platonic substance.

Miksa and Reppert apparently think worldviews are total systems of knowledge (or belief) that are based on or even synonymous with our prior religious faith commitments. If so, we cannot isolate and subject to critical analysis our religious faith commitments without also subjecting our whole worldview to the same analysis. Miksa and Reppert apparently think that religious faiths are equivalent in every relevant sense to worldviews such that what we think about metaphysics, economics, politics, epistemology, science, law, and art is totally dependent on them. Perhaps they think that a change of one's religious faith results in a totally different worldview that results in an overturning of one's positions on every issue, every subject, to some significant degree. Perhaps they think theology is the queen of the sciences, the paragon of knowledge, and final judge of everything else we think is true, which is an outmoded and antiquated idea, given the demonstrated efficacy of modern science. This seems to lie behind such an objection, since we probably cannot doubt everything we know or think we know. It's doubtful that even Descartes did that, although we might be able to do so quite extensively.

So what is a worldview? A worldview is our total view of the world, including everything we know or think we know about everything, based on the totality of our experiences and what lessons we have learned from them. It is not merely one's religious faith. It is a total system of thought that is all-encompassing. Everyone has one, and they are all different by degrees. So there are probably as many worldviews as there are people. They also change incrementally with every new experience and lesson learned. With each change of opinion we adopt a slightly different worldview. We do not switch from one whole worldview to another one all at once. They change every day, incrementally.

Christian philosopher James Sire, in his book *The Universe Next*

Door, makes a worldview out to be a set of specific, somewhat arbitrary assumptions about the world. He then proceeds to define them as having to do with a list of notions about God, man, ethics, history, death, and so forth.[19] Norman Geisler and William D. Watkins, in their book *Worlds Apart*, do the same thing.[20] However, Brian Walsh and J. Richard Middleton, in their book *The Transforming Vision*, show this understanding to be an utterly incomplete view. Walsh and Middleton are Christians who show that one's worldview affects everything, including education, healthcare, legal institutions, environmental concerns, arts, family, religious institutions, and politics. To a large extent, worldviews are also culturally shared. In each different culture, the authors tell us, "we can observe different modes of recreation, different sports, transportation and eating habits. Each culture develops unique artistic and musical life."[21] Culturally held worldviews even affect how we bathe our babies. They contrast how Japanese and Canadian babies are bathed by their mothers. While the Japanese rituals reflect gentleness, obedience, submission, and dependence by the closeness of the parent to the child, the Canadian rituals reflect a distance between mother and child because the child is on his or her own. As such, Canadian bathing of babies places an emphasis "on independence, assertiveness and the development of power."[22]

When it comes to religion within a worldview, Ninian Smart, a pioneer in the field of secular religious studies, provides an important analysis. As a first principle he states that "civilizations are importantly interwoven" with religions. "Whether you believe them or not is beside the point. Western culture is bound up with Catholicism and Protestantism; Sri Lankan civilization with Buddhism; the modern West with humanism; the Middle East with Islam; Russia with Orthodoxy, India with Hinduism, and so on. These are facts."[23] Professor Eller explains that whereas the Christian faith can Christianize cultural worldviews, it is in turn affected by them. He argues that "cultural integration is a two-way street: culture adapts to and is suffused with religion, but religion also adapts to and is suffused with culture. In other words, not only does religion replicate itself through the many parts of culture, but culture replicates itself through the religion, recasting a religion like Christianity in the culture's own image."[24] Religion always embeds itself into culture, and as it does, a culture embeds itself within religion. For most people, religion is an extremely important part of their cultural worldview. That's why Eller says, "Christians, like other religionists, are not so much convinced by arguments and proofs as colonized by assumptions and premises. As a form of culture, it seems self-evident to them; they are not so much indoctrinated as enculturated."[25] Since Christianity can take on different cultural forms depending on the culture it embeds itself in, cultural worldviews are larger and more encompassing than religious faiths and creeds. And since individually held worldviews are not always in complete agreement with dominant socially constructed cultures, individual worldviews are larger and more encompassing than cultural worldviews.

Even believers within the same religious culture will have different worldviews depending on which religious sect they were raised in; how old they are; their gender, race, and sexual orientation; their social status in life; how much wealth they have; and their own individual experiences in life. Can we explain why people of different color can be Christians and yet have different attitudes when it comes to politics? Does the fact that one is a Christian woman mean she will think like a Christian man? Does a Christian from New York City see the world exactly like a Christian from Mexico? H. Richard Niebuhr's book *Christ and Culture* even shows that there are different Christian responses to cultures stemming from the New Testament itself.[26]

Christians have had a wide variety of opinions about a wide variety of issues down through the centuries, and they continue to have widely divergent opinions. Bare-bones creeds like the Apostles' Creed or the Nicene Creed are not in themselves expressions of a worldview. They say little about how Christians should interpret those creeds, how Christians should think about economic and political issues outside of those creeds, and how Christians should behave based on those creeds. Christians do not all share the same opinions on significant issues, yet even with their divergent individual views, they all still claim to be, or still are, Christians. Worldviews must therefore be larger and more encompassing than a mere identification with the Christian faith. There are many Christian worldviews, many Christianities, not just one. Christians arbitrarily select a set of "essential" doctrinal issues and then go on to say that anyone who agrees on them shares the same worldview, and that's it. Other religious believers could arbitrarily select a different set of "essential" doctrinal issues, if they select any at all, and claim that represents a worldview, too.

So while we probably cannot subject whole worldviews to the OTW as complete outsiders, we can subject certain beliefs, traditions, rituals, values, and laws to critical analysis separately, one at a time. We do it all the time. This is what the OTF seeks to do with regard to a wide diversity of religious faiths. Can we really extract a religion from a cultural worldview in order to do this? I see no reason why not, even though doing so may require extracting for examination a large set of ideas within one's worldview.

I see no reason why we must doubt everything we think is true at the same time in order to doubt one item within our total worldview. Take for instance questions concerning whether beauty is in the eye of the beholder, or questions concerning epistemology, or questions about the correct basis for ethical theory. Resolving those questions might call into question a lot of what we think, but they wouldn't require doubting everything. How would a resolution of these issues affect what we think about economic questions, like capitalism versus socialism, poverty, discrimination, wealth, inequality, work, or the causes of unemployment? How would a resolution of these issues affect what we think about homosexuality, feminism, racism, slavery, human rights, overpopulation, contraception, cloning, pornography, prostitution, adultery, marriage and divorce, abortion, euthanasia, suicide, welfare, war, the environment, capital punishment, and a host of other subjects? Depending on how those questions are resolved, it might affect a great deal of what we think in some minimal ways, but there is no reason why we cannot isolate and subject for critical analysis one idea that makes up our total worldview.

This is being done in various places in Europe, most notably in Sweden, Denmark, and England, without a loss of other aspects of culture. David Perfect's "Religion or Belief," a paper distributed by the *Equality and Human Rights Commission,* has some interesting statistics on the decline of religion in England.[27] It shows that 55.3 percent of respondents between the ages of eighteen and twenty-five claim to have "no religion" while only 22.1 percent of respondents sixty-five and older claim to have "no religion." And, while someone might argue that people simply become more religious as they get older, the declining rates of religiousness and church attendance over the past few decades says that it's a real decline—34.4 percent of all respondents in 1985 claimed no religion while 43.4 percent of all respondents in 2008 claimed no religion. The paper also shows that between 1990 and 2008 the percentage of people who "believe and always have" declined. During the same period, the percentage of those who "don't believe and did before" increased. Meanwhile, the percentage of those who "don't believe and never have" also increased. The percentage of those who "believe and didn't before" has remained steady, accounting for less than 6 percent of total poll respondents. The numbers show that by 2008 people were three times more likely to say that they "don't believe and did before" than to say that they "believe, but didn't before." And, while this is taking place, there are a great many cultural traditions and ideas that remain the same, allowing England to continue to be basically the same society.

Nonetheless, if we want to subject whole worldviews to critical analysis it takes something different than the OTW, but we can do this. The only proper way to analyze whole worldviews is to become anthropological or phenomenological in our "worldview analysis" by adopting what Ninian Smart describes as "informed empathy." This is best done by the "suspension of our own beliefs." Smart says, "We should understand . . . foreign beliefs and values, not imposing our own beliefs and judgments on the other. . . . It is like trying to understand cricket through base-

ball: 'Is that guy the pitcher?' Yes, but the rules are quite different."[28]
Worldview analysis of this kind "conveys a sense of attempted objectivity, and indeed it is for that reason a relatively modern phenomenon
... since the 1960s."[29] The first thing to go when adopting Smart's
approach to worldview analysis is the idea that there is one true religion,
and anthropology professor Eller tells us why:

> Nothing is more destructive to religion than other religions; it is
> like meeting one's own anti-matter twin ... other religions rep-
> resent alternatives to one's own religion: other people believe in
> them just as fervently as we do, and they live their lives just as suc-
> cessfully as we do ... the diversity of religions forces us to see reli-
> gion as a culturally relative phenomenon; different groups have
> different religions that appear adapted to their unique social and
> even environmental conditions. But if their religion is relative, then
> why is ours not?"[30]

WHAT ABOUT EPISTEMIC CONSERVATISM?

Victor Reppert has argued that "a certain natural conservatism with
respect to changing our minds about matters of worldview, or any
other issue for that matter, is both natural and rational."[31] I understand
this. We do have a propensity to conserve rather than overthrow what
we have come to accept as true. What I don't understand is what
C. S. Lewis scholar Steve Lovell said: "If I suspend belief in all those
things which 'I wouldn't believe if I weren't a Christian' then ... I'll
be left with almost nothing."[32] Lovell argues that he cannot eject his
religious faith from his whole worldview and start over from scratch.
All that anyone can expect of him, he says, is to change one plank at
a time in his boat of beliefs. This process is naturally and rationally
conservative with respect to what we know or think we know. The
boat analogy on which he relies was first used by philosopher Otto
Neurath:

Imagine sailors, who, far out at sea, transform the shape of their clumsy vessel from a more circular to a more fishlike one. They make use of some drifting timber, besides the timber of the old structure, to modify the skeleton and the hull of their vessel. But they cannot put the ship in dock in order to start from scratch. During their work they stay on the old structure and deal with heavy gales and thundering waves. In transforming their ship they take care that dangerous leakages do not occur. A new ship grows out of the old one, step by step—and while they are still building, the sailors may already be thinking of a new structure, and they will not always agree with one another. The whole business will go on in a way that we cannot even anticipate today. That is our fate.[33]

Since the OTF is emphatically not about examining whole worldviews, it doesn't ask that believers question everything they think is true at the same time. So Neurath's boat analogy is a perfect one despite the fact that Reppert and Lovell brought it up. The OTF is about questioning one's religious faith, representing just one plank in a boat of beliefs, a big one, but just one. If believers think the OTF is asking them to question everything at the same time, they're dead wrong. Worldviews are larger than religious faiths. Believers may abandon their religious faith without it affecting the rest of what they accept from their culture. When I left the Christian faith I didn't leave my culture, language, or most of the rest of what my culture led me to think about history, democracy, geography, science, love, friendship, work, or what makes me happy. I am a testament to the fact that you can reject your religious faith and retain most everything else you accept from your cultural upbringing. So the OTF isn't asking anyone to do the impossible.

I certainly agree then that accepting epistemic conservatism is natural with respect to not wanting to change one's handed-down traditions, values, and ideas. It's so natural that people will go to some extreme lengths to defend them. But they should accept what they were led to conclude *only* if those conclusions have been derived by a highly reliable method for grasping the truth. Only then is epistemic conservatism warranted. When handed-down traditions, values, and ideas have not been derived by a reliable method, epistemic conservatism has no demonstrable warrant. In short, religious traditions that have never passed any measure of the OTF deserve no conservative respect at all. I see nothing about this conservatism that is justified at all.

8
DOES THE TEST UNFAIRLY TARGET RELIGION?

This type of objection first originated with Christian philosopher Victor Reppert during our interactions in the blog world. He claims it would be cheating "to have a test and just mark our religious beliefs as the beliefs to be tested,"[1] so he offered some other examples that I might consider testing in the same way. Reppert objected that since we were brought up in the West to accept a material world, we should test this conclusion with an outsider test, too. I'll call this the *Outsider Test for Ideas* (OTI). After all, if someone born in India, who was brought up believing the world of experience is *maya*, or an illusion, should take the OTI, then why shouldn't Westerners do likewise? In the previous chapter I defended the notion that there is a material world, not from faith but from scientific reasoning. Not only was I taught to think there is a material world, I experience it daily. In fact, to deny the existence of a material world would require denying everything I personally experience throughout every single day of my life. And denying this would deny science—the very thing that has produced the modern world. I think it's a categorical mistake to equate the nonverifiable religious view that there is no material world with the scientific view that there is one. The scientific method and the consensus findings of scientific inquiry have already passed the OTI. Religious people who deny a material sensory world must subject their beliefs to the OTI, since saying there is a material world that causes our experiences is not an extraordinary claim. But denying it is. And the OTI, just like the OTF, is a test for extraordinary religious claims.

WHAT ABOUT AN ANTI-RAPE ETHIC?

Reppert further asks whether any moral and political beliefs would survive an outsider test: "I think that rape is wrong. If I had been brought up in a certain culture, I'm told, I would believe that rape is okay if you do it in the evening, because a woman's place is at home under her husband's protection, and if she is gone she's asking for it. So my belief that rape is wrong flunks the outsider test."[2]

Seemingly without so much as thinking about it Reppert claims an anti-rape ethic would flunk the test. My argument is that when adults examine any belief we learned on Mama's knees we should do so with the informed skepticism of outsiders. But I know of no informed skeptical person in today's world who would ever want to morally justify rape. Beliefs like the acceptability of rape (and honor killings) are based on religious faiths and ancient texts. Since the nature and origin of such beliefs are religious, they must be scrutinized with the informed skepticism of an outsider, a nonbeliever. The perceived strength of Reppert's argument collapses when this is understood.

Christian philosopher Thomas Talbott says I have no reason to think rape is wrong based on the informed skepticism of an outsider, a nonbeliever. He claims that Victor Reppert's "previously expressed arguments are pretty decisive."[3] Talbott offers three criticisms of what I have written on this issue.

Talbott's first criticism is that "the issue is not whether some skeptical persons 'would ever want to morally justify rape.' The issue is whether the belief that rape is morally wrong passes the Outsider Test; and if so, how."[4] So let's make some important distinctions before proceeding. First, there are people who think rape is morally wrong yet do it anyway. In fact, this describes nearly all rapists. Perhaps one way to explain this is that, like other people who have addictions, some rapists cannot restrain themselves from acting on desires they know are wrong. Second, there are people who think God commands rape and have raped people because of this. I find this horrific and barbaric to the core. The fact that some religions justify this practice is one of the reasons I am opposed to faith-based reasoning. Third, there are billions of decent, civilized folk around the world who condemn rape. By far they outnumber the people who would seek to justify it.

So how skeptical should I be of an anti-rape ethic? Given these differences, the burden of proof is on a person who seeks to justify rape. Rational, civilized, decent people all oppose it. Others know it's wrong even if they do it anyway. Furthermore, an anti-rape ethic is not an extraordinary supernatural claim akin to believing in the elves of Iceland, the trolls of Norway, and the power of witches in Africa. The OTF calls upon people to be more skeptical of these types of extraordinary claims.

Talbott's second criticism is that "the number of irreligious soldiers who have thought it quite acceptable to rape the women of a conquered people probably numbers in the millions (if not tens of millions) over the course of human history."[5] But we're not talking about times of war. In times of war soldiers rape women. The Christian Crusaders did so because they were raised under the influence of the cultural norms of a past era, which differ dramatically from the norms of our era. Morality evolves. That's my claim. I am arguing against the religious-based nature of these crimes in a modern nation of peaceful, democratic, civilized people. Remove the religion, and you remove a great deal of the violence, as Hector Avalos has argued in his book *Fighting Words*.[6]

Talbott ends with a third criticism, saying, "One could easily appeal to cultural relativism and construct an argument that parallels exactly Loftus' initial four step argument; and in this argument, the third step would read: 'Loftus' belief that rape is morally wrong is probably false.'"[7] In other words, if cultural relativism obtains then it's probably false for me to say rape is morally wrong. But he failed to notice that with the words "overwhelming" and "overwhelmingly" in my argument for the OTF I am not claiming cultural relativism— that all our religious beliefs are culturally dependent—only that this is overwhelmingly the case. I have purposely excluded that from the discussion. Besides, Talbott apparently doesn't even know what cultural relativism is. One cannot say, given cultural relativism, that the dominant cultural opinion on an ethical issue is "probably false."

Talbott also says, "Loftus fails to cite a single example of an ancient religious text that, as he interprets it, justifies rape . . . he can hardly deny that many religions condemn it."[8] But this baffles me. Let me help him out. According to Deuteronomy 21:10–12: "When you go out to battle against your enemies, and the LORD your God delivers them into your hands and you take them away captive, and see among the captives a beautiful woman, and have a desire for her and would take her as a wife for yourself, then you shall bring her home to your house." According to Numbers 31:15–18: "Moses said to them, 'Have you spared all the women? Behold, these caused the sons of Israel, through the counsel of Balaam, to trespass against the LORD in the matter of Peor, so the plague was among the congregation of the LORD. Now therefore, kill every male among the little ones, and kill every woman who has known man intimately. But all the girls who have not known man intimately, spare for yourselves.'"[9]

But to the point, can an anti-rape ethic be justified with an OTI? Yes, most assuredly. Why is rape wrong? (1) Because of the nature of the act itself. As an act of violence against another innocent human being it harms people, mostly women. Harming innocent people is wrong. (2) Because fathers, husbands, brothers, and sons would retaliate and probably kill someone caught raping their daughter, wife, sister, or mother. (3) Because of a social contract between rational people that allows our daughters, wives, sisters, and mothers to live in an environment in which they do not need to fear for their safety. The absence of such an environment would create a great deal of social dysfunction. Who in their right mind would try to justify a rape ethic? We all have mothers. If we all had daughters, sisters, or a wife then we would not try justifying a rape ethic. That ethic would allow others to rape the women closest to us. This would be an utterly barbaric society if a rape ethic were accepted. Finally, but not exhaustively, rape is wrong because (4) we should not treat people as means to an end, as Immanuel Kant argued. If I were an outsider to an anti-rape ethic I would quickly embrace it, easily. It passes the informed skepticism of the OTI, even against any hedonistic preferences for wanting to embrace it, since I want the women I love to be able to walk the streets unmolested. *And if I were a woman this would be an absolute no-brainer, and women account for more than half the population of the world.*[10]

I have offered reasons for an anti-rape ethic that an overwhelming number of people accept, and that is good enough. What if a few people still think otherwise? So what? Why should it be required that I need to convince them they are wrong? Why should it matter at all if people disagree with an anti-rape ethic? No ethical view is agreed upon by everyone. An argument does not have to convince everyone for it to be a good one. I have offered good reasons based on the OTI. That should be sufficient.

One thing we know is that *one of the main reasons there is moral diversity is because there is religious diversity.* Likewise, *one of the main reasons people in today's world might seek to justify a rape ethic is because of their religious views.* That's what the OTF is meant to do, offer a way to examine which religion is true, if any of them are, and along with it any religiously based morality. In the absence of religions that justify rape, people worldwide would be able to reach an overwhelming consensus against it.

ON JUSTIFYING CULTURALLY DERIVED BELIEFS

The common objection then, coming from Reppert, Talbott, and others, is that it's unfair to single out religious faith for this kind of test, that the OTF unfairly exempts other things we hold dear. Why not treat all "beliefs" in the same way? So Talbott asks, "Just what, exactly, would count as passing an outsider test in any context, whether it be moral, political, metaphysical, or religious?"[11] Reppert, for instance, thinks "representative democracy is a better form of government than monarchy." He claims, "If I lived in sixteenth-century Europe, or in other parts of the globe, I probably would not believe that. So my belief in democratic government flunks the outsider test."[12] And yet he holds representative democracy dear and sees no reason to think differently than he does. Reppert's argument is a version of an argument that Christian professor Randal Rauser made by charging that

> if you were born into Afghanistan or North Korea or Saudi Arabia do you think you'd have been an advocate of representative democracy? The fact is that political theories are also largely distributed over geographic areas. So if I accept your outsider test in religion then it applies here as well and you need to test your political convictions with the outsider test as surely as does the Afghani, North Korean or Saudi Arabian.[13]

I've admitted that believers are correct to apply the equivalent OTI to ethics and to politics. Indeed, one of the principle causes of social strife, confusion, and misery is a failure to examine moral and political ideas skeptically and critically. That includes the rightness of representative democracy. But only religious believers in today's world are defending the notion of a theocracy, both in Muslim countries and among the Christian Reconstructionists in America. So in order to apply the OTI believers must first apply the OTF to their own religions to see if the religious ethics and politics based on them have any warrant. If they don't, then ethics and politics must be based on scientific reasoning as best as possible.

In a very well-written comment on my blog a Catholic doctoral student in philosophy at Princeton who calls himself "EricRC" sums up what he calls the "fundamental objection" to the Outsider Test for Faith (OTF):

> We have to distinguish what's essential to the OTF from what's accidental. What's essential, as far as I can tell, is the notion that similar truth claims should be held to similar epistemic standards when

we reason about them, for if you're using different epistemic standards for different truth claims that are in the same category, then you're acting in a way that's minimally epistemically suspect, and most likely epistemically illegitimate. So, when you look at the epistemic standards you hold a claim C to, they should be in accord with the epistemic standards you hold to claim C if C is in the same category of claims (however we establish the boundaries) as C.

However, we all know that when human beings reason, they often apply different standards to truth claims they accept from those they reject. So, one way to think about applying the same standards would be to suggest that someone who accepts C on rational grounds consider C from the perspective of someone who rejects C on rational grounds. That is, if you take C to be true on rational grounds, and you want to see if you're applying the epistemic standards that led you to the truth of C consistently, then you should, as far as this test goes, adopt an outsider perspective with respect to C and evaluate the rational grounds for it from there. Further, you should examine the grounds on which you reject C1 etc. to see if you're acting consistently. When faith claims are at issue, we call this sort of test the OTF.

Note, the OTF just is a particular way of going about asking whether you're applying the same epistemic standards to truth claims in similar categories (let's call this principle N). That is, what's essential to the OTF is just this notion, viz. the same standards should be applied to the same sorts of claims. What's particular is that it's about faith claims. But again, note that N *is not* faith specific. That is, there's nothing that precludes the application of N to other categories. Hence, *if* there is a legitimate OTF, then there are, ineluctably, outsider tests for other claims in the same category, e.g. moral claims or political claims. Therefore, everything that you claim follows from the application of N to F by way of assuming the position of an outsider—that is, from the OTF—follows for claims in these other categories as well.

Again, this is, as far as I can see, inescapable. But then this gives us an outsider test for the outsider test, as it were: If we apply N to other categories of claims by adopting the position of an outsider to those claims, do your skeptical conclusions vis-à-vis the OTF follow?

Well, it seems to me that they do. We've been through this

all before: equally intelligent and equally well informed people disagree about all sorts of moral and political claims, moral and political positions are heavily correlated with the time and place in which one is born and raised, and so on. Further, when we adopt moral and political positions, we affect thousands if not millions of people in a variety of ways—some of them coercive. Hence, we have good reasons to question whether N obtains as people go about reaching their moral and political conclusions, and we have good reasons for desiring N to obtain. So, we have as good a set of reasons, both epistemic and practical, for formulating an outsider test for M (morality) and P (politics) as we do for F (faith).

But, as you know, very few moral and political claims could pass the OTM and the OTP. Hence, given the OTF, and given what you claim follows from it—viz. the imperative of skepticism—it follows that moral and political skepticism follow from the OTP and the OTM. But that strikes us as absurd. Indeed, you've tried (unsuccessfully, in my judgment) to avoid this implication of the OTF on numerous occasions. However, as the argument sketched above concludes, these implications are unavoidable—again, given the OTF in its current form. But then the OTF fails its own outsider test.

As I see it, issues of this sort are what predominate concerns with the OTF. You may disagree, but I don't think you can say that the grounds I've provided above are irrational or poorly thought out. They are, I think, serious objections, and they're motivated not by a desire to avoid the OTF, but by a desire to understand it by taking it seriously enough to think it through.[14]

I do appreciate EricRC's taking the time to think through the OTF and treat it seriously. The truth is that there are a great many political and moral beliefs we think are essential to a human society that are not in fact necessary at all. Democracy is one of them. People have done fairly well without democracy from the beginnings of human society until its creation in ancient Athens in the fifth century BCE.

There is a whole range of issues that admit of diversity in the moral and political areas based to an overwhelming degree on "accidents of birth." Caucasian American men would've believed with

President Andrew Jackson in manifest destiny, America's God-given mandate to seize Native American territories as part of the westward expansion of the United States. Up through at least the seventeenth century we in the West would have believed that women were intellectually inferior to men, and consequently we would not even have allowed women to become educated in the same subjects as men. Like Thomas Jefferson and most early Americans, we would've considered black people intellectually inferior as well, while if we were born in the South, we would have cited the Bible to justify slavery.

If we were born black in contemporary America and were also football fans, we would probably have believed O. J. Simpson was not guilty of murder because of our distrust of white police officers, who have had a history of arresting us and railroading us in the legal system as scapegoats for crimes they cannot solve. If we were born in the Palestinian Gaza Strip, we would probably hate the Jews and want to kill them all. If we were born in France, we would probably have opposed the war in Iraq to oust Saddam Hussein.

These kinds of moral, political, religious, and cultural beliefs, based upon specific cultural conditions, can be extended into a lengthy list of ideas we would've had if we had been born in a different time and/or place. There is a whole range of issues like these, including how we dress, what foods we like, what music we listen to, and even the criteria for what kinds of people we consider beautiful. So let me respond to this in three ways.

First, there are three significant differences between religious faiths and moral/political views.

There are some similarities to be sure, since people not only disagree with each other about religion, they also disagree with each other on moral and political issues. But there are three significant differences to consider, deriving from demographics, the extraordinary nature of religious claims, and the fact that moral/political views are forced upon us whereas religious faiths are not.

1. The demographical data. Let's say we created a world map of moral and political views based on demographics similar to world maps showing how religions are situated geographically into separate regions of the globe. Would such a map show the same type of similarities in geographical distribution we see when looking at the various religious faiths? The answer is both yes and no. Yes, there would be some similarities, but no, the similarities would not be relevant. In some cases specific moral duties and political views are necessitated by a particular culturally dominant religion (such as wanting a theocracy, wearing burkas, male chauvinism, female circumcision, anti-homosexuality, and so forth). So the similarities are not relevant overall because religious diversity produces moral and political diversity. Religious diversity stands in the way of achieving a moral and political global consensus. If trends tell us anything, when people revolt it is because they want more democracy, and when they vote with their feet they come to countries with democracies. It would seem as if democracies are the wave of the future. That people want political freedom can best be seen in the fall of the Berlin Wall in November 1989 and in the Muslim world with the ousting of Egyptian president Hosni Mubarak in February 2011. Setbacks occur only as Muslim believers, in Egypt's case the Muslim Brotherhood, demand a return to their religion.

When it comes to morality I agree with C. S. Lewis that overwhelming numbers of people agree about a number of basic ethical duties.[15] Almost everyone thinks we should care for our family and friends and neighbors, for instance. We agree that murder and torturing innocents is wrong, that lying is bad, that we should be merciful to those who show mercy, that honesty is a good policy, that hard work is good for us, that we should seek justice for the helpless, and so on. So, in the end, the demographical data are not similar in the same relevant sense between religious faiths and moral/political views. We do not see global moral/political diversity to the same extent that we see global religious diversity. If we were to produce a world map of basic ethical duties, I think we would see a worldwide consensus about them. If we were to have a map of political views divorced from religious beliefs there just might develop a consensus embracing some form of democracy. The same thing will probably be true of economic views. Perhaps in the long run a worldwide consensus could develop based on empirical results. If it does develop it will do so based on science not faith.

2. *The extraordinary nature of religious claims.* Belief in supernatural forces or beings and their workings in the world through answered prayers and miracles (like divinely inspired texts, virgin births, and resurrections) are in a different category from moral/political views. There is no consensus about them, nor can there be, because they are faith-based claims. There is therefore a significant difference between the nature of religious views, on the one hand, and moral/political views, on the other. Moral, political, and economic views can and do have empirical evidence for them. Let's take the obvious. We can test economic theories by how well they produce jobs and growth within a society. If one theory doesn't do what it's supposed to do then the evidence of a depression shows that it was wrong. The same thing can work when it comes to morals and politics, although testing these things can be hard to do, as we know.

3. *Moral/political views are forced upon us, whereas religious faiths are not.* Contrary to William James's claim that religion is a forced option, the reality is that moral/political views are forced upon us. To be in a society demands that we have rules for living. We have no choice if we want to live in a society, any society. We must have them. In some ways it's better to have bad rules than none at all. So long as most people agree, or so long as these rules are forced upon us by a dictator, we will have them. We'll have them whether we like them or not, whether they can be justified or not, and whether we agree with them or not. By contrast, when it comes to religious faiths, we do not need them for morality or politics. We can have morality and a good government without religion, as even most Christian philosophers admit. They argue that morality and good government are based on God, not that we need to believe in God for us to act morally or to

have a good government. The fact is that there have been a lot of good societies that weren't influenced by Christianity, like Ancient Greece, the Roman Empire, China, and Japan. They did just fine by the world standards in their own times.

Second, what exactly is the skepticism of the outsider?

The outsider's skepticism is doubt, reasonable doubt. It is the adult attitude, the scientific attitude. What is reasonable doubt? An informed skepticism, as I have previously argued, is one that people of faith use when examining the religions they reject. They should apply that same level of doubt to their own religion. Otherwise they have a double standard. The outsider looks at the data to determine the probability of a claim. The insider takes a leap of faith beyond the probabilities. The outsider doesn't claim more than what the probabilities can show. We should never go beyond what the probabilities show when assessing a truth claim about matters of fact such as the origins, nature, and workings of the universe. And the probabilities are set by scientific reasoning, which is based on empirical evidence. We need sufficient evidence in order to accept a truth claim. Skeptical thinking is the hallmark of scientific reasoning. This is most emphatically not a radical type of unjustified skepticism.

With this in mind, *we should be skeptical about everything* to some degree, so I welcome this same type of reasonable skepticism about moral and political views. I welcome the day when believers will look at the evidence showing that people are born gay, that there really is global warming, that women are not inferior to men, that we do face an overpopulation crisis, and so on. There is evidence that we can provide healthcare for everyone, that parents do not need to hit or spank their kids to get them to obey, that antismoking laws in public places are just, and so forth. And we should look at the evidence when it comes to economics, the value of democracy, and political freedom, too. Only if we do can we hope to achieve any global consensus.

Third, what if skepticism leads us to cultural relativism?

So what? Why should this be considered a criticism of the OTF? People who criticize cultural relativism usually do not understand it. Most atheists are cultural relativists because that's where the evidence leads. This criticism of the OTF is little different than rejecting arguments against the existence of God because a consequence of doing so means that when we die there is no hope for an afterlife. But whether we think the arguments for God's existence succeed is not dependent on the mere hope of an afterlife. If God doesn't exist then bite the bullet. So it goes for cultural relativism. If this is a consequence stemming from applying skepticism across the board to moral and political views, then bite the bullet. Learn what cultural relativism is and learn to embrace it.

Moreover, if a consistent application of the OTF to moral and political views leads to cultural relativism then it will have doubly helped us in our quest for the true religious faith, if there is one. For if cultural relativism obtains then it takes away one of the main supports theists have for the moral argument for God's existence. Without a universal, unchanging, absolute morality that argument cannot even get off the ground.[16]

SCIENCE ONE MORE TIME

Incredibly, Thomas Talbott and others suggest that informed skeptics should examine our own scientific understandings with the same level of skepticism we use when examining nonscientific beliefs. He wrote, "Is there any reason whatsoever why modern scientists, for example, should restrict themselves to evidence that might appeal to some outsider, such as an African Bushman?"[17] In a review for *Philosphia Christi*, Christian philosopher Matthew Flannagan said the same thing when he wrote:

Given that the RDPT [2] is inferred from the RDVT [1], if Loftus' argument is valid then analogues of [2] must apply to Loftus et al's own moral, epistemological and scientific beliefs. But then parity of reasoning would entail that their readers should adopt the same skepticism towards science and critical history as they hold towards the myths and superstitions of primitive cultures. . . . This conclusion is obviously absurd.[18]

Randal Rauser suggests a radical skepticism based on the OTF whereby we should even doubt our own sensory inputs![19] Really? Wow!

Which brings us back to science, again. One cannot doubt empirical evidence, for it is the strongest evidence we can have about something. To join Talbott in suggesting that we should question science from the perspective of an African bushman actually gives the game away. For it shows the depths to which a believer will go in order to defend his or her faith no matter what. It shows the disingenuousness of Talbott's arguments, for behind them all he is throwing up smoke screens in order to deflect the force of the OTF. In order to do this he finds it necessary to denigrate science. That's typical of believers, as we've seen before. All believers must denigrate science in some places in order to believe. Science gives us the tools to be rationally skeptical. Science has overthrown superstitious thinking since its inception. It is a given. At the very least the only science that one needs in order to become an informed skeptic is the kind I mentioned in chapter 1 and defended in the next two chapters: sociological data, brain biology, anthropology, and psychology. That's all. Christian apologists need to provide a reason why we should not trust that kind of science, which is the minimum requirement to become an informed skeptic. And I don't see any believer disputing that science except to say it's still possible that it is wrong.

Flannagan has come up with a *reductio ad absurdum* (reduction to absurdity) type of argument against the OTF, whereby he asks us to consider the following alternative propositions to the OTF:

(1) The scientific diversity thesis: that people from different cultures adopt different scientific beliefs.

(2) The scientific dependency thesis: the scientific beliefs one adopts are overwhelmingly dependent on cultural conditions.

Flannagan asks, if the OTF is a good argument then why isn't this alternative argument equally good for the results of science? Why shouldn't we be skeptical of modern science based on the same type of argument? He challenges that "either we reject modern science or the argument for the OTF is invalid."[20]

I have tried to disabuse Flannagan of this argument with no success at all. He touts it as a refutation of the OTF without so much as considering anything else I have to say. What he is oblivious to is that the OTF is based on science, the same kind of science he accepts in a vast number of areas except those rare ones that conflict with his faith. As an outsider, a nonbeliever in other religions, Flannagan either accepts the results of DNA evidence that Native Americans are not descendants from Semitic peoples, contrary to the belief of Mormons, or he does not. He either accepts the results of science that blood transfusions are necessary and helpful in saving lives, contrary to the belief of Jehovah's Witnesses, or he does not. He either demands scientific evidence for the Scientologist's claim that 75 million years ago Xenu, the dictator of the "Galactic Confederacy," brought billions of his people to earth, stacked them around volcanoes, and blew them to bits with hydrogen bombs, or he does not. If he does, then as an outsider he's admitting scientific evidence is decisive evidence for all religious faiths. If there is any inconsistency at all it's in his refusal to apply the OTF to his own evangelical faith.

The problem is that both (1) and (2) are false, and obviously so. Just look at the World Distribution of Modern Science map provided in the appendix of this book. Scientists don't have different conclusions in a vast number of areas. Their conclusions are based on evidence, and so they are accepted cross-culturally. Science is cross-cultural in scope. Science in Russia is the same as science in Europe, *science is cross-cultural in scope. Science in Russia is the same as science in Europe, which is the same as science in the U.S., China and Saudi Arabia. The situation as to concensus about scientific truths is, however, different when dealing*

with cutting edge science, where there may well be a diversity of scientific opinions because such science is concerned with unsolved mysteries. It is appropriate to be skeptical about science on the cutting edge where concensus does not yet exist

which is the same as science in the United States, China, and Saudi Arabia. It's the same as science in his own country, New Zealand.

There is, however, a difference that should be noted. It's between the consensus of scientists in a vast number of areas and frontier science on the cutting edge. Cutting-edge science in every generation contains a diversity of scientific opinions, since cutting-edge science is concerned with unsolved mysteries. So there is nothing wrong with being skeptical about science on the cutting edge. In fact, since a diversity of opinions exist in these areas, skepticism is required until the evidence for one theory brings about a consensus among scientists. But just because there are mysteries left unsolved does not mean the various religious faiths can insert their own mysterious answer. A mystery, as philosophy professor John Shook explains, "by definition is awareness of the absence of knowledge." He adds that substituting a religious mystery for a scientific mystery "is not any sort of satisfactory explanation, since mere substitution of mysteries does not increase understanding." Mystery substitution, he argues, is "not really any sort of explanation at all." For it should be obvious that "it really cannot be a simple and easy matter to credit god with 'explaining' mysteries of nature when the god 'explanations' themselves additionally require such an immense labor to explain as well." By contrast, a "genuine explanation is able to increase knowledge about reality by connecting what we know together with what we want to know. Scientific explanation is the most careful intellectual form of genuine explanation yet invented."[21] Furthermore, "Scientists can honestly admit when they don't yet have a scientific explanation for something. But no scientist should proclaim that science could never explain some natural phenomenon, since that very claim would require scientific evidence in support, the sort of evidence which everyone admits is obviously lacking too."[22]

What's not to understand about this? I think Christian apologists simply see all science as controversial because they focus on the frontiers of science while maintaining amnesia about the lessons we've learned from the history of science. That's a gross misunderstanding of science. It's also a gross ignorance of the advances of science.

MY RESPONSE TO ALL THESE OBJECTIONS

Let's just respond to all these objections this way: either the OTF is a fair way to assess the truth of religious faiths or it is not. If it is not a fair test, per the above objections, then why do believers use it to reasonably examine the religious faiths of others? That they do is clearly evident. When believers criticize the faiths they reject, they use reason and science to do so. They assume these other religions have the burden of proof when it comes to their extraordinary claims of miracles. They assume that their holy book(s) are written by human not divine authors. They assume a human not a divine origin of their faiths. Believers do this when rejecting other faiths. So this dispenses with all the red herrings about ethics, politics, science, and a material universe, for the OTF simply asks believers to do unto their own faith what they already do unto other faiths. All it asks of them is to be consistent. If there is any inconsistency at all, it is in how *they* assess truth claims. But if the OTF is a fair test, why do believers have a double standard, one for their own religious faith and a different standard for the religious faiths they reject? Let them use reason and science to examine their own faith. Let them assume their own faith has the burden of proof when it comes to their extraordinary claims of miracles. Let them assume human rather than divine authors of their holy book(s).

There is therefore something clearly wrong with these Christian objections to the OTF. Here's what I think. The OTF is the name of an argument. The name I gave to this argument is not the argument itself. The word "outsider" in the argument is an example that illustrates a skeptic, a doubter, a nonbeliever. Such a person is an outsider because he or she is not an insider. An insider is a believer and an outsider is a nonbeliever. The insider believes in a particular religious sect. The outsider does not. The insider has faith. The outsider doubts. The insider makes extraordinary claims. The outsider makes no claims. The insider has a belief in search of data. The outsider is a doubter who is examining the data.

So one could just as easily substitute the word "skeptical" and call it the "Skeptical Test for Faith." For that matter, it could be called the "Scientific Test for Faith" or the "Consistent Test for Faith" or the "Golden Rule Test for Faith" or the "Objective Test for Faith" or even the "Burden of Proof Test for Faith." It could even be simply called "A Test for Faith." But because of this misunderstanding, Christian defenders have constructed all kinds of wildly improbable outsider-type scenarios. They think of an outsider as a person who has a radical skepticism. Hey, why not be an outsider to love, too, or life, they might add. Who has that kind of radical skepticism? Not me, that's for sure. And I doubt very much anyone does. So they end up rejecting the OTF because they falsely attribute to it a radical skepticism *and then use that as an excuse for not being skeptical at all,* which is one reason why I think Christianity is a delusion.

Almost all the objections to the OTF are red herrings placed in the road to sidetrack us from getting at the truth. Christian apologists fail to understand the perspective of an outsider, or they grossly misrepresent it in favor of faith. The outsider perspective is not about being antiscientific, or some Martian, or a sociopath, or a lunatic, or a rapist. It is the perspective of science, which is the same standard believers use when rejecting other religions.

If Christians wish to avoid the charge of hypocrisy, they cannot reject the OTF while continuing to use it. They must admit either that they have a double standard for examining religious faiths, one for their own faith and a different one for others, or that their God did not make their faith to pass the OTF in the first place. The bottom line is that, given the facts that form the basis of the OTF, doubt is the adult attitude. One cannot subject this doubt to further testing. It is what makes testing our ideas possible in the first place. Doubt is a filter that strains out the wheat of what's true from the chaff of what's false. By contrast, all religions have the same faith-based foundation. When faith is the foundation anything can be believed. Science is the only antidote to an unexamined faith.

Doubt C

9

DEBATING CHRISTIANITY BASED ON THE TEST

The Outsider Test for Faith (OTF) is primarily a self-diagnostic test for believers who want to honestly examine whether their culturally adopted religious faith is true. There is no teacher who can say that you passed it except yourself, so you have to be brutally honest by recognizing how irrational human beings are at justifying what we think.

That being said, Christian professor Steve Lovell, just like several other Christians, argues that his particular set of religious beliefs passes the OTF. In a veiled criticism of the OTF Lovell wrote:

> If, when I examine them, trying to put myself in the position of someone outside Christianity but rationally open-minded about it, I find that my faith is reaffirmed, I think I've done everything that can be reasonably asked of me. Now since you clearly believe that all those who take the test find that their faith fails, you would also seem to be committed to saying that either the above is not a sufficient test, or that I haven't really done as I describe above. Your options are limited:
>
> (1) Say that, although I think I've taken the test I haven't really. That would be the pre-theoretic commitment you say you don't have.
> (2) Say that some religious belief passes the outsider test after all.
> (3) Say that while I've done the above, that isn't all that the test requires. It requires something more stringent.

Your only good option seems to be (3). But then I'm back to my original question: "What else are we being asked to do?"[1]

The answer to his question is nothing. I'm not asking believers to do anything more than examine their own religious faith as an informed skeptic would. But given the fact that psychological data shows us that most believers cannot think rationally in assessing their culturally inherited faith, the OTF also serves a dual purpose in that it sets a standard for all future debates about religion. After agreeing that the OTF is neither unfair nor faulty in any way, and that it doesn't unfairly target religion, the debate can really begin. For if believers claim to have taken and passed the test then at that point we have agreed upon the standard whereby they can no longer punt to faith to defend what they believe. With an acceptance of the OTF everyone can share common ground about what a religion should be like in order to be accepted as true.

This chapter and the next one represent stage-three arguments based on an acceptance of the OTF. I argue that any believer who claims to have successfully taken and passed the OTF has not done so properly, so I embrace Lovell's option (1). This doesn't involve any pretheoretic commitment on my part though. My conclusions come as a result of applying the OTF. Whether I can convince any believer of this is a separate issue that needs to be weighed on its own merits. So just because I conclude that no religion passes the OTF does not entail that I have any pretheoretic commitment to the test's outcome, just as scientists do not have pretheoretic commitments to the outcome of experiments conducted dispassionately according to acceptable procedures. But it is my conclusion.

I have offered some very good grounds for starting out as an informed skeptic, given the RDVT and the RDPT. Informed skepticism is the basis for the OTF. Methodological procedures are those procedures we use to investigate something. How we go about investigating something is a separate issue that must be justified on its own terms, and I have done so. I have argued that the OTF offers us the only hope for solving the problem of religious diversity in the world. So someone cannot say of the OTF that I ought to be just as skeptical of it as I am about the conclusion(s) I arrive at when I apply the test, since I have justified this test independently of my conclusions based on the test. So let me once again say that the methodological procedure of the OTF most emphatically is not self-defeating. J. L. Schellenberg deals with this type of objection in these words: "Now this objection can be sound only if my arguments do indeed apply to themselves, and it will not take much to see that they do not."[2] He distinguishes between "bold, ambitious, and risky metaphysical beliefs," on the one hand, which tell us that "active investigation should cease," since "the truth has been discovered," and "the belief that some such bold, ambitious, and risky metaphysical belief is unjustified."[3] The latter merely claims that such bold and ambitious metaphysical beliefs "have not successfully made their case; it bids us to continue investigation . . . because skepticism is always a position of last resort in truth seeking contexts."[4]

I have already written and edited several books against Christianity, so my readers can find my arguments there. Just as people would be better informed about their purchases if they were to consult *Consumer's Digest*, in a similar sense, to be an *informed skeptic*, one would desire to read books authored by those who disagree with one's faith. I argue that if Christian believers really want to take the OTF they should be eager to read books like mine. If they claim to be open-minded they should actively seek out such books. My aim is to drive a wedge between the Bible and the brain of the believer. I argue over and over that one cannot reasonably accept the Bible and the theology based on it. The question is what Christians would believe if I could show this to be the case. My claim is that they probably wouldn't believe at all.

Since a book like this would be deficient without providing some examples of how outsiders think, I have included them. I must confess, though, that I have kicked this dead horse so many times, it's hard to know where and how hard to kick it again. What I intend to do is show

how an informed skeptic, an outsider, a nonbeliever, or a non-Christian sees the Christian faith, so I'll focus on those type of arguments. By using a variety of arguments utilizing the OTF I intend to show that no reasonable outsider could ever embrace Christianity. Now I know in advance that many Christians who read this will still disagree. But I don't think they can reasonably do so. This will be the longest chapter in this book, because I want to argue as effectively as I can.

THE INEFFECTIVENESS OF THEISTIC EXPLANATIONS AND ARGUMENTS

When it comes to arguments on behalf of faith like Alvin Plantinga's Reformed Epistemology, William Lane Craig's argument for the "inner witness of the Spirit," divine hiddenness arguments, Pascal's Wager, or William James's argument for faith, the Christian believer must think of them just as an outsider or a nonbeliever would. As far as I can tell there are a number of different religions, and each one could utilize these same arguments. They probably have their own versions leading to their own respective faiths. How would it sound to evangelical Christians if they heard Mormons claim that Mormonism is "properly basic" or that the inner witness of the Spirit self-authenticates their faith? Just think how it sounds to Christians when Muslims explain the lack of belief in Allah because Allah is a hidden God? The "many gods" objection to Pascal's Wager destroys the wager's force, since we must first decide from among the various gods which one to wager on. And William James's argument for faith can be used to justify most any religion, since the religious "hypothesis" people think is a "live option" that they are to "meet halfway" will already be the one they think is more probable than not.

Many of these types of arguments can be easily dismissed if you evaluate them as an outsider would. They have absolutely no force at all. That's because they are not so much arguments to one's religion but rather *explanations* for having it. Explanations can be used as arguments, but the primary strength of these particular arguments are that they explain why Christians believe what they do. To outsiders these Christian explanations are completely dependent on arguments, positive arguments, for why there is a Trinitarian God who sent his son to die for our sins and why this God raised Jesus from the dead. That's why all the so-called beneficial arguments to a particular God of one's choice are ineffective as arguments. They may help in some meager way to defeat objections to Christianity or to help to keep believers in the fold, but at best these explanations simply do not have any force in leading informed skeptics to faith.

What about the arguments to the existence of a particular kind of God? There are arguments to God from morality, design, the cosmos, reason, religious experience, and a conception of the greatest conceivable being. But when we examine them more closely as an outsider, an informed skeptic, or a non-Christian would, it's crystal clear that each type of argument can easily be used by other religions to support their deities as well. Let me very briefly show you how this is done.

When it comes to the ontological argument, if we were to ask Easterners what they conceive to be the greatest conceivable being, their conceptions will start off being different from those of Westerners from the get-go. I think Anselmian arguments, including those of Hartshorne, Plantinga, and Malcolm, all begin with Occidental not Oriental conceptions of God, and their Western conceptions of God are theirs by virtue of the prevalence of the Christian Gospel in the West. If ontological argumentation is sound, then the Eastern conceptions of God will entail that their God (or the One) also exists. Since these two conceptions of God produce two mutually exclusive conclusions about which kind of God exists, the ontological argument fails to do what it's supposed to. It does not lead us to believe in the Christian God. An Easterner might even start off by saying that the greatest conceivable being is the One, which cannot be conceived. Where do you go with the ontological argument from here? Orthodox Jews and Muslims also use ontological arguments to their own God, so ontological arguments for the existence of God aren't specific to Christians.

When it comes to the moral argument, believers of any religion could use it in defense of their own faith. Even militant Muslims could have used the moral argument to Allah's existence just before boarding planes on 9/11 to kill infidels, since in their minds Allah's nature calls for such violence. The same is true of arguments to a particular god based on design, the cosmos, reason, or religious experience. For instance, I once skimmed through a massive book on intelligent design that argued for Allah's existence. I don't know of any theist who could not use all these arguments in defense of one's faith. Even deists who merely believe that a distant creator God exists can use all of them except for the argument from religious experience.

My point is that none of these arguments to God's existence, even if we grant them, solve the problem of religious diversity. After all, the very nature of religion is that all of them are based on believing in supernatural beings or forces, something they have always agreed about. At best, even if we grant that the arguments to God's existence succeed, they only show that such a god is consistent with the God that each religious believer already accepts. Therefore, demonstrating the existence of a generic god of the philosophers does nothing to help us decide which religion is true.

Not only this, but these arguments support countless other god-hypotheses that believers have probably never considered before. For example, these same arguments are equally consistent with a god who created this world as nothing more than a scientific experiment, a god who thinks of us as rats in a maze, one who wonders what we will conclude about it all and how we will live our lives. Such a god may be nothing more than a divine tinkerer who is learning as he goes by creating one successive universe after another. Or perhaps some supernatural force may merely have had the power to create what Edward Tryon and Stephen Hawking both describe as a "quantum wave fluctuation"[5] before committing deicide. That is, perhaps this supernatural being or force had to die in order to create the quantum wave fluctuation. It's also possible that this god is guiding the universe ultimately toward an evil purpose, disguising himself as benevolent so as to trick us. If such a trickster god exists then all the evidence Christians use to conclude their good God exists would have been planted there to deceive us by that very same trickster god. Based on this alternative god-hypothesis alone there is no way believers can go on to reasonably conclude anything else. I can see no reasonable objection to these other God-hypotheses once we allow them into our equations. They are just as possible as what any Christian believes. For this reason, arguments to the existence of God don't work in showing which religion is true, if any of them are true at all.

Contrast this with a scientific understanding.[6] When it comes to the explanation of the origin of the universe we are faced with basically two options, that (1) something—anything—has always existed, or (2) something—anything—popped into existence out of nothing. Either choice seems extremely unlikely—or possibly even absurd. There is little in our experience that can help us choose. But one of them is correct and the other is false. We either start with the brute fact that something has always existed or the brute fact that something popped into existence out of nothing. So the simpler our brute fact is, the more probable it is, per Ockham's razor. All that scientists have to assume is equilibrium of positive and negative energy and the laws of physics. This is as close to nothing as science can get. But grant it and physicist Victor J. Stenger argues, "the probability for there being something rather than nothing can actually be calculated; it is over 60 percent." As such, "only by the constant action of an agent outside the universe, such as God, could a state of nothingness be maintained. The fact that we have something is just what we would expect if there is no God."[7]

I find it implausible that a Triune God (3 persons in 1) has always existed (what's the likelihood of even one eternal God-person?) and will forever exist (even though our entire experience is that everything has a beginning and an ending) as a fully formed being (even though our entire experience is that order grows incrementally) who knows all true propositions (and consequently never learned any new ones), possesses all power (but doesn't exercise it like we would if we saw a burning child in need of rescue), and is present everywhere (and knows what time it is everywhere in our universe even though time is a function of movement and bodily placement). How is it possible for this being to think or make choices or take risks (things that all involve weighing alternatives)? How could this being have freely chosen who he is and what his values are, since there was never a previous time before he was who he is?

Undeterred by this, believers will fallaciously use the augments to their own particular god-hypothesis by additionally arguing that in a world inhabited by a supernatural being, their particular miracle claims are more probable than not. So in this way Christians argue for their own distinct natural theology just as other theists do. But there is no reasonable way to tell in advance if these arguments point to their particular God. How do they know which god these arguments lead them to in advance of looking at the historical evidence for their particular religion? They simply cannot reasonably assume these arguments lead to their particular God. Therefore they cannot approach their own miracle claims as having any more probability than the miracle claims advanced by other religions, even granting that the theistic arguments work, which I don't.

In other words, the arguments to God's existence simply do not grant believers any *priors*, or relevant background knowledge prior to examining their own particular religious faith. They must still look at the raw, uninterpreted data to determine if a miracle took place, that is, *without using a potentially false presumption that their particular God performed the miracle under investigation.* This line of reasoning destroys natural theology in one fell swoop. In philosophical circles, this is known as *Hume's Stopper,* and it stops natural theology dead in its tracks. Even if there is a god of some kind, believers still have no reason to think their particular God did the miracle under investigation. For if Allah exists then Jesus was not raised from the dead, and we all know that the Jews rejected the Christian claim that Yahweh raised him from the dead.

Let this sink in. The Jews of Jesus' day were theists who believed in Yahweh (and that Yahweh performed miracles), and they knew their scriptural prophecies. Yet the overwhelming majority of them did not believe Jesus was raised from the dead by Yahweh, even though our best estimate is that there were eight million Jews in the known world at the time of Jesus. Catholic New Testament scholar David C. Sim argues: "Throughout the first century the total number of Jews in the Christian movement probably never exceeded 1,000 and by the end of the century the Christian church was largely Gentile."[8] The Christian response is that these Jews didn't want to believe because Jesus was not their kind of Messiah, a king who would throw off Roman rule. But then, where did they get that idea in the first place? They got it from their own Scriptures. And who supposedly inspired them? Yahweh. If they were theists and they were there and they didn't believe, why should anyone in our day, as outsiders, believe? I see no reason to do so.

To Christians who respond that the arguments to God's existence open up the possibility of miracles, I simply ask them if they would ever seriously consider the Christian miracles if they were Muslims or Orthodox Jews? Theism does not entail that your particular miracles have any more probability to them than other miracle claims. I suspect Muslims and Orthodox Jews, even as theists themselves, are no more open to Christian miracle claims than I am as a nonbeliever, so Christians should not see such connections as reasonable either. There is simply no reasonable way to privilege one's miracle claims over the miracle claims of other believers.

This has an unfortunate downside, for upon accepting the existence of a supernatural being and realizing that no miracle claims have any special privilege, theists would find themselves in the strange position of equally considering all miracle claims. In such a position, it would be much more difficult to be skeptical of different miracle stories, and as such, believers would be susceptible to following after any guru, priest, minister, and/or huckster out to bilk them out of their money. Gone would be some of their critical thinking capacities for spotting false miracle claims. Gone would be the full potential for being rationally skeptical adults.

WHAT THEN OF THE RESURRECTION OF JESUS?

When it comes to the miracle of the resurrection of Jesus from the grave all that Christians have is ancient testimony, which has the same authority (or lack of authority) as the evidence available to those who claim Muhammad flew through the night, or Balaam's ass talked, or Jonah was swallowed by a great mythical fish, or a pillar of fire directed the Israelites by night, or the Red Sea parted, or the pool of Siloam healed people, and so on. But ancient testimony ain't worth a thing when it comes to any of these things.

German critic Gotthold Lessing's "ugly, broad ditch" destroys any reasonable chance of concluding that Jesus rose from the dead. Lessing wrote: "Miracles which I see with my own eyes, and which I have opportunity to verify for myself, are one thing; miracles, of which I know only from history that others say they have seen them and verified them, are another." But, he continued, "I live in the 18th century, in which miracles no longer happen. The problem is that reports of miracles are not miracles . . . [they] have to work through a medium which takes away all their force." He asks, "Is it invariably the case, that what I read in reputable historians is just as certain for me as what I myself experience?"[9]

Lessing admits that someone might object that miracles like the resurrection of Jesus from the dead are "more than historically certain" because these things are told to us by "inspired historians who cannot make a mistake." But Lessing counters that whether or not we have inspired historians is itself a historical claim, which is only as certain as history allows. This, then, according to Lessing, "is the ugly broad ditch which I cannot get across, however often and however earnestly I have tried to make the leap. . . . Since the truth of these miracles has completely ceased to be demonstrable by miracles still happening now, since they are no more than reports of miracles, I deny that they should bind me in the least to a faith in the other teachings of Christ."[10]

The fact is that there are a lot of things that happen to people that go against the overwhelming odds. Let's take the example of Oprah Winfrey's disclosure in November 2010 that she has a half sister named Patricia who was given up for adoption by her mother shortly after being born. What are the odds of someone discovering late in life that she has a half sister? I don't know, but surely it's extremely rare. It wasn't a miracle, that's for sure. Things like that do occur from time to time. By contrast, if Jesus rose from the grave, such a thing was a miracle. As such, it has an even lower probability of happening by far than a woman discovering she has a previously unknown half sister.

The point is that incredibly rare events within the realm of the natural world take place all the time, like people getting struck by lightning, winning the lottery, finding a bottle with a note in it that washes up on a beach, or living through a disaster that should have killed them. Yes, these things are all extremely rare, but they happen all the time. Therefore a natural explanation for the resurrection claim should always be preferred over any claim that Jesus rose from the dead, so long as it has even a minimal degree of plausibility. It's the rational thing to conclude. Even if we cannot produce a natural explanation of what actually happened from the so-called evidence, it's still far more reasonable to say we don't think Jesus rose from the dead. Why? Because incredible events against overwhelming odds happen within the natural world all the time.

In what follows I'll offer a very brief natural explanation of the claim that Jesus was resurrected. Compare it with the claim that he physically rose from the dead. You cannot say my natural explanation lacks plausibility because I already admit that it does. As I said, incredible things happen all the time. What you should say, based on a rational assessment of the probabilities, is that my natural explanation is *more* implausible than the claim that Jesus physically rose from the dead.

My natural explanation is that the early disciples were visionaries; that is, they believed God was speaking to them in dreams, trances, and thoughts that burst into their heads throughout the day. Having had their hopes utterly dashed following the crucifixion of Jesus, they began having visions that Jesus had risen from the dead. They began preaching this to people who subsequently had these same kinds of visions. In these visions disciples thought Jesus was speaking to them, so they began preaching what they learned from him (Acts 2:17–21; 1 Cor. 14; 2 Cor. 12:1–10). The most obvious of these revelations was Paul's claim that he learned the Gospel and of the Lord's Supper directly from Jesus himself, not from men (Gal. 1:11–12; 1 Cor. 11:23). The author of Revelation wrote down seven dictated letters from Jesus as the result of a vision (Rev. 2–3).

They "saw" a "resurrected" Jesus in visions. They preached what he "revealed" to them. There was no objective evidence for any of this, so there is no reason why we should take their word. After all, these visions were private, subjective experiences. With such subjective visions as a basis for their faith, they could believe and teach anything as though it had the authority of Jesus speaking from heaven. All one needs to do is compare this phenomenon with the rise of Mormonism.

In such a visionary environment it could also be believed that there was an empty tomb on the basis of a vision from someone who is thought to have received this revelation from Jesus himself. We call such visionaries "liars for Jesus," and we know plenty of believers who have claimed they found Noah's Ark. In fact, there are many documented lies by the church down through the ages, from forged New Testament and extra-biblical texts to forged insertions in Jewish historian Josephus's writings, and the alleged "Donation of Constantine." So even if Christianity is true, and even if these lies are not God's fault, it destroys the credibility of Christianity. Since that's the case, a reasonable God should know that reasonable people cannot believe. And a reasonable God could not reasonably send anyone to hell for not believing.[11]

My natural explanation for the resurrection requires neither a conspiracy nor that Jesus didn't die on the cross. All it requires is one liar for Jesus, and I think this liar is the author of Mark, the first Gospel. He invented the empty tomb sequence. That's it. The rest is history among superstitious people who desired hard evidence for their claim and believed Mark's Gospel based upon the testimony of a visionary. Just think of Joseph Smith, who started the Mormon church. It's the same claim.

Stranger things have happened. But miracle claims are more incredible than my natural explanation, by far. Therefore no reasonable person should believe Jesus rose from the dead. Just as it was incredible but nonmiraculous that Oprah Winfrey discovered she had a half sister, so there is no reason to punt to a miracle when it comes to the claim by the early church that Jesus physically rose from the grave. And if my natural explanation doesn't work, there are a number of others, any one of which is more probable than that Jesus physically rose from the dead.

Christian, your only recourse is your "priors." And in your bag of priors is the assumption that God exists. Upon the supposition that God exists it becomes more probable than not that God raised Jesus from the dead. But, as I have argued, those so-called priors are ineffective when examining the evidence itself. From where do you get your priors? Since the evidence for the resurrection cannot be established from the raw historical data alone, you must approach said evidence from a prior that you cannot have yet. The evidence from the raw historical data must lead you to believe that your God did this particular miracle. But there are plenty of theists who do not think God raised Jesus from the dead, even though they are theists. My contention is that Christians accept the evidence for the resurrection because they were raised to believe, and that's pretty much it. It's the only explanation that fits, since the evidence simply is not there. Let the following statement fully sink in: *Someone must first start out believing in the God to whom this particular miracle is attributed before he or she can find the evidence convincing, since the evidence is circular, viciously so.* The evidence of a biblical miracle cannot reasonably convince someone that such a God exists unless said person already believes in the God to whom the miracle is attributed. My contention is that the basis for all miracle claims in the ancient past is faith, which is an irrational leap over the probabilities. When faith is the basis, anything can be believed. *When faith is involved, probabilities are in the eyes of the beholder.* So although Christians think the resurrection of Jesus is more probable than not, I can see why other theists would disagree. If faith is the means by which the truth of miracle claims is assessed, then any one of them can be seen as better evidenced than the others.

WHO ANSWERS PRAYERS?

What I'm arguing isn't true only of god-hypotheses and miracle claims. It's also true of petitionary prayers. When an astounding event matches a prayer the believer always attributes the answer to his or her own particular god. Christians maintain that any prayer request granted for believers in other religions is done by the Christian God out of compassion, because only one God exists, theirs. The reason Christians think this, despite the fact that only prayers offered in Jesus' name are to be prayed, is because their own answered prayers are no better evidenced than are the answered prayers of others. So the Christian God becomes the explanation for the answered prayer of a Muslim, or an Orthodox Jew, or a Fred Phelps, or a Roman Catholic, or a liberal Christian, or a Jehovah's Witness, or a Mormon, or a Satanist, or a Hindu. But believers in these other religions will take answered prayers as evidence that their faith is true. This means God, the Christian God, is providing confirming evidence against the truth of Christianity to believers of false religions who will be condemned to hell. So, Christian, either give up the belief that your

God answers the prayers of other believers or admit that your God is actively deceiving believers in other religions. And, if you give up the belief that God is answering the prayers of other believers, show us why your own answered prayers are better evidenced than theirs.

A comment on my blog put this another way:

> A Muslim man prays to Allah to have his cancer cured. The prayer is answered, and the Muslim man is strengthened in his faith in Allah. After all it was Allah who he was praying to, and who healed him right? And so the man, as a devout Muslim, endorses stoning of adulterers, killing of apostates and cutting limbs off of thieves. . . . This is the issue right here. When Christians say that it is their God who answers all prayers in the world, they are basically saying that the Christian God intentionally mystifies people from other religions into believing their false religions even more (and in their faith making sins, that will never allow them to be saved). In other words, the God who answers all prayers supports the violence/sins in the name of other religions.[12]

THE INHERENT UNFALSIFIABILITY OF THE CHRISTIAN FAITH

Theistic believers use what I call the *Omniscience Escape Clause* to defend their faith, and it makes their faith unfalsifiable (in that nothing can conceivably be counted against their faith). It makes believers resilient to any and every argument showing their faith claims are misguided and false. We've heard this excuse far too many times. It's the stock-in-trade for apologists. "My ways are not your ways," an ancient, superstitious, canonized biblical text says of God. So an apologist chimes in, "How do we know what an omniscient God might do or how he might reveal himself?" He might communicate to us in ways that are indistinguishable from anything else we see in the ancient world, or through the tragedy of the Haitian earthquake, or through a child suffering and soon to die from leukemia. We're asked over and over, how can we judge an omniscient God's ways?

The implied answer is, "We can't." However, the answer is obvious. We must be able to understand enough of God's ways to know that his ways are good and that he knows what he's doing. It's that simple. If God does not act as a loving person would, or if he does not reveal himself in ways that are distinguishable from other so-called revelations in the ancient world, then all we can reasonably conclude is that God is not acting as a reasonable or loving person.

It doesn't matter what the particular problem is for a person's faith. Conceptualizing God as omniscient solves it. It could be the intractable and unanswerable problem of ubiquitous suffering, or how a deity could simultaneously be 100 percent God and 100 percent man, or how the death of a man on a cross saves us from sins, or why God's failure to better communicate led to massive bloodshed among Christians during the French Wars of Religion and the Thirty Years' War. It just doesn't matter. God is omniscient. He knows best. Therefore, punting to God's omniscience makes faith unfalsifiable, which allows believers to ignore the probabilities and disregard what reason tells them.

When we take an inventory of the times Christians argue that the evidence supports their faith and make a comparison to the times they are forced into explaining the evidence away, we find something very interesting. Most of the supposed evidence they claim supports their faith doesn't actually support their particular Christian sect. It's only consistent with it. Much of the same evidence can be used by other believers to support their particular faith, too. And of the supportive evidence, at some point along the way Christians must use the Omniscience Escape Clause. That's basically all they've got. The rest of what they do is to explain away the contrary evidence by claiming it's still possible to believe despite that evidence.

There is only one way to convince believers in an omniscient God that their faith is false. They must be convinced their faith is impossible before they will consider it to be improbable, and that's an utterly unreasonable standard. So think on this: Given that there are so many different, mutually exclusive faiths, each having the same

Omniscience Escape Clause, believers should seriously entertain that their own God might be false. Sure, an omniscient God might exist (granted for the sake of argument), but how we judge whether or not he exists cannot rely over and over on his omniscience, since that's exactly how other believers defend their own culturally inherited faith.

The concept of God's omniscience is not the only thing that makes theistic faith unfalsifiable. So also does the concept of hell, since believers must be certain there is no hell before they will abandon their faith in order to overcome the force they feel from Pascal's Wager. With the concept of an omniscient God and the threat of hell it is nearly impossible for believers to doubt their faith and then walk away from it. The thought never crosses the Christian mind that if Allah exists there is a hell threat they have not considered before, a threat that makes Muslims deathly afraid to question their faith as well.

Believers must be forced to acknowledge that other believers in different religions (or sects within their own) who have the same concepts have the same problems when it comes to reasonably evaluating their own faith. This is the type of reasoning believers reject when it comes to evaluating the probability of other faiths. They reject other religions even though other religions have their own threats of hell and use the Omniscience Escape Clause to save their faith from refutation. Why is it that they don't reject this same reasoning when it comes to their own faith?

WHAT IF CHRISTIANS WERE TO GO ON STRIKE?

To make this point clearer let me offer an argument that seems reasonable to accept when it comes to other faiths but is rejected when it comes to one's own faith. This argument was provoked online by a blog poster who used the name "Walter." Consistent with the pervasive need felt by Christian apologists to argue against skeptics so that others are not led away from the faith, he asked, "Aren't Christians supposed to be guided to the truth by the Holy Spirit? Are John's arguments more powerful than the Third Person of the Trinity?"[13]

Workers go on strike when they are overworked and underpaid. So I got to thinking, what would happen if Christian believers from around the world went on strike. This strike would be against having to do all the evangelistic and apologetic work themselves. What if they stopped praying for others to be saved? What if they stopped telling others about Jesus? What if Christians stopped evangelizing and arguing on behalf of Christianity? What if all evangelists, missionaries, and apologists went on strike and instead let the Holy Spirit do the work?

I'm serious. What would happen? I know Christians think they have a commission mandate to do missionary work, so this will never happen. Consider it a thought experiment instead. Can God do this work himself? If he can, then why does he need Christians do this work at all? If he cares, really cares for people, then he should do something himself. Would God step in and show he cares if they were to go on strike? Would he do what is right because it is the right thing to do regardless of whether Christians helped him? Would Christianity survive and even thrive into the future because God would be forced to get involved? Or would Christianity die out as God lets the world and its people go to hell? If God sits back and does nothing while the world goes to hell, then he cannot be a good God, or perhaps he's just too lazy.

If Christians were to go on strike there should be no cause for concern. If God is really inside the Christian faith then it cannot fail. The theme of the book of Revelation is God's victory in the end. So the faith response is to relax, since God's victory is assured. "Be still and know that I am God," believers are told. Actually, the Hebrew in Psalms 46:10 is better translated, "Cease, and know that I am God." So don't be frustrated. Don't lose any sleep over it either. God is winning and will win in the end. After all, in Matthew 11:30 Jesus reportedly said, "My yoke is easy and my burden is light." Imagine that, me, offering devotional advice!

It seems to me believers feel they must argue against me in order to keep others from being persuaded by what I write. "Oh," I imagine them saying to themselves, "I must say something lest others be led astray." That's because they don't believe God can keep people away from my arguments. They don't believe that God can give believers an extra jolt of the God juice or that he is able to answer a prayer in a spectacular way in order to mitigate my arguments or that God can speak to believers or appear to them, if needed. They simply do not believe God can blind people to blogs or books like mine. They don't believe God can change the search-engine results so that susceptible believers will not find skeptical websites. They do not believe God can keep any thought of reading something by a skeptic out of the minds of susceptible believers. They do not believe God can take away critical thinking skills so that susceptible believers will not be led astray if they do happen to come upon skeptical blogs or literature.

Believers act and talk as if God isn't helping them at all, as if God doesn't care to do anything if they don't do it themselves. They really do not believe the parable of the lost sheep applies to God, that he will do everything he can to shepherd his sheep. Christians claim to "pray as if it's all up to God, but act as if it's all up to us." But it appears as if Christians do not even think prayers to God will work. Christians really do not believe God can defend himself. They don't believe their God will take the necessary steps to defeat arguments against his existence and his plan of salvation. It proves to me that their God needs human beings to do this work because he doesn't exist at all.

If Christians all went on strike then Christianity would go out of existence. That's *my* prediction. You know it. I know it. Everyone who is not a Christian knows it. The Christian faith needs people of faith who proselytize. This is true of every religion. Without people of faith any given religion would die out because there is no deity behind any of them. That's what Christians think of other faiths. That's what they should think of Christian faith as well.

What's your prediction?

In order to suppose that the Christian faith would not die out Christians need to provide some objective evidence that God is doing something now that would help convert people even if Christians stopped sharing the Gospel. So, what, objectively, is God doing now?

Christian apologist Randal Rauser replied to this argument, saying that it was a "new one."[14] I doubt that's the case, since there have been many skeptics who have asked why God needs human beings to propagate the faith. If there is a new aspect to it then it's probably my proposal that Christians should go on strike. In any case, in one of his responses he said that if the church died out "it would still be fully compatible with the existence of the Christian God." It seems Rauser uses that kind of escape way too often, which goes to show that I must prove his faith is impossible before he will ever consider it to be improbable. Let me show something by simply inserting the letter *x* in his sentence. Let it now read: "X would be fully compatible with the existence of the Christian God." Now replace *x* with the following words and phrases one by one, things Rauser himself has said on different occasions in defense of his faith:

Evolution

The evolution of concepts about God

The evolution of morality

That the Bible is indistinguishable from God not revealing himself at all

So I asked him to get serious with me. No more playing games. I asked him to answer the late Antony Flew's question. "What would count against your faith?" You know what he said?

"The bones of Jesus."

Rauser is a master at playing word games. He will not entertain that his faith is false. He's actually so good at it that he's deceiving himself and doesn't know it. There isn't anything that counts against his faith. No matter what the problem is, it's compatible with his faith, if by "compatible" he means it's still possible his faith is correct until it's been proven false.

The bones of Jesus? Really? You and I and everyone else know we will never find them, and even if we did there would be no way of knowing they were really his bones. This demand places too high a demand upon nonbelievers. It places his faith beyond the reach of reason and science. His faith is untouchable, unfalsifiable, and delusional. My claim is that the more believers are educated in their faith, the *more*, not *less*, deluded they can be. Rauser is exhibit A for this.

COGNITIVE BIASES

This brings me to cognitive biases. From what I can tell, the basis of all the logical informal fallacies of Christian apologists resides in a wide assortment of cognitive biases that human beings all share, which have been more than amply documented. It's quite possible that if you can think of an informal fallacy there are Christians who depend on it to defend their faith. We have biases that cause us to adopt ideas that cannot be reasonably justified. We have biases that cause us to justify those unreasonable ideas. We have biases that prohibit us from being objective with the facts. We have biases that cause us to neglect relevant data. We have biases that cause us to confirm what we prefer to be true. We have biases that can even cause us to become more entrenched in what we think even after our cherished concepts have been refuted. These are the facts. No one can dispute them. Even knowing these facts, most of us will claim to be exceptions to them, even though it's impossible for so many of us to be the one exception.

I've mentioned some of these biases in this book, especially in chapter 3. But here are some other relevant ones. Confirmation bias is the overarching term that describes the strong tendency we have for seeking to interpret information in a manner that confirms our expectations. We do it. All of us. Most of us don't know how to think differently. We seek to confirm rather than disconfirm what we believe. That's why most believers will not read a skeptical book. Instead, they'd rather read an apologetics book that confirms what they believe. Muslims will read books defending Islam. Scientologists will read books defending Scientology. And Mormons will read books defending Mormonism. Very rarely will believers step outside and read the opposition. Very rarely will believers seek to disconfirm what they believe even though disconfirming evidence is decisive evidence.

For instance, I actually saw the Pool of Siloam in Jerusalem for myself when I visited there in 1988. What follows from this? The archaeological evidence is consistent with the Gospel stories about Jesus sending the blind man there to wash (John 9:1–7). But it does nothing to show Jesus healed the man. Roswell, New Mexico, is an actual city, too. Is this evidence of the existence of aliens? Both cases are equivalent. The existence of the Pool of Siloam and the City of Roswell are what we would expect to find if such claims were true, but that's all they can show. This is called confirming evidence. Confirming evidence confirms while disconfirming evidence disconfirms. At best, then, what Christians have are archaeological findings regarding the Pool of Siloam that are consistent with what they believe in the same way that the existence of the City of Roswell confirms the existence of aliens or the existence of Bethlehem confirms that Jesus was born of a virgin. But this kind of evidence is negligible at best. That's because confirming evidence is easy to come by. It can be found at every corner. Disconfirming evidence, however, is decisive evidence. It only takes a small amount of disconfirming evidence to discredit something. Confirming evidence is not entirely irrelevant, but it takes a whole lot of it to confirm something when there is no evidence to the contrary. Therefore we should pay more attention to disconfirming evidence and even actively seek it out. Of course this is what the OTF is all about, being reasonable skeptics who seek out the appropriate kind of evidence.

We have many other biases. There is an expectation bias, which is the tendency to believe data that agree with our expectations and to disbelieve data that conflict with those expectations. We sometimes perceive what we expect to perceive despite what the data shows. This is akin to observational bias, whereby we have a tendency to count the hits and discount the misses. This is especially true when it comes to considering answers to petitionary prayers. The more prayers that believers pray to the god of their choice then the more often some of those prayers will seem to have been answered in amazing ways simply because of the odds alone. These biases also cause believers to take personal anecdotes as evidence when they're not evidence at all. Clinical studies offer the strongest evidence beyond reasonable doubt for whether prayers enhance healing. By comparing groups of people with the same ailment based on whether or not prayer was part of the clinical intervention, the most methodologically rigorous of these studies have demonstrated that prayer does not enhance patient outcomes. Then there are similar biases, like the knowledge bias, which is the tendency of people to choose the option they know best rather than the best option. There is the mere-exposure effect, which is the tendency to have an undue fondness for things merely because of familiarity with them. And there is the illusion-of-truth effect, whereby people are more likely to believe a familiar statement than an unfamiliar one. These biases get right to the heart of the need for the OTF. There are many others.

Cognitive dissonance is a discomfort caused by holding conflicting views or ideas or values simultaneously. When faced with cognitive dissonance, people will feel surprise, dread, guilt, anger, or embarrassment. It tells us that people have a motivational drive to reduce this uncomfortable feeling by altering their ideas or values or by adding new ones in order to create a consistent system of thought. People have a strong bias for consonance among their ideas and values. So we seek to reduce cognitive dissonance in any way we can, sometimes in defiance of the facts. If this cannot be done satisfactorily we have a strong tendency to deny or reject the new information that causes the discomfort. And because we also have a conservatism bias, we will usually reject the new information if we cannot resolve the dissonance that comes with it. There is also the ostrich effect, which is to ignore painful or potentially negative or falsifying situations or evidence.

Because of these cognitive biases, we often fail to be Bayesians in our thinking, which is the best way to reason about the evidence for any religious faith claim. To be Bayesians in our thinking means we should think exclusively in terms of probabilities. Bayes's Theorem is a mathematical model for evaluating empirical theories with the available evidence by attributing probabilities to the various factors involved and then comparing the probability to that of alternative theories. We need not concern ourselves with the math itself, since explaining it fully would be too time and space intensive for the scope of this book. Very loosely and imprecisely put for the average reader, Bayes's Theorem states that the probability that our explanation of the evidence is true is equal to the following factors: (1) how typical or usual our explanation is, given the evidence, multiplied by (2) how likely or probable the evidence is if our explanation is true, divided by (3) how typical or usual it is that our explanation is false, given the evidence, times (4) how likely or probable the evidence is if our explanation is false.

Richard Carrier explains that, with Bayes's Theorem, "instead of myopically working out how we can explain all the evidence 'with our theory,' we start instead by asking how antecedently likely our theory even is, and then we ask how probable all the evidence is on our theory . . . and how probable all that evidence would be on some other theory."[15] Only then "can we work out whether our theory is actually the best one. If we instead just look to see if our theory fits the evidence, we will end up believing any theory we can make fit." So, "the question must be which explanation, among all the viable alternatives, is actually the most likely. And that's where Bayesian reasoning enters in."[16] This is the point of Bayesian reasoning. We must consider the prior probabilities and weigh them not just with the probability of the evidence for our theory, but also weigh them against the probability of the evidence for alternative theories.

When I was a believer I was infected with a lot of confirmation bias. I wanted my faith to be true. I had invested a great deal of time and effort into defending my faith. But I was shocked and dismayed that even with this bias my faith was a sham. It was heartbreaking and completely contrary to what I had expected. I have not heard from any former Christian who describes it any other way. None of us wanted to conclude what we did. We went kicking and screaming into unbelief.

Listen to what ex-minster Dan Barker said about leaving the fold:

> It was like tearing my whole frame of reality to pieces, ripping to shreds the fabric of meaning and hope, betraying the values of existence. . . . It was like spitting on my mother, or like throwing one of my children out a window. It was sacrilege.[17]

Is there anything comparable for this when an atheist becomes a Christian? I think not. Not by a long shot. What does being a nonbeliever offer us in return? Nothing but nonexistence. We simply had to follow reason no matter what we concluded.

The bottom line is that the OTF is the only antidote to confirmation bias. It demands that one must approach his or her religious faith as if it has the burden of proof. It should make us all think in terms of Bayesian reasoning. It means taking disconfirming evidence seriously.

THAT WHICH DISCONFIRMS UFOs ALSO DISCONFIRMS GOD'S EXISTENCE

The best and only way to avoid cognitive bias then is to actively seek out disconfirming evidence, which is what the OTF encourages believers to do as *informed skeptics*. In 1971 a NASA space orbiter named *Mariner 9* discovered that the canals on Mars were illusory. This discovery strongly disconfirmed the claim that there was intelligent life on that planet. Before this discovery many people claimed they encountered Martians. Afterward, Martians stopped visiting us and we instead started receiving visitors from Venus. Then after the surface of Venus was found to be hot enough to melt lead, Venusians stopped visiting us, too. Now visitors from space come from far more distant places in our universe. What best explains this? It's because there were never any Martians or Venusians who visited earth.

When we examine the messages from UFOs we see that they have always been addressed to the fashions of a particular time period. None of them conveyed any new scientific information, even though visitors from other planets should be far more advanced than us. Before the Cold War was over the messages warned of nuclear war, then later they warned us about the degradation of our environment. Carl Sagan, in his masterful treatment of this phenomena in his book *The Demon Haunted World*, asked why UFOs didn't warn us about ozone depletion in the 1950s or about the HIV virus in the 1970s, "when it might really have done some good? . . . Can it be that aliens know only as much as those who report their presence?"[18]

Now apply this same critical thinking to the Bible and its God. You don't believe Martians or Venusians visited earth. Why? Because we discovered some facts about these planets (yes, I know we've discovered water on Mars). You also don't believe they visited us because the messages these aliens supposedly communicated were not the kind we would expect, offering us nothing new and changing with the fashions of the times.

That's why you shouldn't believe in the God of the Bible.

First, when we discovered that the gods didn't live in the mountains believers then proposed that they lived in the sky. As we gradually discovered how huge the sky was, the God of faith got bigger, too, until believers claimed he lived in an entirely different realm.

Second, Christian, why didn't your God tell us that drinking polluted water would kill us, as would lead poisoning? Why didn't he tell us which poisonous plants and creatures would kill us if we ate them or they bit us? Many people, mostly children, had to die in every part of the planet for humans to learn what would kill us. Where in the Bible can we find your God telling us how to discover penicillin or a vaccine for tuberculosis or polio? Some basic information during the tragedy of the Black Death plague in the fourteenth century, where up to 50 percent of European Christians died, would have been helpful, such as information about the efficacy of quarantining people, which was first learned as a result of this plague. And with God's help scientists could've created a vaccine for the worldwide Spanish Influenza outbreak of 1918, which killed an estimated 50 million people.

But no. We find none of this from God in the Bible, and that's only the beginning. Come on now. Can you actually believe that an omniscient, perfectly good being withheld this kind of information, things that the ancients just didn't know? You don't believe in Martians. Why do you believe in the biblical God? The *only* explanation that fits the data is that a perfectly good, all-powerful God doesn't exist.

TESTING RELIGIOUS EXPERIENCES BY THE OTF

Let me offer how outsiders to a personal religious experience might think about it, not having experienced it for themselves. Religious experience offers a believer the most psychologically certain basis for believing in a particular religion or divine being. When a believer has a religious experience it is really hard, if not psychologically impossible, to argue him or her away from that belief. How then is it possible for a believer who claims to have had such an experience to look at his experience as an outsider, as the OTF demands?

We can point out that the brain often deceives us and provide many examples of this phenomenon (brainwashing, wish fulfillment, cognitive dissonance, the power of suggestion). But believers will maintain that their particular religious experience is *real* because they experienced it, despite the odds that their brains are deceiving them about it.

We can point out that many people of other faiths have claimed to have had similar religious experiences (for example, Mormons, Muslims, Catholics, or Jews), but believers will say their experience is *true* because they experienced it, despite the odds that make it seem obvious they could be wrong. Because of these things, at the very minimum, believers should not take their so-called religious experiences at face value.

Sometimes in the face of such an experiential claim I simply say to believers, "If I had that same experience I might believe, too. But I haven't. So why not? Why doesn't your God give me that same religious experience?" At this point believers must blame me and every living person on the planet for not being open to such a religious experience. Depending on the religion in question, that might include most everyone, up to seven billion of us. But even this realization doesn't affect believers who claim to have had such a religious experience. Some of them will simply say that God doesn't want various people to have a saving religious experience. It never dawns on them that if this is true, the Christian God they love and worship is a mean-spirited, barbaric God, especially if he will send people to eternal punishment because they have not received such an experience.

There are other ways to test religious experiences as an outsider. Let me offer one example from a conversation I had with a friend I'll call "Matt." Matt told me he knows there is an afterlife because he had a vivid dream of his father and grandfather talking to him from beyond the grave. To him this dream was very real. His dad had died ten years earlier and his grandfather had died fifteen years earlier. But here they were, talking face-to-face with him from beyond the grave!

Now if there is one thing about dreams that everyone should know by now, it's that they can seem very real. You may actually feel like you're riding a horse or that you are in a gun battle during World War II. So the fact that dreams seem real does not mean they are real. Dreams are the result of normal brain functioning. This is what our brains do when we are asleep. We dream vivid dreams during REM sleep. So one way for Matt to understand the truth about his dream is to learn what science teaches us about the sleeping brain. Such a study should cause room for plenty of doubt. As scientific understanding gains ground among the scientifically illiterate we should see dreams being used less and less to support religious beliefs.

Back to Matt. I asked him how he knew it was actually his dad and grandfather talking in the dream. "Well," he said, "they told me things that only they could know." "Really?" I questioned, "How does that show you anything at all? If the people in your dream tell you something that you already knew about them before they died, then they're not telling you anything new. This information was already stored in your brain. There is at least one other person in that dream who knew the same things you heard them say, and that person is the one doing the dreaming . . . you! For this dream to be considered evidence that you were actually talking with them they would have to tell you something you didn't know that could be confirmed after you awoke."

Matt replied, "But I am sure it was them. The evidence was that I know what I experienced!"

Then I asked Matt what they each looked like. He said they looked like he had remembered them. "Were they wearing the same kinds of clothes you knew them to wear?" "Yes," he said. "Had they aged any?" "No," he admitted. Then I asked him if people in the afterlife would always look the same, wear the same clothes, and stay the same age? "What are the odds that they were really in your dream versus the odds that you merely had a dream about them based on what you knew them to be?"

At this point he began having some doubts, but then he replied, "Maybe they came back to me looking like this so I could recognize them?"

Wow, isn't this something? What does it take? I don't know sometimes. But evidence? Who needs that when you have an experience? An outsider with this kind of "insider" experience would simply have to admit he or she just doesn't know if the experience was real or a delusion. But a delusion it was.

RELIGIONS DEBUNK THEMSELVES

When it comes to Christianity, I agree with the Protestant criticisms of the Catholics as well as the Catholic criticisms of the Protestants. I agree with the fundamentalist criticisms of the liberals as well as the liberal criticisms of the fundamentalists. In addition, I agree with the Hindu, Muslim, and Jewish criticisms of Christianity as well as the Christian criticisms of Hinduism, Islam, and Judaism. When they criticize each other, I think they're all right.

When Orthodox Jews argue against the Christian belief that Jesus rose from the dead, I agree with their conclusions and quite probably with their reasons as well. When Christians argue against Muhammad flying through the night on a winged horse or the divine inspiration of the Koran, I agree with their criticisms, too. When these different religions use an *informed skepticism* to reject other mutually exclusive extraordinary religious claims of supernatural powers, answered prayers, and miracles, I agree with them all. It doesn't mean, nor should it, that I both agree and disagree with the claim that Jesus did not die on the cross, as Muslims and Christians disagree on this. I cannot possibly accept all of what these mutually exclusive religions believe.

When it comes to liberalism I don't say much by way of criticizing it because I don't have to do so. Christian fundamentalists do that for me. Their criticism of the liberals is my criticism, which centers on one question: Why do they even bother with the Bible at all? Why not the Koran, the Bhagavad Gita, or Mary Baker Eddy's *Science and Health with Key to the Scriptures*? Or, why not just receive direct inspiration from God? Or "listen to their heart"? If believers no longer accept the historical underpinnings of their faith, they should look for a different one, or they should abandon faith altogether. It's the intellectually honest thing to do. To me, liberalism is a pretend game, much like M. Night Shyamalan's movie *The Village*. In my opinion, liberals should stop pretending.

Liberals should openly recognize that they did not come to their conclusions without a fight against the goads. They were forced against their preferences into accepting what science and biblical criticism led them to think. Now all they do is pick and choose which parts of the Bible to believe with no solid criteria for distinguishing the believable parts from the unbelievable parts other than their shared evolving consensus—and, since it's an evolved consensus, they don't need the Bible to inform it. Liberals don't accept anything the Bible says just because it says it. So they can quite easily dispense with it altogether as irrelevant for their lives, as Hector Avalos has effectively argued.[19]

Evangelicals even do the work of debunking themselves. Just take a look at the "four/five views" books published by Zondervan, InterVarsity Press, and Baker Books. As but one example, just look at the book *The Nature of the Atonement: Four Views*, edited by James Beilby and Paul R. Eddy (IVP Academic, 2006). I agree with the criticisms each author presents of the others, for the most part. They debunk themselves. All I have to do is read what they say and then report it to others.

CHRISTIANITY IS DEBUNKED BY SCIENCE

Since science is the basis for the OTF I should say something about how it debunks Christianity. "God is dead," said Friedrich Nietzsche over a century ago. No, God did not die. We just came to the realization that he never existed in the first place. We no longer need him to explain what needs to be explained. We now have better natural explanations of the existing phenomena. Science explains more without recourse to the ad hoc theories that supernatural explanations offer believers. Theologians came to realize this in the 1960s. The cover of *Time* for April 8, 1966, asked what killed him? The answer? Science.

Philology first undermined religion when it was learned that texts could be dated based on grammar, vocabulary, and dialect. Lorenzo Valla used it in the fifteenth century to show that the Donation of

Constantine decree was a forgery. In this forged decree the Emperor Constantine transferred authority over Rome and the western part of the Roman Empire to the pope. From the science of philology we've learned that there are many forgeries in the canonized Bible (2 Isaiah, the pastoral epistles, 2 Peter, and so on) and that certain other books in the Bible reveal an evolutionary history. That's science, baby; kick against the goads all you want to.

The next big hit came from astronomy. The Copernican astronomical revolution, as defended later by Galileo, showed that we do not live in a geocentric universe. Never did. The biblical viewpoint, supposedly coming from a divine mind, did not understand this basic fact. The earth revolves around the sun. And we exist on a spiral arm in one galaxy out of billions in the universe. The Catholic Church took a big hit on this one and lost credibility in the eyes of scientists.

An even bigger hit came from biology, specifically but not limited to Darwinian evolution. The Catholic Church learned from the debacle in Galileo's day and came to embrace evolution as a fact. Evangelicals still denounce it, even though it is slowly winning over the best and the brightest among them. But with evolution we no longer need a creator, for there is nothing left to explain by means of the supernatural hypothesis. Completely obliterated is the literal Genesis account of origins and along with it the need for a redeemer from the supposed original sin of Adam and Eve in the Garden of Eden. Since that's the case, why should anyone think there is any divine mind behind the writings in the Bible at all? No one should.

Everything after this was a forgone conclusion. The Bible was nothing more than a human product. There was no need to look for a divine mind behind the human authors. If God revealed himself to human beings he did so in ways that are indistinguishable from him not revealing himself at all.

Other sciences came into play as well.

Archaeology has debunked many stories in the Bible. Archaeologists have discovered several ancient Mesopotamian texts that predate the ones in the Bible and tell similar superstitious stories of the origins of the universe. It has also shown us there was no exodus of the Israelites out of Egypt.

Psychology shows that we are largely products of our environment, that we often think illogically, that we believe what we prefer to be true, that we are not evil so much as ill. Psychology shows that we are largely shaped by our social environment. It discredits the notion that there is a wrathful God who will punish us forever because of what we believe.

Anthropology shows that there are many different cultures around the globe as well as a great deal of religious diversity. It shows that there are many rational ways to understand our place in this world. Human beings get along just fine living in these so-called different universes. As a result many people are embracing multiculturalism. This is contrary to equating Christianity with the absolute standard for judging cultures. Such a parochial notion is absolute hogwash.

Neurology shows that there is an extremely close relationship between our beliefs and physiological processes in our brains, which can be influenced by drugs or surgical procedures. There is therefore no need for the supernatural explanation of the soul.

In fact, these and other sciences have repeatedly pummeled religion for centuries. The fact that there are still believers is a testament to the stubbornness of belief and the almost willful ignorance that results from the psychological need to believe. This need to believe is most clearly seen in the mind of the believer when we consider the massive amount of ubiquitous worldwide suffering and the lack of any satisfactory theodicy explaining why a good, omnipotent God allows it. The only explanation that can account for continued belief in the presence of this suffering is wish fulfillment.

God is dead. We do not need him. It's time to give up childish things and think as adults. Become scientifically literate. Become informed. Grow out of religious belief just as you grew out of belief in the Tooth Fairy, Santa Claus, and the Easter Bunny.

THE DANGER OF FAITH IS THINKING
YOU BELIEVE WHAT GOD DOES

Finally, I want believers to understand something very significant. What an outsider learns when examining the various religions and sects within them are that every single believer thinks that what they believe is what their god believes. This should cause us some serious concern about not only the truth of what they think but also how they might behave and justify their behavior. A study done by Nicholas Epley, from the University of Chicago, tells us that every believer thinks their God agrees with them on a host of nonrelated issues. According to an article by Ed Young describing these findings,

> Epley asked different groups of volunteers to rate their own beliefs about important issues such as abortion, same-sex marriage, affirmative action, the death penalty, the Iraq War, and the legalization of marijuana. The volunteers also had to speculate about God's take on these issues, as well as the stances of an "average American," Bill Gates (a celebrity with relatively unknown beliefs) and George Bush (a celebrity whose positions are well-known).
>
> For many religious people, the popular question "What would Jesus do?" is essentially the same as "What would I do?" Through a combination of surveys, psychological manipulation and brain-scanning, he has found that when religious Americans try to infer the will of God, they mainly draw on their own personal beliefs.
>
> Epley surveyed commuters at a Boston train station, university undergraduates, and 1,000 adults from a nationally representative database. In every case, he found that people's own attitudes and beliefs matched those they suggested for God more precisely than those they suggested for the other humans.[20]

If this study shows us anything at all it should make believers less certain of what they pontificate about. It confirms Ludwig Feuerbach's famous argument that we made God in our image. In fact, this study falsifies faith itself, for there is no independent way to determine what God thinks, if he exists at all. Believers simply create their own religion, their own Gospel, and their own God in their own image. This is also a recipe for disaster, since believers will claim they have a divine mandate for anything they think is the case, something I think is dangerous in a world with weapons of mass destruction that is already on the brink of a number of potential environmental disasters.

10
WHY SHOULD ANYONE BELIEVE ANYTHING AT ALL?

I will argue in this chapter that faith by its very nature cannot pass the Outsider Test for Faith, and this means neither can Christianity. I think this is a reasonable conclusion. In fact, even if God exists we should not have faith in him. Why? Because faith is an irrational leap over the probabilities. Because reasonable faith is an oxymoron. Faith is an attitude or feeling whereby believers attribute a higher degree of probability to the evidence than what the evidence calls for. Faith is a cognitive bias that causes believers to overestimate confirming evidence and underestimate disconfirming evidence. So if we have to have faith in order to please God then we are being asked to do something no reasonable person should do. If God created us as reasonable people then he took away our ability to give him what he demands, faith.

This chapter might be a hotly contested one. I'm going to argue that no one should believe anything at all, that when it comes to truth propositions about reality we should think exclusively in terms of the probabilities. So I should reiterate that this chapter, like the last one, represents stage-three types of arguments, where we argue our conclusions based upon accepting the OTF. Readers should understand that objecting to the main argument of this chapter does nothing to undermine the test itself. It is a conclusion I have come to based on the test, but my conclusion is not necessitated by the test.

THE PROBLEM IS FAITH ITSELF

Dr. Victor Reppert wrote: "If what it is to be skeptical is just to entertain skeptical questions about one's beliefs, to subject them to scrutiny, to take seriously possible evidence against them and to ask what reasons can be given for them, then I have been performing the outsider test since 1972."[1] But has he? I don't think so at all. I don't think any religion can pass the OTF, especially any of the so-called revealed religions.

Michael Shermer did some extensive research on why people believe in God and other weird things. Nine out of ten people said that other people are influenced by nonrational factors to believe in weird things, and yet these same respondents turned around and said they were the exceptions to the rule. How is it possible for nine out of ten respondents to be the exceptions to what nine out of ten of them recognize to be the rule? Logically they cannot all be correct about this. Either 90 percent of them came to their conclusions rationally, which we *know* is not the case from psychological studies, or the respondents are simply deceiving themselves and are no different from other people. As human beings we have what Shermer calls an *intellectual attribution bias*, "where we consider our own actions as being rationally motivated, whereas we see those of others as more emotionally driven. Our commitment to a belief is attributed to a rational decision and intellectual choice; whereas the other person's is attributed to need and emotion."[2] And Shermer goes on to explain that "smart people, because they are more intelligent and better educated, are better able to give intellectual reasons justifying their beliefs that they arrived at for nonintelligent reasons," even though "smart people, like everyone else, recognize that emotional needs and being raised to believe something are how most of us most of the time come to our beliefs."[3]

So upon what basis do nearly all believers around the world, including Reppert, think they are the exceptions? Believers are simply in denial when they claim their religious faith passes the OTF. Psychology has repeatedly shown us that people, all people, seek to confirm what they believe, and we also have an intellectual attribution bias to explain away what we intuitively know to be true. We do not come to our conclusions based solely on rational considerations. Because of these biases, *believers should be just as skeptical that their particular religious faith passes the OTF as they reasonably are when other believers in different religions claim the same thing.*

Rather than subjecting his own religious faith "to scrutiny," as Reppert claims to have done, if he had instead subjected his faith to the same level of reasonable skepticism that he applies in assessing the other religious faiths he rejects, that would be more impressive to me. Instead, Reppert, like most Christians, has adopted St. Anselm's motto, "faith seeking understanding" (*fides quaerens intellectum*). Theirs is a faith that calls upon believers to subsequently understand, confirm, and defend what they believe. In fact, most Christian thinkers, from Tertullian to Luther to William Lane Craig, have disparaged reason in favor of faith. Faith is the warp and woof of Christian theology and apologetics. Faith is belief in search of data. Faith seeks to confirm itself. But such a faith attitude is not conducive to testing what one believes, so long as believers have faith in the first place. Until believers repudiate such a faith stance, they cannot claim with a straight face that their faith has passed the OTF. Faith is an irrational cognitive bias. *Faith is not something Christians can have while seeking to examine the religion that was given to them, since that is not how they approach any of the other religions they reject.*

This is the conclusion I have come to even after reading a great many Christian justifications for faith from Christian philosophers and apologists such as Alvin Plantinga, Richard Swinburne, William Lane Craig, and others. In my years of blogging there is nothing I have written that elicits more of an adverse response from Christian believers than when I have denounced faith in favor of scientifically based reasoning. I can write against the resurrection, miracles, or the inspiration of the Bible, but when I write against faith the blog world lights up (well, those who read my blog anyway). Why? George H. Smith tells us in his book *Atheism: The Case against God*: "In order to understand the nature of a philosophical conflict one must grasp the fundamental differences that give rise to the conflict." True enough. Applied to debates between atheism and Christianity he identifies what it is: "The conflict between Christian theism and atheism is fundamentally a conflict between faith and reason. This, in epistemological terms, is the essence of the controversy. Reason and faith are opposites, two mutually exclusive terms: there is no reconciliation or common ground. Faith is belief without, or in spite of, reason."[4] As such, "for the atheist, to embrace faith is to abandon reason."[5]

There was a time when I thought Smith was foolish, ignorant, and at best philosophically naïve. But not anymore. Smith is right. There is a good reason why atheists are described as nonbelievers. In fact, Smith goes on to say: "I am not merely arguing, as a matter of historical fact, that all attempts to reconcile reason and faith have failed. My position is stronger than this. I am asserting that all such efforts must fail, that it is logically impossible to reconcile reason and faith. The concept of faith itself carries a 'built in' depreciation of reason; and without this anti-reason element, the concept of faith is rendered meaningless."[6] "I am arguing that faith as such, faith as an alleged method of acquiring knowledge, is totally invalid—and as a consequence, all propositions of faith, because they lack rational demonstration, must conflict with reason."[7] Smith concludes, "With the preceding groundwork, we now arrive at what may be termed the central dilemma of faith: Insofar as faith is possible, it is irrational; insofar as faith is rational, it is impossible."[8]

Christian philosophers will scoff at these statements like I did at one time. They will say such a view is naïve at best. They will say that if I embrace such a view I can no longer be taken seriously. Okay. Let them. I cannot convince them of much anyway. It's a conclusion I have come to based on all that I know, and I cannot say all that I know. If they disagree with me then maybe they can explain why Norman L. Geisler, arguably one of the biggest names in Christian apologetics, along with cowriter Frank Turek, say in their book *I Don't Have Enough Faith to Be an Atheist,* "The less evidence you have for your position, the more faith you need to believe it (and vice versa). Faith covers a gap in knowledge." Their whole argument in that book is that "the atheist has to muster a lot more faith than the Christian."[9] Implicit here is the assumption that faith adds something to the mix, that it takes off where the probabilities end. My question is, was, and always will be, what does faith add to the probabilities? As far as I can tell leaping that gap is irrational.

DEFINITIONS OF FAITH

Christians themselves have an evolved understanding of what faith is, and they cannot agree among themselves. Malcolm Ruel in his book *Belief, Ritual and the Securing of Life,* discusses this evolved understanding. In *Introducing Anthropology of Religion,* David Eller offers a useful summary, noting that Ruel

> demonstrates that the concept of belief in Western civilization and Christianity has evolved, from a kind of "trust" in god(s) to specific propositions about God and Christ to the notion of "grace" based on the personal experience of and commitment to God and Christ to a conception of belief as an "adventure of faith" which does not have any particular destination or make any specific claims. The evolutionary trajectory of belief in Christianity is, then, distinctively "local" and historical—that is, culturally and religiously relative— and not to be found in every religion. Many religions do not have any "creed" of explicit propositions about their supernatural worlds, and many do not mix fact, trust, and value in the English/Christian way. Ruel concludes that the English and Western concept of belief is "complex, highly ambiguous, and unstable." It "is demonstrably an historical amalgam, composed of elements traceable to Judaic mystical doctrine and Greek styles of discourse."[10]

So let me share some of the skeptical definitions (or descriptions) of faith that I've found and contrast them with what Christians would say about other faiths, a sort of outsider test for faith definitions.

There are plenty of them to be found. Skeptics all seem to share the same basic view about faith.

Voltaire: "Faith consists in believing, not what appears to be true, but what appears to our understanding to be false. Only by faith can Asiatics believe in the voyage of Mohammed to the seven planets, the incarnation of the god Fo, or Vishnu, of Xaca, of Brahma, of Sammonocodom, etc. etc. etc."[11]

Mark Twain famously defined faith as "believing what you know ain't true."[12]

Sam Harris: "Faith is the license religious people give themselves to keep believing when reasons fail."[13]

Richard Dawkins: "The whole point of religious faith, its strength and chief glory, is that it does not depend on rational justification. The rest of us are expected to defend our prejudices."[14]

Matt McCormick, in selected quotations from chapter 11, "The 'F' Word," in his book *Atheism and the Case against Christ*:[15]

"To take something on faith or to believe by faith is to believe it despite contrary or inadequate evidence. It is to believe anyway when there's not enough support from evidence and reason to clear the way."

"If someone's reaction to my arguments against the resurrection and other religious beliefs is that she has faith, then she is conceding the central point. In effect, she is acknowledging that in order to believe those religious doctrines, one must ignore the inefficiencies in the evidence and believe anyway."

"If there is sufficient evidence to justify the conclusion, then faith isn't needed. So to suggest that faith and evidence jointly justify is acknowledging that the evidence by itself isn't enough, and I will ignore that gap and believe anyway."

"In fact, the need to invoke faith to bridge the gap affirms the inadequacy of the evidence."

"In effect, the faith response amounts to, 'I'm going to believe anyway, despite those objections.' That's just dogmatic irrationality, not a serious consideration that the critic must give some further objection to."

Victor J. Stenger, from the preface to his book *God and the Folly of Faith*:[16]

"Faith is belief in the absence of supportive evidence and even in the light of contrary evidence."

"Theology is faith-plus reason, with some observation allowed. Science is observation-plus reason, with no faith allowed."

"Science and religion are fundamentally incompatible because of their unequivocally opposed epistemologies—the separate assumptions they make concerning what we can know about the world."

"The differences between science and religion are not merely matters of different points of view that might be harmonized with some effort. They are forever irreconcilable."

Anthropology professor David Eller:

"Knowing is not believing." According to him "knowledge is about reason" while "belief is about faith." He says, "the two are logically and psychologically utterly different and even incompatible."[17]

A. C. Grayling succinctly summarizes this view: "Faith is a negation of reason. Reason is the faculty of proportioning judgment to evidence, after first weighing the evidence. Faith is belief even in the face of contrary evidence."[18]

Bertrand Russell said: "We may define 'faith' as a firm belief in something for which there is no evidence. Where there is evidence, no one speaks of 'faith.' We do not speak of faith that two and two are four or that the earth is round. We only speak of faith when we wish to substitute emotion for evidence."[19] He says, "I think faith is a vice, because faith means believing a proposition when there is no good reason for believing it. That may be taken as a definition of faith."[20]

W. L. Reese, in his massive *Dictionary of Philosophy and Religion: Eastern and Western Thought*, defines faith as "an attitude of belief which goes beyond the available evidence."[21]

Now to help Christians see why skeptics have come to this conclusion all we have to do is randomly insert various religious faiths into these statements. Let me do this for just a few of them:

"Faith is the license Mormons give themselves to keep believing when reasons fail."

"The whole point of the Orthodox Jewish faith, its strength and chief glory, is that it does not depend on rational justification. The rest of us are expected to defend our prejudices."

"The Scientologist faith is an attitude or feeling whereby someone attributes a higher degree of probability to the evidence than what the evidence calls for."

"The Hindu faith is an irrational leap over the probabilities."

"Reasonable faith in Haitian voodoo is an oxymoron."

"The overcoming of doubts or counter-evidence is the essential feature of the Shinto faith."

"The Muslim faith is belief in the absence of supportive evidence and even in the light of contrary evidence."

Perhaps it might seem clearer now to Christian philosophers who think such a view is philosophically naïve. Christians reject the faiths of other religions precisely because they are faith-based. They just do not understand that their own religion or sect shares that same foundation. If the problem is not faith itself, then what is it?

Christians will object that faith is a reasonable trust in a person, their God, even when it might seem he is untrustworthy. Faith is trusting God in the face of contrary evidence, just as we might still trust a person after identifying some reasons for not doing so. The problem, however, is that believers have never personally met God; that is, they have never shook his hand and held him tight. All they have are personal, private, subjective religious experiences, and that's it, experiences that believers in other deities likewise claim. The only way someone can objectively place a reasonable trust in the existence of one's deity, and that he cares, is with sufficient evidence that he exists and that he cares. There is no other way. There must be sufficient evidence for this trust. Faith has nothing to do with this. Probabilities are all that matter.

I don't expect believers to agree until they reject faith, but it is crystal clear to the rest of us that faith is irrational. Just as the religious faiths of others are considered irrational to Christians, so also is their own faith. Just as Christians think other religious faiths are held despite the cold hard evidence, so also is their own faith. The problem is faith. All religions share the same fundamental basis: faith. With faith as a basis anything can be believed, and anything can be denied. With faith the probabilities are all in the eyes of the beholder.

WHY FAITH IS IRRATIONAL

David Eller, probably more than anyone else, has explained what religious believers do and why skeptics reject faith of any kind as fundamentally incompatible with scientifically based reasoning. Eller claims that if believers "can drag down real knowledge to their level and erase any distinctions between the true and the false, the known and the merely felt or believed or guessed, they can rest comfortably in their own undeserved self-certainty."[22] Since the English language has the words *belief* and *faith* in our lectionaries we instinctively use them when others words would be better. No scientifically minded person should say, "I believe the earth is round" or "I believe our universe began with a big bang," or "I believe two parallel lines do not intersect." That is a misuse of the word, a word inherited in the Christian Western world. We know these things to be the case. When someone says, "I believe it will rain tomorrow" or "I believe the sun will rise tomorrow morning," these are predictions. Predictions are either based on good evidence or they are not. So the proper way to speak would be: "I predict it will rain tomorrow." When it comes to the sun rising we should say: "I know the sun will rise tomorrow." The same thing goes for the sentence, "I believe that the accused is innocent of the crime." One could be intending to say "I hope" or "I trust" or "I desire that he is innocent of the crime." If the person has solid evidence to back it up then he can say, "I know he's innocent." Then we can evaluate the evidence.

Eller explains, "So, clearly, most of the time when we say that we 'believe that' something, we are really engaging in some other activity than belief."[23] Eller writes that in "situations where the evidence is inadequate and the question is unsettled, it is wise for us to neither believe nor disbelieve but to wait for more information . . . if the evidence warrants a positive conclusion, accept it as true; if the evidence warrants a negative conclusion, reject it as false; if the evidence warrants no conclusion, postpone arriving at a conclusion while pursuing more information. But at no point is belief warranted, necessary or helpful." He continues, "Belief can never be anything better than premature arrival at a conclusion (figuratively 'jumping to a conclusion') and can often be much worse, like accepting an unjustified and more-than-likely false conclusion."[24] Eller rightly concludes, "There is knowledge and there are other kinds of things—opinions, hypotheses, theories, preferences, predictions, hopes, values, and wishes—but belief quite emphatically and thoroughly has no place in our mental world."[25]

Saying that I have "faith" or a "belief" requires nomenclature I reject, given a proper understanding of what those words mean. Most definitions of these words are a result of the prevalence of the Gospel in the Western world, which demands "belief unto salvation." So I do not have *any* beliefs at all about matters of fact; or, more precisely, I *shouldn't* have any beliefs at all about them. If someone thinks this conclusion is silly then, if nothing else, they should realize that the definitions of words are always evolving. Dictionaries only tell us how people *currently* use words; they do not weigh in on whether the definitions of words are sufficiently precise for nuanced arguments like the ones presented in this book. Because Christianity, in my judgment, fails the OTF, and because the definitions of *belief* and *faith* are inextricably bound into the web of meanings Christianity has cast upon Western civilization, I follow Eller in rejecting the use of these words to characterize the relationship human beings ought to have with propositions about the reality in which we live.

Let me explain further. Let's just take the following five propositions:

1. Yogi Subbayah Pullavar levitated into the air for four minutes on June 6, 1936.
2. Swedish poet and author Barbro Karlen is Anne Frank reincarnated.
3. Wearing magic underwear protects Mormons from all sorts of harm.
4. Alien Body Thetans live inside us because of an incident caused by an ancient galactic dictator named Xenu.
5. Jesus ascended from the earth into the sky, where heaven is located.

Each of these propositions is a knowledge claim subject to an assessment of whether or not it is probable. I'm reminded of the title of Tina Turner's song "What's Love Got to Do With It." However, here I'm asking, what's faith got to do with it? Each of the above knowledge claims is either improbable or not. What's faith got to do with accepting them? What does faith add when assessing them? Nothing that I can see. Nothing at all. If these five propositions are improbable, as we must reasonably admit, then faith is irrelevant, unnecessary, unhelpful, and can lead people to believe in absurdities against the probabilities. Hitchhiking on a line from Tina Turner's song, faith is a second-hand emotion.

Christians retort that I have faith in reason, in skepticism, in science, in my senses, and in the evidence, but what can they possibly mean? Could trusting them be conceivably wrong at times? Yes, of course. We even know this. But there simply is no alternative but to trust them. Faith provides no remedy to this at all. It has no method. It solves no problems. It isn't a reasonable alternative. Having provided evidence for a finding, you will never hear a scientist say to others, "The rest you must take on faith" or "where the evidence is lacking you must have faith." A good scientist will never claim more than what the evidence shows.

Another Christian retort is to say, "The reliability of reason cannot be proven because to do so is circular and therefore fallacious." By contrast, consider the reliability of faith as an alternative. It has given us nearly forty-five thousand different religious sects, none of which can agree on anything more than that there are supernatural forces and/or supernatural beings and that the reliability of reason cannot be proven. So let's just use their own words against them, inserting the word *faith*: "The reliability of *faith* cannot be proven because to do so is circular and therefore fallacious." Clearly, they have two different standards, one for faith and one for reason. They are demanding that reason must be "proven" to be reliable before they will ever consider their method of faith to be unreliable. Do they seek to prove the reliability of faith? If not, they should not demand the same concerning reason, especially since there is such a deep disconnect between the two in terms of reliability and demonstrated efficacy. In the hands of human beings reason has its flaws, but in conjunction with science it is the only game in town. All that faith can do is sit on the sidelines and watch. It offers us nothing at all by comparison.

To be clear, when I say faith is an irrational leap over the probabilities I'm not saying that people who take the leap of faith are irrational people, only that it's irrational to take that leap. But once believers have taken the irrational leap of faith they often make rational judgments based on it. Having accepted faith as a foundation, it's rational to conclude, as Pat Robertson does, that national disasters are God's judgment for our sins. The problem isn't that his utterly ignorant conclusion isn't rational. The problem is his faith. Faith is irrational. It's also rational for Fred Phelps and the Westboro Baptist Church to argue that "God hates fags." The problem isn't that their utterly ignorant conclusion isn't rational. The problem is their faith. Faith is irrational. The establishment of the Inquisition was a rational action taken by the Catholic Church. The Church believed heresy was a leavening influence in society and, as such, was the worst crime of all. It could send others to hell. So they concluded that heretics must die. The problem wasn't that their utterly ignorant conclusion wasn't rational. It was their faith. Faith is irrational.

FAITH AGAINST THE PROBABILITIES

Faith is a parasite on the mysterious. Without mystery, faith couldn't exist. Wherever there is mystery there will always be room for faith because humans seek an explanation for the mysterious. For believers, their particular God-concept fills in the mysterious gaps. Believers require solutions to nearly all mysteries before they will consider their faith unreasonable, and that's an unreasonable epistemic standard, since there will probably always be mysteries. One should conclude only what the probabilities show, and one should never assert more than what the evidence leads us to think is probably the case. Otherwise, as Stephen Law has argued, "anything based on faith, no matter how ludicrous, can be made to be consistent with the available evidence, given a little patience and ingenuity."[26]

To see this for what it is, consider the story of the man who thought he was dead. He went to his doctor, who tried to reason with the man, pointing out that he was really still alive. Finally the doctor asked the man, "Do dead men bleed? If you cut a dead man, does he bleed?" The man replied, "No. The heart is not beating, there is no blood pressure, so if you cut a dead man, he does not bleed." The doctor then took a scalpel and nicked the man on his finger, and his finger began to bleed. As the blood continued to come forth, the doctor said to the man, "See, you are bleeding. What does that tell you?" And the man answered, "Well, I guess dead men do bleed after all."

This anecdote illustrates what skeptics see over and over again, and why faith is irrational. Believers will either deny the evidence or they will reinterpret their faith to adjust to the evidence. Only a very rare few of them will ever seriously question faith itself.

This is what I know about faith:

1. Faith has no method.
2. Faith cannot settle differences between believers.
3. Faith does not lead to new discoveries.
4. Faith cannot solve any problems.

5. Faith cannot explain anything.
6. Faith depends on mysteries.
7. Faith can and does lead to a denial of the evidence.
8. Faith is pretty much immune from debunking.
9. Faith is rooted in fear and ignorance.
10. With faith as a foundation anything at all can be believed or denied.

The problem is that practically nothing is certain. But accepting some conclusion because it's merely possible is irrational. We should never do that. I suppose it's possible a man could jump off a building and fly, right? After all, he could instantaneously grow wings or a huge burst of air could keep him afloat or a supernatural force could propel him through the air. It's even possible that the man could be dreaming, and in the dream he can fly, or that there isn't a material world, and in the world of his mind he can fly. Okay, I understand all this. All these scenarios are remotely possible, I suppose, but because they are so remote I consider them virtually impossible.

By contrast, consider the opposite scenario. It's probable that if the man jumps off a building he will fall to the ground. How probable is this? Well, since it's possible he won't fall (per our examples above), we cannot say with certainty that he will fall. But it's virtually certain that he will. In between these extremes there are a lot of different odds for something, stretching from extremely improbable, very improbable, improbable, and slightly improbable to even odds, slightly probable, probable, very probable, and extremely probable. As I have said, we should think exclusively in terms of probabilities. We don't have a word to differentiate between the odds on that continuum stretching from virtually impossible to virtually certain. But does anyone really want to suggest the word *faith* applies to these different probabilities such that there is the same amount of faith required to accept any one of them? If so, that is being irrational.

If believers want to say that more faith is required to accept something that is virtually impossible and less faith is required to accept something that is virtually certain, what can they possibly mean? What is faith at that point? Faith adds nothing to the actual probabilities. Having more of it or less of it does not change anything. If it's possible to accept a virtually impossible conclusion by having more faith, that's irrational. And if we have a virtually certain conclusion then we don't need faith at all.

What about something that is only slightly probable, one might ask. What if we accept something that has only a 60 percent chance of being true? I still don't see where faith can change the actual probabilities. Faith cannot change a thing, you see. Faith adds nothing. Accepting faith as a basis for knowledge is irrational. Who would fill in the probability gap with anything more than what the probabilities actually show us?

Not me.

The *only* sense I can make of the way believers use the word *faith* is that it's an irrational leap over the probabilities. Believers fill in the actual probabilities with faith in order to call an improbable conclusion extremely probable, and that is quite simply irrational. A probability is a probability is a probability. When it comes to propositions about entities that exist or events that may have taken place, we must think exclusively in terms of probabilities.

DOES ALL KNOWLEDGE HAVE A FAITH ELEMENT?

Christians have been thinking about faith for a very long time, beginning with Jesus' disciples and continuing with the apostle Paul, Augustine, Anselm, Aquinas, Calvin, and others. So Christians have framed the debate in the Western world. The reason this issue is so important to believers is because, well, they are believers. I am a doubter, a skeptic. I think this is the direction science leads thinking people. It leads us to doubt and to come to conclusions based on sufficient evidence. It's what we should do, so it doesn't matter if we don't always do it.

Christians claim that all knowledge has a faith element and that, since nothing is certain, people must assume some things based on faith in order to come to any knowledge at all. I do not deny that at any given time we must assume some things, since we cannot place on the table everything we think is true and examine it all at the same time. This is especially true of our most basic notions: that we exist, that we communicate with other people, that our memories represent the past, that there was a past, that there is a material world, that our senses give us accurate input, that we are not dreaming right now, and so on. What I deny is that we accept any of these things by faith. We might be wrong, but faith isn't what allows us to accept such things. Scientific reasoning based on probabilities is.

Christian philosopher Randal Rauser thinks what I've written applies to us all, not just to believers: "The fact is that everyone can be guilty of holding a belief beyond what the evidence warrants. You can have an irrational commitment in your favorite sports team, or the rightness of your nation's foreign policy, or your own intellectual prowess."[27] However, such things as rooting for a sports team are different. Rooting for a team is fun. It bonds people together; we can win bragging rights or even a bet. So we do it. We hope our team wins. I do it. When it comes to hoping to win the affections of a lover, or hoping to do a good job at something, or even hoping our arguments are good ones, hope is often a prerequisite for achievement. Except in the case of dumb luck, one cannot achieve what one does not hope to achieve. *A person can reasonably hope beyond the actual probabilities when that person can achieve more with such a hope than without it.* Hope helps people overcome the odds because positive thoughts and actions help change them. If a boy hopes to be a professional baseball player, that hope may mature into a commitment to rigorous training, which will make it more likely that he will succeed. Positive thinking and positive acting work because they help us overcome the odds. And people most often react positively to someone who acts positively. Therefore, hoping against low odds is a reasonable thing to do in many cases. *Hoping against the odds changes the actual probabilities because the person doing the hoping is part of the odds.*

But hoping to change facts that do not involve the person doing the hoping is irrational. Either a virgin had a baby or she did not. Either Jesus rose from the dead or he did not. Hope has nothing to do with these concrete examples.

Rauser calls this *John's BS* (belief stricture) and asks how I can know that probability is all that matters, as if I need a metajustification for what seems obvious, or I need to prove it. But I never said this conclusion is a certain one derived from a deductive argument. It's an inductive conclusion. Probability is what makes for scientific progress and for good, sound reasoning, so therefore, unless someone can show why I should accept a less-than-probable conclusion, I should still base my thinking on the probabilities. If Rauser wants to hang his hat on possibilities then it's possible he's a poached egg!

Christians will continue to argue that there is such a thing as misplaced faith, so there must also be a well-founded or reasonable faith; which is to say, faith is not always irrational. I argue that people simply misjudge the probabilities, and that's it. Faith should have nothing to do with this process. Why would anyone believe something against the probabilities?

Rauser thinks it's easy to define *faith*. He defines it as "assent to a proposition that is conceivably false."[28] By doing so he's lowered the bar so far that everyone could be thought to have faith. On the basis of this self-serving definition he can go on to claim Christians are doing nothing more than what all other people do. Faith, then, is equally involved when it comes to trusting our short-term memories, our senses, and even scientific conclusions that are based on an overwhelming amount of physical evidence.

Now I don't doubt for a minute that all propositions are conceivably false. What I deny is that mere possibilities count as anything significant. The more something is considered conceivably false, the less we should pay attention to it, for if we were to treat every proposition as being equally likely to be false, simply because any fact is *conceivably* false, we would all be paralyzed and unable to accept any proposition as true. This is what I object to.

Let's just focus on one example, the fact that the sun will rise tomorrow morning over the horizon where I live in Indiana. Given that the sun has risen every day of the earth's existence, and given that the earth has existed for about 4.5 billion years, the odds that it will rise again tomorrow are about 1.643 trillion to 1. So when I say I know the sun will rise today I can say this with a great deal of certainty. The odds are virtually certain the sun will rise over the horizon (even if clouds might hide it from view).

The question is whether I need to be absolutely certain that the sun will rise tomorrow. I think not, obviously so. I don't need this gap to be filled. I don't need to be certain the sun will rise tomorrow. I am quite comfortable going with the odds, the probabilities. I could be wrong, but so what? Probability is all that matters. We should think exclusively in terms of probabilities. Faith adds nothing to my calculations at all. This goes for everything else I think is probably true.

Is faith used to calculate the very probabilities I use to conclude the sun will rise tomorrow? How so? That a great deal of background knowledge from personal experience is used to calculate the probabilities is granted, and most all of it could conceivably be false, too. So? This background knowledge has the weight of probability; at least, we accept it as more probable than not overall. We cannot do otherwise. What else do we have for judging our background knowledge except the probabilities? I trust my background knowledge not because of faith, but because it is built up based on the evidence of personal experience one layer at a time from birth. Trust is based on the probabilities, which are in turn based on the evidence of past experience, that's why faith is not the same as trust. If it were the same, Rauser would be equivocating on the meaning of the word *faith*, for faith would become equivalent to trusting the probabilities, which is the very thing for which I argue. Therefore, to say we need faith to think the sun will rise tomorrow is at best superfluous, completely unnecessary, utterly irrelevant, and at worst irrational.

Christians will typically respond that faith is what is required to uphold the things we believe are most probable. How does faith do that? Imagine flipping a quarter. The probability of getting heads is equal to the probability of getting tails. Where is faith? What does it do here? How does having faith change the odds? Imagine a lottery in which you have a 1 in 80 million chance of winning. Where is faith? What does it do here? How does having faith change the odds? Imagine a sports contest, say a boxing match. Gamblers place their bets on who will win based on the odds. Where is faith? What does it do here? How does having faith change the odds?

When it comes to providing scientific evidence that we should think exclusively in terms of probabilities we must think in Bayesian terms. The two hypotheses to be compared are: (1) science helps us arrive at the truth and (2) faith helps us arrive at the truth. Since faith has no method, solves no problems, and reaches conclusions contrary to probabilities that are calculated based on the evidence generated by objective observation and experimentation, the probability that it helps us arrive at the truth is extremely low.

The really intriguing cases have to do with a host of hypothetical scenarios, the ones Rauser and other apologists focus on, the ones I examined in chapter 8. Am I really typing these words in September 2012? There is faith involved, they argue, since it's conceivable that I'm not. For all I know, it's currently 2032 and a mad scientist, having just extracted my brain, is now pouring chemicals over it so that I'm merely remembering that I typed these words twenty years in the past. There is a host of scenarios like these. Perhaps our universe is nothing more than a raindrop in a thunderstorm that's taking place in a much larger universe. Perhaps. Perhaps.

I have argued that none of these hypothetical scenarios are probable, but that's beside the point here. Let's call these scenarios possible explanations for our mundane experience of life. Rauser claims that anyone who assents to the proposition that they are probably false has faith. But what Rauser has failed to provide in his definition is the continuum by which he judges something as conceivably false. Is everything conceivably false to the same degree? Or are there some things that are more or less probable?

So he has a choice to make. Either (a) he must say there is no way at all to judge between the probabilities of these scenarios, including our mundane experience of life, which means all the scenarios are equally probable, or (b) he must admit he's thinking about all of them exclusively in terms of the probabilities after all. In either case, Rauser doesn't have a soapbox to preach on, for it follows that (a) requires Rauser should be a skeptic, a real skeptic, a nonbeliever, and, beyond this, potentially an epistemological solipsist, while (b) dispenses with the need for, and the value of, faith itself. So in the end Rauser is playing a Christian language game, one that no one needs to accept.

But wait! Don't change the channel. There's more.

Let's say we are living in the matrix or dreaming right now. It still doesn't change the fact that we should think exclusively in terms of the probabilities inside the matrix or the dream. If reality is up for grabs, with no way to assess any probabilities at all, then we might as well take a gun and shoot ourselves in the head. After all, perhaps there isn't a bullet in the gun? Perhaps the bullet won't fire even if it exists? Perhaps there isn't really a gun in our hand? Perhaps we'll miss if we pull the trigger? Perhaps it won't hurt even if it hits our head? Perhaps our head will heal instantly even if it hurts us? What's the probability we'll die? We might just be dreaming instead. And we might as well rob a bank, too. Hey, why not? What's the probability we might get away with it? What if we're merely brains in a vat and we already got away with it or we already paid the price in prison twenty years ago? What difference does it make now?

So even if we're inside the matrix or we're dreaming or our brains are in a vat, we should still assess Christianity based on the probabilities. Probabilities are all that matter. Faith adds nothing to the probabilities, nothing at all. Rauser's definition of faith is therefore utterly irrelevant to whether Christianity is true. It's a Christian language game, pure and simple.

WHAT ABOUT THE INFINITE REGRESS ARGUMENT?

Just look at the contortions Rauser has to go to in order to deny what seems obvious. He wrote: "If John's view is that every belief has to be shown to be probable before one can assent to it then he has to show that that belief is probable before he can assent to it."[29] I don't deny that it's possible I accept propositions that are improbable without knowing it. But my view is that I *should* only hold to propositions that are probable. Rauser wants to say this view is self-defeating, but I don't see it at all. Again, all we have to do is ask what is the alternative, believing against the probabilities? If that's what he wants, my definition of faith as an irrational leap over the probabilities fits him perfectly.

Rauser argues that my view commits me to an impossible infinite regress, that any accepted proposition requires a probability calculus, which in turn requires a probability calculus, and so on, infinitely. Therefore, I am committed to the impossible task of providing an infinite number of justifications for what I've concluded, like a child who asks "why?" over and over again to any answer a parent provides. But this is simply not how the brain works. We are not machines. We do not compute chess moves as if every chess move has equal merit. We see patterns. We see the whole, which helps justify the pieces of the whole. And the whole of that which we think is true forms our background knowledge. I have amassed a great deal of it in my life. It forms the basis for what I think is probable. I learned it through my studies and experiences. But Rauser resorts to characterizing me as a radical skeptic. He even asks if I have to recompute what I think is probable every morning when I wake up. But that's just silly. It's very probable that my short-term memory is correct. Unless he can show me that my memories are improbable I'll continue to think I'm probably right about my background knowledge. I cannot think any other way, even if I am wrong. Ultimately, he's asking me to prove with certainty that probability is all that matters. Well, nothing is certain, as I've stated. No one can criticize any viewpoint simply because it cannot be shown to be certain. I'm only talking about probabilities. While I can't be absolutely certain that probability is all that matters, I can say it is virtually certain that probability is all that matters.

So this infinite regress argument does not work at all. The questions peter out as fast as they do when reflecting on our own consciousness, and then reflecting on that reflection, and so forth. Assenting to the infinite regress argument would be agreeing that we cannot ever know we are conscious human beings. And yet we do. This isn't my problem. It's the problem of the infinite regress requirements. Our background knowledge is where the infinite regress of justifications ends. It is the basis for what we think is probable. The fact is that what we think is probable extends all the way down, built up from the center of all that we've learned empirically through experience coupled with any genetic capabilities built into us.

The OTF shows us this. Faith is shown to be irrational. Faith-based reasoning is irrational. Science-based reasoning about matters of fact is all that matters, and such reasoning is based upon probabilities.

CONCLUSION

The problem this book addresses is the massive amount of worldwide religious diversity, the reason for its existence, and how it can be solved, if it can be solved at all. My claim is that if we keep on doing the same things we will get the same results. Nothing has worked so far because believers have not considered what their faith looks like to an outsider, a nonbeliever in their particular religion.

This book presents a sustained case that the only way to settle this problem is with the Outsider Test for Faith. We cannot have a Milquetoast test when it comes to the truth of religion. If we merely ask believers to critically examine their faith, almost all of them will say that they have done so and that their faith is sure. But ask them instead to test their faith with the same level of reasonable skepticism they already use when examining the other religious faiths they reject, and that will get their attention like nothing else.

Believers can respond to the OTF in four ways: (1) object to (or mitigate) the facts of the RDVT and the RDPT that form the basis for the test or (2) object to the OTF by arguing that it is faulty or unfair in some relevant manner and, along with objections (1) and/or (2), also (3) provide a better alternative to reasonably judge between religions. Or believers can (4) subject their religion to the test, in which case their religion either (a) passes or (b) fails the OTF. It's that simple. If in the end believers can neither find fault with the OTF nor propose a better alternative, then intellectual honesty demands they use it to test their faith. It also demands that all future religious debates should be based on it. And if they find that their religious faith is irrational, as I've argued in the last two chapters, they should just bite the bullet and abandon it.

Throughout this book we have seen Christians object to various things concerning the OTF. I have shown that none of these objections have any merit at all. Believers who object to it do so because they intuitively know their faith will not pass the test, even though this tacitly concedes the whole argument. If their faith were able to pass the test, they would be the first ones embracing the test and pushing it on everyone else. Instead, they argue against it, which is like arguing against the need for a fair and impartial ruling coming from a fair and impartial judge or jury in a court case. No fair-minded person would ever want this, much less publicly argue for it. Believers will retort that it is impossible to not be biased, but this is the very thing I admit, which is why I've proposed the OTF in the first place. Again what is the alternative?

I suspect that, after reading this book, believers who no longer object to the OTF will endeavor to argue that their particular sect within their religion actually *does* pass the test. They've used their best mental contortions to deny the test; now they'll have to use them to try to show that their religious faith passes the test. If they change their minds it will prove yet again that they'll say practically anything to defend their faith. This will be interesting to watch. In any case, we now have a basis for all future debates about religion.

Let the debates begin.

WORLD MAPS

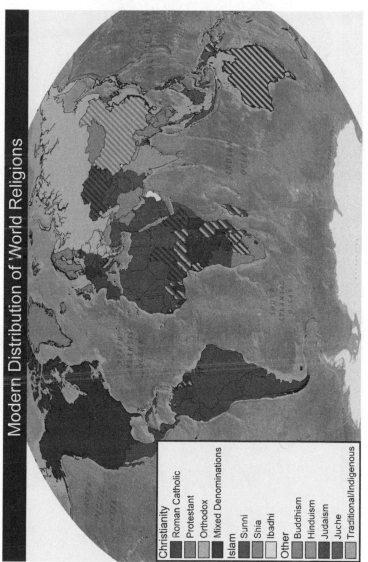

Modern Distribution of World Religions

Created by Adam Smith

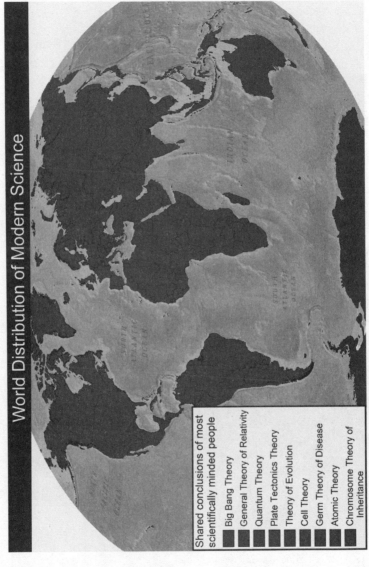

World Distribution of Modern Science

Shared conclusions of most scientifically minded people

- Big Bang Theory
- General Theory of Relativity
- Quantum Theory
- Plate Tectonics Theory
- Theory of Evolution
- Cell Theory
- Germ Theory of Disease
- Atomic Theory
- Chromosome Theory of Inheritance

Created by Adam Smith

NOTES

CHAPTER 1. WHAT IS THE OUTSIDER TEST FOR FAITH?

1. Richard E. Petty and John T. Cacioppo, *Attitudes and Persuasion: Classic and Contemporary Approaches* (Dubuque, IA: William C. Brown, 1981), pp. xviii, 184. See also Robert B. Cialdini, *Influence: The Psychology of Persuasion* (New York: William Morrow, 1993).

2. On this see Michael Shermer, *The Believing Brain: From Ghosts and Gods to Politics and Conspiracies—How We Construct Beliefs and Reinforce Them as Truths* (New York: Times Books, 2011); Pascal Boyer, *Religion Explained* (New York: Basic Books, 2010); and Jesse Bering, *The Belief Instinct: The Psychology of Souls, Destiny, and the Meaning of Life* (New York: W. W. Norton, 2011).

3. Scott Atran, *In Gods We Trust: The Evolutionary Landscape of Religion* (Oxford: Oxford University Press, 2002); Jack David Eller, *Introducing Anthropology of Religion: Culture to the Ultimate* (London: Routledge, 2007), and *Cultural Anthropology: Global Forces, Local Lives* (London: Routledge, 2009). See also David Eller's chapters on the topic in my books *The Christian Delusion* (Amherst, NY: Prometheus Books, 2010) and *The End of Christianity* (Amherst, NY: Prometheus Books, 2011).

4. This kind of science is discussed in Gary Marcus, *Kluge: The Haphazard Evolution of the Human Mind* (New York: Mariner Books, 2009); Carol Tavris and Elliot Aronson, *Mistakes Were Made (but Not by Me): Why We Justify Foolish Beliefs, Bad Decisions, and Hurtful Acts* (Orlando, FL: Harvest, 2007); Ori Brafman and Rom Brafman, *Sway: The Irresistible Pull of Irrational Behavior* (New York: Broadway Books, 2009); Christopher Chabris and Daniel Simons, *The Invisible Gorilla: And Other Ways Our Intuitions Deceive Us* (New York: Crown, 2010); and Cordelia Fine, *A Mind of Its Own: How Your Brain Distorts and Deceives* (New York: W. W. Norton, 2008). See also my edited volume *The Christian Delusion*, particularly the early chapters by Valerie Tarico, Jason Long, and myself.

5. Some sociologists even go so far as to make the claim that reality itself is a social construct in what is called the "Sociology of Knowledge" thesis. There is extensive literature on this subject, but one place to start is the classic by Peter L. Berger

and Thomas Luckmann, *The Social Construction of Reality: A Treatise in the Sociology of Knowledge* (Garden City, NY: Anchor Books, 1966). See also Peter L. Berger, *The Sacred Canopy: Elements of a Sociological Theory of Religion* (Garden City, NY: Anchor Books, 1990).

6. For this evidence, see Simon G. Southerton, *Losing a Lost Tribe: Native Americans, DNA, and the Mormon Church* (Salt Lake City, UT: Signature Books, 2004).

7. For readers who think I've introduced for the first time that an informed skepticism is required by the OTF, they need to read my chapter "The Outsider Test for Faith *Revisited*" in *The Christian Delusion*, pp. 85–86. There I described two methods Christians use to reject religion, which are basically the same two types of skepticism I just described. And like here, where I argue for a science-based skepticism, so I also did there.

8. Robert Burton, *On Being Certain: Believing You Are Right Even When You're Not* (New York: St. Martin's, 2008), p. xi.

9. Rene Descartes, *Meditation I*, http://www.duke.edu/web/secmod/primary texts/Descartes.pdf (accessed November 26, 2012).

10. David Hume, "Origin of Theism from Polytheism," section 6 of *The Natural History of Religion*, http://www.davemckay.co.uk/philosophy/hume/hume .php?name=the.natural.history.of.religion.06 (accessed November 26, 2012).

11. Merrill D. Peterson, ed., *Thomas Jefferson: Writings* (New York: Library of America, 1994), pp. 900–906.

12. Robert Green Ingersoll, "The Gods," http://www.infidels.org/library/ historical/robert_ingersoll/gods.html (accessed November 26, 2012).

13. Thomas Huxley, "Letter to Charles Kingsley, September 23, 1860," in *Life and Letters of Thomas Henry Huxley*, ed. Leonard Huxley (London: MacMillan, 1900), p. 219.

14. Henrietta A. Huxley, ed., *Aphorisms and Reflections from the Works of T. H. Huxley* (London: Macmillan, 1908), p. 35.

15. G. K. Chesterton, *The Everlasting Man*, Project Gutenberg Australia, http:// gutenberg.net.au/ebooks01/0100311.txt (accessed November 26, 2012).

16. Antony Flew, *God, Freedom, and Immortality: A Critical Analysis* (Amherst, NY: Prometheus Books, 1984).

17. Flew called on his readers to return to the original meaning of the word *agnosticism*, which was first introduced by Thomas Huxley and was described differently by Bertrand Russell in his famous 1953 *Look Magazine* article, "What Is an Agnostic?" Russell said, "An agnostic thinks it impossible to know the truth in matters such as God and the future life with which Christianity and other religions are concerned. Or, if not impossible, at least impossible at the present time." Bertrand Russell, "What Is an Agnostic?" *Look Magazine*, November 3, 1953, http://

atheistempire.com/mm_dl/text/Russell,%20Bertrand%20-%20What%20is%20an
%20Agnostic.pdf (accessed November 29, 2012).

18. J. P. Moreland and William Lane Craig, *Philosophical Foundations for a Christian Worldview* (Downers Grove, IL: InterVarsity Press, 2003), p. 156.

19. There are other precursors. One precursor might be akin to the "original position" argued by John Rawls for impartially evaluating fundamental principles of justice, only extended to the investigation of religious faiths. We could imagine ourselves in the "original position" behind a Rawlsian *Veil of Ignorance,* one where we know some general facts about psychology, economics, biology, and other social and natural sciences, but we don't know in advance our own personal, social, or historical circumstances in life. Most importantly, we don't know when in history or where on earth we'll be born. Then, from behind the veil, tell us how you would objectively test the religious options available. See John Rawls, *A Theory of Justice* (Cambridge, MA: Belknap, 1971). Mathematics professor James East suggested a thought experiment in which we're told that when we wake up tomorrow, we'll be randomly changed into a person with a different religious view or even an atheist. But before we go to bed we're allowed to write a letter to ourselves offering some general advice on how to investigate the religious options without saying anything about which one to accept. He asks, "How would you advise yourself?" See Reasonably Faithless, "The Outsider Test for Faith and the Veil of Ignorance," *Reasonably Faithless,* http://skepticink.com/reasonablyfaithless/2012/11/10/the-outsider-test-for-faith-and-the-veil-of-ignorance/ (accessed November 29, 2012). While I recommend these two ways of looking at the problem of religious diversity, without the non–double standard that the OTF provides, people will more than likely sneak in their own sectarian views as much as they can.

Stephen Maitzen deserves an honorable mention, since he argued that religious diversity, or the "uneven distribution of theistic belief around the world," counts against Christians who argue on behalf of divine hiddenness. In arguing for the best explanation of this data, Maitzen claims theistic answers to this problem "are less plausible" than naturalistic ones: "Even judged on their own terms, theistic explanations of the geographic lopsidedness of belief look farfetched compared to naturalistic explanations." See Stephen Maitzen, "Divine Hiddenness and the Demographics of Theism," *Religious Studies* 42 (2006): 177–91, and Stephen Maitzen, "Does Molinism Explain the Demographics of Theism," *Religious Studies* 44 (2008): 473–77. While he uses the problem of religious diversity, I'm making a different case with regard to global religious diversity itself. I'm arguing that because of it, believers should approach all religious faiths, including their own, with the non-double-standard skepticism of an outsider, a nonbeliever.

20. Albert Bigelow Paine, *Mark Twain: A Biography,* http://ebooks.adelaide.edu.au/t/twain/mark/paine/chapter295.html (accessed November 26, 2012).

21. This quote is widely attributed to Stephen Roberts, but I cannot find the original source.

22. I thank professor Matt McCormick for these terms, which can be found in chapter 1 of his book *Atheism and the Case against Christ* (Amherst, NY: Prometheus Books, 2012).

CHAPTER 2. THE FACT OF RELIGIOUS DIVERSITY

1. "Religions by Adherents," Adherents.com, http://www.adherents.com/Religions_By_Adherents.html (accessed November 26, 2012). This site says that "a major source for these estimates is the detailed country-by-country analysis done by David B. Barrett's religious statistics organization, whose data are published in the *Encyclopedia Britannica* (including annual updates and yearbooks) and also in the *World Christian Encyclopedia* (the latest edition of which—published in 2001—has been consulted). Hundreds of additional sources providing more thorough and detailed research about individual religious groups have also been consulted."

2. Jack David Eller, *Cultural Anthropology: Global Forces, Local Lives* (London: Routledge, 2009), p. xiii.

3. David Eller, *Atheism Advanced: Further Thoughts of a Freethinker* (Cranford, NJ: American Atheist Press, 2007), pp. 13–15.

4. Eller, *Cultural Anthropology*, p. xiii.

5. Eller, *Atheism Advanced*, p. 15.

6. Ibid., pp. 27–28. See also Eller's chapter 1, "The Culture of Christianities," in *The Christian Delusion*, ed. John W. Loftus (Amherst, NY: Prometheus Books, 2010).

7. "Predominant Religions," Adherents.com, http://www.adherents.com/adh_predom.html (accessed November 26, 2012).

8. Robert McKim, *Religious Ambiguity and Religious Diversity* (Oxford: Oxford University Press, 2001), p. 131.

9. Ibid, p. 151.

10. Ibid. p. 152.

11. Ibid.

12. See Richard Feldman, "Reasonable Religious Disagreements," in *Philosophers without Gods*, ed. Louise M. Antony (Oxford: Oxford University Press, 2007).

13. Hilary Kornblith, "Belief in the Face of Controversy," in *Disagreement*, ed. Richard Feldman and Ted Warfield (Oxford: Oxford University Press, 2010), p. 31.

14. Ibid., p. 46.

15. Peter van Inwagen, "We're Right. They're Wrong," in Feldman and Warfield, *Disagreement*, p. 28.

16. David Marshall, "John Loftus and the Outsider Test for Faith," in *True Reason: Christian Responses to the Challenge of Atheism*, ed. Carson Weitnauer and Tom Gilson (Englewood, CO: Patheos, 2012).

17. McKim, *Religious Ambiguity*, p. 131.

18. John W. Loftus, "It's Preposterous That Victor Reppert and David Marshall Believe in Allah," *Debunking Christianity*, http://debunkingchristianity.blogspot .com/2012/03/its-preposterous-that-victor-reppert.html (accessed November 26, 2012).

19. Thomas Talbott, "The Outsider Test for Faith: How Serious a Challenge Is It?" p. 14, http://www.willamette.edu/~ttalbott/Loftus%20OTF2.pdf (accessed November 26, 2012).

20. Marshall, "John Loftus and the Outsider Test for Faith."

21. See William Lane Craig, "Politically Incorrect Salvation," in *Christian Apologetics in the Post-Modern World*, ed. T. P. Phillips and D. Ockholm (Downers Grove, IL: InterVarsity Press, 1995), pp. 75–97.

22. Ibid.

23. This view is known as Molinism, which is disputed by evangelicals themselves. See *Divine Foreknowledge: Four Views*, ed. James K. Beilby and Paul R. Eddy (Downers Grove, IL: InterVarsity Press, 2001), in which Craig defends his view against three other evangelicals.

24. William Lane Craig, "Middle Knowledge, A Calvinist-Arminian Rapprochement," in *The Grace of God, The Will of Man*, ed. Clark H. Pinnock (Grand Rapids, MI: Zondervan,1989), pp. 141–64.

25. William Lane Craig, "Politically Incorrect Salvation."

26. See Dennis L. Okholm and Timothy R. Philips, eds., *More Than One Way: Four Views on Salvations in a Pluralistic World* (Downers Grove, IL: InterVarsity Press, 1995).

27. Alvin Plantinga, "Pluralism: A Defense of Religious Exclusivism," Carnival Sage, http://www.carnivalsage.com/articles/plantinga-alvin-pluralism-defense-of -religious-exclusivism.html (accessed November 26, 2012).

28. John Hick, *An Interpretation of Religion: Human Responses to the Transcendent* (New Haven, CT: Yale University Press, 1989), p. 2.

29. Huston Smith, *Why Religion Matters* (New York: HarperSanFrancisco, 2001), pp. 205–206.

30. Phil Zuckerman, "Atheism: Contemporary Rates and Patterns," in *Cambridge Companion to Atheism*, ed. Michael Martin (Cambridge: Cambridge University Press, 2007), pp. 56–57. I'll confess that I'm puzzled as to why China didn't make it into the top thirty.

31. Just compare the ranking of atheist countries with the scientifically literate

ones found at "Education Statistics," NationMaster.com, http://www.nationmaster
.com/graph/edu_sci_lit-education-scientific-literacy (accessed November 26, 2012).

32. Zuckerman, "Atheism," p. 61.

33. Ibid., p. 59.

34. Nigel Barber, "A Cross-National Test of the Uncertainty Hypothesis of Religious Belief," *Cross-Cultural Research* 45, no. 3 (August 2011): 318–33.

CHAPTER 3. THE FACT OF RELIGIOUS DEPENDENCY

1. Michael Shermer, *The Believing Brain: From Ghosts and Gods to Politics and Conspiracies—How We Construct Beliefs and Reinforce Them as Truths* (New York: Times Books, 2011), p. 5.

2. Ibid., pp. 88–89.

3. See Pascal Boyer, *Religion Explained* (New York: Basic Books, 2010); Scott Atran, *In Gods We Trust: The Evolutionary Landscape of Religion* (Oxford: Oxford University Press, 2002); Jesse Bering, *The Belief Instinct: The Psychology of Souls, Destiny, and the Meaning of Life* (New York: W. W. Norton, 2011); and Nicholas Wade, *The Faith Instinct: How Religion Evolved and Why It Endures* (New York: Penguin, 2009).

4. Shermer, *Believing Brain*, p. 88.

5. Randal Rauser, *The Swedish Atheist, the Scuba Diver, and Other Apologetic Rabbit Trails* (Downers Grove, IL: InterVarsity Press, 2012), chap. 6.

6. Philip Wheelwright, ed., *The Presocratics* (New York: Odyssey, 1966), p. 33.

7. John Hick, *An Interpretation of Religion: Human Responses to the Transcendent* (New Haven, CT: Yale University Press, 1989), p. 2.

8. Richard Dawkins, "The 'Know-Nothings,' the 'Know-Alls,' and the 'No-Contests,'" *Nullifidian*, December 1994.

9. David Eller, *Natural Atheism* (Cranford, NJ: American Atheist Press, 2004), pp. 121–22.

10. Ibid., pp. 124–25.

11. David Eller, *Atheism Advanced: Further Thoughts of a Freethinker* (Cranford, NJ: American Atheist Press, 2007), p. 270.

12. Eller, *Natural Atheism*, pp. 127–28.

13. David Eller, "The Cultures of Christianities," in *The Christian Delusion*, ed. John W. Loftus, (Amherst, NY: Prometheus Books, 2010), p. 26.

14. Ibid. p. 44.

15. John W. Loftus, "Professor David Eller Responds to Randal Rauser," *Debunking Christianity*, http://debunkingchristianity.blogspot.com/2010/06/professor-david -eller-responds-to.html (accessed November 26, 2012).

16. Shermer, *Believing Brain*, p. 5.

17. Michael Shermer, *Why People Believe Weird Things*, 2nd ed. (New York: Henry Holt, 2002), pp. 283–84.

18. Robert McKim, *Religious Ambiguity and Religious Diversity* (Oxford: Oxford University Press, 2001), p. ix.

19. Shermer, *Why People Believe Weird Things*, p. 299.

20. Valerie Tarico, *The Dark Side: How Evangelical Teachings Corrupt Love and Truth* (Seattle: Dea, 2006), pp. 221–22.

21. Valerie Tarico, "Christian Belief through the Lens of Cognitive Science," in Loftus, *Christian Delusion*, p. 51.

22. This science is also discussed in Christopher Chabris and Daniel Simons, *The Invisible Gorilla: And Other Ways Our Intuitions Deceive Us* (New York: Crown, 2010); and Cordelia Fine, *A Mind of Its Own: How Your Brain Distorts and Deceives* (New York: W. W. Norton, 2008). See also Loftus, *Christian Delusion*, particularly the early chapters by Valerie Tarico, Jason Long, and myself.

23. Carol Tavris and Elliot Aronson, *Mistakes Were Made (but Not by Me): Why We Justify Foolish Beliefs, Bad Decisions, and Hurtful Acts* (Orlando, FL: Harvest, 2007), p. 2.

24. As reported by Joe Keohane in "How Facts Backfire," *Boston Globe*, July 11, 2010, http://www.boston.com/bostonglobe/ideas/articles/2010/07/11/how_facts_backfire/ (accessed November 26, 2012).

25. Gary Marcus, *Kluge: The Haphazard Evolution of the Human Mind* (New York: Mariner Books, 2009), p. 1.

26. Ibid., p. 2.

27. Ibid., p. 41.

28. Ibid., p. 42.

29. Ibid., p. 53.

30. Ibid.

31. Ibid., p. 68.

32. Ibid., p. 174.

33. Ori Brafman and Rom Brafman, *Sway: The Irresistible Pull of Irrational Behavior* (New York: Broadway Books, 2009), p. 55.

34. Ibid., p. 56.

35. Ibid., p. 63.

36. Ibid., p. 30.

37. Ibid., p. 75.

38. Ibid., p. 88.

39. See Jim West, "Whoring after Her Lovers: The Quest for Power, Control, Exploitative Domination, and the Industry of Accreditation—Or, How Academic Manipulators Have Become the New Magisterium," *The Bible and Interpretation*,

http://www.bibleinterp.com/articles/lover357908.shtml (accessed November 26, 2012).

40. Dan Ariely, *Predictably Irrational: The Hidden Forces That Shape Our Decisions*, rev. ed. (New York: Harper Perennial, 2010).

41. Matt Flannagan and Madeleine Flannagan "True Reason: Christian Responses to the Challenges of Atheism," *M and M*, http://www.mandm.org.nz/?s=True+Reason%3A+Christian+Responses+to+the+Challenges+of+Atheism (accessed November 26, 2012). The Flannagans link to Larry Laudan, "Science at the Bar—Causes for Concern," https://webspace.utexas.edu/kal698/science at the bar.pdf.

42. I've written on this subject briefly in my *Why I Became an Atheist*, 2nd ed. (Amherst, NY: Prometheus Books, 2012), p.139. Hector Avalos has done so as well, in *The End of Biblical Studies* (Amherst, NY: Prometheus Books, 2007), pp. 113–15. For a detailed, up-to–date, and accessible book-length scholarly discussion of the problem of induction, one can start with Colin Howson, *Hume's Problem: Induction and the Justification of Belief* (Oxford: Oxford University Press, 2003).

CHAPTER 4. THE PERSPECTIVE OF THE OUTSIDER

1. Thomas Talbott, "The Outsider Test for Faith: How Serious a Challenge Is It?" p. 16, http://www.willamette.edu/~ttalbott/Loftus%20OTF2.pdf (accessed November 26, 2012).

2. Randal Rauser, *You're Not as Crazy as I Think: Dialogue in a World of Loud Voices and Hardened Opinions* (Colorado Springs, CO: Biblica, 2011), p. 4.

3. Ibid., p. 8.

4. Ibid., p. 11.

5. Ibid., p. 100.

6. James McGrath, "Miracles and the Golden Rule," *Exploring Our Matrix*, April 8, 2009, http://www.patheos.com/blogs/exploringourmatrix/2009/04/miracles-and-the-golden-rule-a-christian-approach-to-history.html (accessed November 26, 2012).

7. For this I thank Jason Long, *The Religious Condition* (New York: iUniverse, 2008), pp. 74–77.

8. Julia Sweeney, "What If It's True?" *Letting Go of God*, disc 2, track 6, Indefatigable, 2006, compact disc.

9. William Lane Craig, "Personal Testimony of Faith," Question 78, Reasonable Faith, http://www.reasonablefaith.org/personal-testimony-of-faith (accessed December 14, 2012).

10. See my chapter 3, "Christianity Is Wildly Improbable," in *The End of Christianity*, ed. John W. Loftus (Amherst, NY: Prometheus Books, 2011), pp. 87–98.

11. Ori Brafman and Rom Brafman, *Sway: The Irresistible Pull of Irrational Behavior* (New York: Broadway Books, 2009), p. 175.

12. David Marshall, "John Loftus and the Outsider Test for Faith," in *True Reason: Christian Responses to the Challenge of Atheism*, ed. Carson Weitnauer and Tom Gilson (Englewood, CO: Patheos, 2012).

13. Tom Gilson, March 15, 2012 (11:48 a.m.), comment on John W. Loftus, "David Marshall on the OTF Again," *Debunking Christianity*, http://debunkingchristianity .blogspot.com/2012/03/david-marshall-on-otf-again.html-comment-466069407 (accessed November 26, 2012).

14. John W. Loftus, "A Brief Review of 'The Loftus Delusion' Book," *Debunking Christianity*, http://debunkingchristianity.blogspot.com/2010/04/brief-review-of-loftus -delusion-book.html (accessed November 26, 2012).

15. David Reuben Stone, *The Loftus Delusion: Why Atheism Fails and Messianic Israelism Prevails* (Raleigh, NC: Lulu.com, 2010), p. 76.

16. Ibid., p. 73.

17. See Robert M. Price, "Jesus: Myth and Method," in *The Christian Delusion*, ed. John W. Loftus (Amherst, NY: Prometheus Books, 2010), pp. 273–90.

18. Talbott, "Outsider Test for Faith."

19. I was a respondent on a panel at the annual meeting of the Society of Biblical Literature in November 2009 concerning Bill Maher's movie *Religulous*. See "My Comments at The SBL on Bill Maher's Movie *Religulous*," at *Debunking Christianity*, http://debunkingchristianity.blogspot.com/2009/11/my-comments-at -sbl-today.html (accessed November 26, 2012).

20. Talbott, "Outsider Test for Faith."

21. Ibid.

22. Ibid.

23. John W. Loftus, "Answering Dr. Randal Rauser's Objections to the OTF (Part 1)," *Debunking Christianity*, http://debunkingchristianity.blogspot.com/2010/06/ answering-dr-randal-rausers-objections.html (accessed November 26, 2012).

24. Ibid.

25. Robert McKim, *Religious Ambiguity and Religious Diversity* (Oxford: Oxford University Press, 2001), pp. 140–41.

26. Ibid., p. 158.

27. Ibid., p. 167.

28. Ibid., p. 187.

29. Ibid., pp. 191–92.

30. I restated these axioms a bit from Yandell's article, "Religious Experience and Rational Appraisal," *Religious Studies* 8 (June 1974): 185–86, which can be found online at http://commonsenseatheism.com/wp-content/uploads/2009/09/Yandell-Religious -Experience-and-Rational-Appraisal.pdf (accessed December 19, 2012).

CHAPTER 5. OBJECTING TO THE FACTS

1. David Reuben Stone, *The Loftus Delusion: Why Atheism Fails and Messianic Israelism Prevails* (Raleigh, NC: Lulu.com, 2010), p. 79.

2. Fred DeRuvo, *The Anti-Christian Bias of Ex-Christians and Other Important Topics* (Scotts Valley, CA: Adroit, 2009), p. 102.

3. Ibid., p. 92.

4. Ibid., p. 102.

5. David Marshall, "John Loftus and the Outsider Test for Faith," in *True Reason: Christian Responses to the Challenge of Atheism,* ed. Carson Weitnauer and Tom Gilson (Englewood, CO: Patheos, 2012).

6. See the Pew Forum on Religion and Public Life, "US Religious Landscape Survey," http://religions.pewforum.org/ (accessed November 26, 2012).

7. See Michael Horton, *Christless Christianity: The Alternative Gospel of the American Church* (Grand Rapids, MI: Baker Books, 2008); Roger Finke and Rodney Stark, *The Churching of America, 1776–1990: Winners and Losers in Our Religious Economy* (New Brunswick, NJ: Rutgers University Press, 1992); and Rodney Stark and William Sims Bainbridge, *The Future of Religion: Secularization, Revival, and Cult Formation* (Berkeley: University of California Press, 1985).

8. Philip Jenkins, professor of history and religious studies at Pennsylvania State University, tells us of this explosive growth in his book *The Next Christendom: The Coming of Global Christianity,* 2nd ed. (Oxford: Oxford University Press, 2007).

9. Philip Jenkins, *The New Faces of Christianity: Believing the Bible in the Global South* (Oxford: Oxford University Press, 2006). This is shown in David Eller's "The Cultures of Christianities," in *The Christian Delusion,* ed. John W. Loftus (Amherst, NY: Prometheus Books, 2010). Missionaries actually modify their marketing specifically to exploit local cultural assumptions to leverage belief, so their success elsewhere is more about the religious dependency thesis and is not evidence against it.

10. Stone, *Loftus Delusion,* pp. 79–80.

11. Ibid., p. 81.

12. See John W. Loftus, *Why I Became an Atheist,* 2nd ed. (Amherst, NY: Prometheus Books, 2012), pp. 242–43.

13. Marshall, "John Loftus and the Outsider Test for Faith."

14. Mark M. Hanna, *Biblical Christianity: Truth or Delusion* (xulonpress.com, 2011), p. 131.

15. See my "The Outsider Test for Faith *Revisited,*" in *The Christian Delusion,* ed. John W. Loftus (Amherst, NY: Prometheus Books, 2010), pp. 99, 102.

16. Hanna, *Biblical Christianity,* p. 30.

17. John W. Loftus, "Professor David Eller Responds to Randal Rauser," *Debunking*

Christianity, http://debunkingchristianity.blogspot.com/2010/06/professor-david
-eller-responds-to.html (accessed November 26, 2012).

18. David Marshall, *The Truth behind the New Atheism* (Eugene, OR: Harvest House, 2007), pp. 27–29.

19. Ibid., pp. 29–30.

20. See John W. Loftus, "Quote of the Day, by David Marshall," *Debunking Christianity,* http://debunkingchristianity.blogspot.com/2012/12/quote-of-day-by -david-marshall_16.html (accessed December 21, 2012).

21. Marshall, *Truth behind the New Atheism,* p. 29.

22. Hanna, *Biblical Christianity,* p. 116.

23. Ibid., p. 132.

24. Paul Feyerabend, *Against Method,* 3rd ed. (New York: Verso, 1993).

25. J. P. Moreland and William Lane Craig, *Philosophical Foundations of a Christian Worldview* (Downers Grove, IL: InterVarsity Press, 2003), p. 313.

26. Paul Kurtz, *The Transcendental Temptation* (Amherst, NY: Prometheus Books, 1991), pp. 55–56.

27. Victor J. Stenger, *God and the Folly of Faith: The Incompatibility of Science and Religion* (Amherst, NY: Prometheus Books, 2012).

28. Ibid., p. 25.

29. Ibid., p. 26.

30. Jerry Coyne, *Why Evolution Is True* (New York: Viking, 2009)

31. Jerry Coyne, "How Can We Justify Science? Sokal and Lynch Debate Epistemology," *Why Evolution Is True,* http://whyevolutionistrue.wordpress.com/ 2012/03/14/how-can-we-justify-science-sokal-and-lynch-debate-epistemology/ (accessed November 26, 2012).

32. Hanna, *Biblical Christianity,* p. 116.

33. Ibid., p. 124.

34. Ibid., p. 117.

CHAPTER 6. IS THE TEST SELF-DEFEATING?

1. There are other things to be said on behalf of the OTF, especially since believers continue to gerrymander around it by coming up with some really odd ways of denying what is obvious. To see the objections and my responses to them, you'll need to read chapters 1 through 4 in John W. Loftus, ed., *The Christian Delusion* (Amherst, NY: Prometheus Books, 2010) and my introduction to John W. Loftus, ed. *The End of Christianity* (Amherst, NY: Prometheus Books, 2011), although I cover most of that territory here. In a post on my blog *Debunking Christianity* (http://www

.debunkingchristianity.blogspot.com/) titled "Debating the Outsider Test for Faith (OTF)," I link to the online discussions and debates I've had about the OTF.

2. Norman L. Geisler and Ronald M. Brooks, *Come, Let Us Reason: An Introduction to Logical Thinking* (Grand Rapids, MI: Baker Academic Books, 1990).

3. Norman L. Geisler, "From Apologist to Atheist: A Critical Review," *Christian Apologetics Journal* 6, no. 1 (Spring 2007): 105.

4. Alvin Plantinga, "In Defense of Religious Exclusivism," in *The Analytic Theist: An Alvin Plantinga Reader*, ed. James F. Sennett (Grand Rapids, MI: Eerdmans, 1998), p. 206.

5. Victor Reppert, "Steve Lovell Comments on the Outsider Test for Faith," *Dangerous Idea*, http://dangerousidea.blogspot.com/2010/06/steve-lovell-comments -on-outsider-test.html (accessed November 26, 2012).

6. Sam Harris, *Free Will* (New York: Free Press, 2012), p. 5. See also Sam Harris, *The Moral Landscape: How Science Can Determine Human Values* (New York: Free Press, 2010).

7. Harris, *Free Will*, pp. 8–9.

8. David Eller "Is Religion Compatible with Science?" in *The End of Christianity*, ed. John W. Loftus (Amherst, NY: Prometheus Books, 2011), pp. 257–78.

9. Geisler, "From Apologist to Atheist," p. 105.

10. Valerie Tarico, "Christian Belief through the Lens of Cognitive Science," in Loftus, *Christian Delusion*, pp. 47–64.

11. Jerry Coyne, *Why Evolution Is True* (New York: Viking, 2009), pp. 222–23. See also Richard Dawkins, *The Greatest Show on Earth: The Evidence for Evolution* (New York: Free Press, 2009).

12. John R. Shook, *The God Debates: A 21st Century Guide for Atheists and Believers (and Everyone in Between)* (Malden, MA: Wiley-Blackwell, 2010).

13. Edward Babinski, "Things Christians Have Been Against," *Edward T. Babinski*, http://edward-t-babinski.blogspot.com/2012/03/list-of-things-christians -have-been.html (accessed November 26, 2012).

14. Geisler, "From Apologist to Atheist," p. 106.

15. Ibid.

CHAPTER 7. DOES THE TEST HAVE HIDDEN FAITH ASSUMPTIONS?

1. Timothy Keller, *The Reason for God: Belief in an Age of Skepticism* (New York: Riverhead Books, 2008), p. xviii.

2. Ibid., pp. xvii–xix.

3. Ibid., p. 20.

4. Ibid., p. xvii.

5. William Lane Craig, "The Witness of the Holy Spirit," Reasonable Faith, http://www.reasonablefaith.org/the-witness-of-the-holy-spirit (accessed November 26, 2012).

6. Randal Rauser, *The Swedish Atheist, the Scuba Diver, and other Apologetic Rabbit Trails* (Downers Grove, IL: InterVarsity Press, 2012), chap. 6.

7. See Michael Martin, *Atheism: A Philosophical Justification* (Philadelphia: Temple University Press, 1990), pp. 35–38.

8. David Mitsuo Nixon, "The Matrix Possibility," in *The Matrix and Philosophy: Welcome to the Desert of the Real*, ed. William Irwin (Chicago: Open Court, 2002), p. 30.

9. Thomas Talbott, "The Outsider Test for Faith: How Serious a Challenge Is It?" http://www.willamette.edu/~ttalbott/Loftus%20OTF2.pdf (accessed November 26, 2012).

10. Ibid, p. 24, n. 23.

11. Ibid., p. 26.

12. Ibid., p. 25.

13. G. E. Moore, "A Defense of Common Sense," Digital Text International, http://www.ditext.com/moore/common-sense.html (accessed December 27, 2012).

14. Talbott, "Outsider Test for Faith," p. 24.

15. See Norman Malcolm, "Dreaming and Skepticism," *Philosophical Review* 65, no. 1 (January 1956): 14–37; Norman Malcolm, *Dreaming* (New York: Routledge & Kegan Paul, 1976); and Bernard Williams, *Descartes: The Project of Pure Enquiry*, rev. ed. (New York: Routledge, 2005).

16. David Eller, *Natural Atheism* (Cranford, NJ: American Atheist Press, 2004), pp. 132–33. For more, read chapters 5 and 11 in his book *Atheism Advanced: Further Thoughts of a Freethinker* (Cranford, NJ: American Atheist Press, 2007).

17. Victor Reppert, "Steve Lovell Comments on the Outsider Test for Faith," *Dangerous Idea*, http://dangerousidea.blogspot.com/2010/06/steve-lovell-comments-on-outsider-test.html (accessed November 26, 2012).

18. Rados Miksa, "The Outsider Test for Faith," March 14, 2012, *Taking Over the Outsider Test for Faith (OTF)*, http://www.theoutsidertestforfaith.blogspot.com/2012/03/outsider-test-for-faith.html (accessed November 26, 2012). Another criticism Rados Miksa levels against the OTF is that the default position should not be agnosticism, or a reasonable skepticism, as I have argued, but rather deism. However, Miksa simply misunderstands deism, saying it represents the particular deist conclusion that there is a creator God. That's not the case at all. Deism began with Herbert Cherbury in England during the seventeenth century as a natural religion, where religious knowledge is acquired solely by the use of reason, as opposed to the Bible or the church or faith. Deists affirmed that reason must support any

theological belief. If it can't, then that religious belief is to be jettisoned. That's the heart of deism, not any particular conclusion arrived at by deists because of their method. Deism went through four different stages and traveled from England to America and France. The final stage is largely of French origin, where God is seen merely as the creator of the universe. God created it and set it in motion but does nothing to intervene in its affairs. It soon evolved into atheism after Darwin published his *Origin of Species* in 1859 because, after all, it was based on reason, not faith. If deism is properly understood, then it is welcomed. Contemporary deists who still hold to the conclusion that there is a creator God are simply not being consistent. After all, as I argue in chapter 10, there is no such thing as reasonable faith or, for that matter, a reasonable religion. See J. O'Higgins, who distinguishes between four types of deism in "Hume and the Deists: A Contrast in Religious Approaches," *Journal of Theological Studies* 23, no. 2 (October 1971): 479, 480, which is summarized in Norman L. Geisler and William D. Watkins, *World's Apart: A Handbook on Worldviews* (Grand Rapids, MI: Baker Book House, 1989), pp. 148–49.

19. James Sire, *The Universe Next Door*, 5th ed. (Downers Grove, IL: InterVarsity Press, 2009).

20. Norman L. Geisler and William D. Watkins, *Worlds Apart: A Handbook on Worldviews*, 2nd ed. (Grand Rapids, MI: Baker Book House, 1989).

21. Brian Walsh and J. Richard Middleton, *The Transforming Vision: Shaping the Christian World View* (Downers Grove, IL: InterVarsity Press, 1984), p. 18.

22. Ibid.

23. Ninian Smart, *Worldviews: Crosscultural Explorations of Human Beliefs*, 3rd ed. (Upper Saddle River, NJ: Prentice Hall, 2000), p. 1.

24. David Eller, "The Cultures of Christianities," in *The Christian Delusion*, ed. John W. Loftus (Amherst, NY: Prometheus Books, 2010), p. 39.

25. Ibid., p. 44.

26. H. Richard Niebuhr, *Christ and Culture* (New York: Harper & Row, 1956).

27. Thanks to Andrew Fakemam for alerting me to the statistics presented in David Perfect, "Religion or Belief," Equality and Human Rights Commission Briefing Paper 1 (London: Equality and Human Rights Commission, 2001), http://www.equalityhumanrights.com/uploaded_files/research/briefing_paper_1_religion_or_belief.pdf (accessed November 26, 2012).

28. Smart, *Worldviews*, p. 5.

29. Ibid.

30. Eller, *Atheism Advanced*, p. 233.

31. Victor Reppert, "Testing the Outsider Test," *Dangerous Idea*, http://dangerous idea.blogspot.com/2009/03/testing-outsider-test.html (accessed December 27, 2012).

32. "Steve Lovell Comments on the Outsider Test for Faith," at Victor Reppert's

blog, *Dangerous Idea*, http://dangerousidea.blogspot.com/2010/06/steve-lovell -comments-on-outsider-test.html (accessed November 26, 2012).

33. Otto Neurath, "Foundations of the Social Sciences," in *International Encyclopedia of Unified Science*, vol. 2, ed. O. Neurath, R. Carnap, and C. Morris (Chicago: University of Chicago Press, 1944), p. 47.

CHAPTER 8. DOES THE TEST UNFAIRLY TARGET RELIGION?

1. Victor Reppert, "Testing the Outsider Test," *Dangerous Idea*, http://dangerous idea.blogspot.com/2009/03/testing-outsider-test.html (accessed November 26, 2012).

2. Ibid.

3. Thomas Talbott, "The Outsider Test for Faith: How Serious a Challenge Is It?" pp. 20–21, http://www.willamette.edu/~ttalbott/Loftus%20OTF2.pdf (accessed November 26, 2012).

4. Ibid., p. 20.

5. Ibid., p. 21.

6. Hector Avalos, *Fighting Words: The Origins of Religious Violence* (Amherst, NY: Prometheus Books, 2005).

7. Talbott, "Outsider Test for Faith," p. 21.

8. Ibid.

9. For a detailed exegesis of these and other passages, let me recommend Susanne Scholz, *Sacred Witness: Rape in the Hebrew Bible* (Minneapolis: Fortress, 2010), and Carol A. Newsom and Sharon H. Ringe, eds., *Women's Bible Commentary: Expanded Edition* (Louisville: John Knox, 1998).

10. For further reading on a nonreligious, skeptical, scientific-based morality, I recommend Walter Sinnott-Armstrong, *Morality without God?* (Oxford: Oxford University Press, 2011), and Greg M. Epstein, *Good without God: What a Billion Nonreligious People Do Believe* (New York: Harper Collins, 2009). I have a whole chapter on this topic in my book *Why I Became an Atheist*, 2nd ed. (Amherst, NY: Prometheus Books, 2012).

11. Thomas Talbott, comment on my blog post "Articulett, A Woman, Responds to Talbott and Reppert on Rape," *Debunking Christianity*, http://debunkingchristianity .blogspot.com/2011/06/articulett-woman-responds-to-talbott.html#comment-230 504645 (accessed November 26, 2012).

12. Reppert, "Testing the Outsider Test."

13. Randal Rauser, *The Swedish Atheist, the Scuba Diver, and Other Apologetic Rabbit Trails* (Downers Grove, IL: InterVarsity Press, 2012), chap. 6.

14. "EricRC," blog comment cited in John W. Loftus, "On the Fundamental

Objection to the OTF," *Debunking Christianity,* http://debunkingchristianity .blogspot.com/2012/03/ericrc-on-fundamental-objection-to-otf.html (accessed November 26, 2012).

15. C. S. Lewis, *The Abolition of Man* (New York: Collier Books, 1947).

16. It might be that our religious, moral, and political beliefs are culturally relative, which is something David Eller's argument in chapter 13 of my edited volume *The Christian Delusion* (Amherst, NY: Prometheus Books, 2010) leads us to think. But one need not go this far to make this case, since even if humans can and do rationally transcend their respective cultures, it changes very little about the odds of doing so.

17. Loftus, "Articulett."

18. Matthew Flannagan, "A Review of *The Christian Delusion: Why Faith Fails,*" *Philosphia Christi* 13, no. 1 (Summer 2011): 231–36.

19. Rauser, *Swedish Atheist,* chap. 6.

20. Matthew Flannagan, "True Reason: Christian Responses to the Challenges of Atheism," March 21, 2012, *M and M,* http://www.mandm.org.nz/2012/03/true -reason-christian-responses-to-the-challenges-of-atheism.html (accessed November 26, 2012).

21. John R. Shook, *The God Debates: A 21st Century Guide for Atheists and Believers (and Everyone in Between)* (Malden, MA: Wiley-Blackwell, 2010), pp. 87–89.

22. Ibid., p. 92.

CHAPTER 9. DEBATING CHRISTIANITY BASED ON THE TEST

1. "Steve Lovell Comments on the Outsider Test for Faith," at Victor Reppert's blog, *Dangerous Idea,* http://dangerousidea.blogspot.com/2010/06/steve -lovell-comments-on-outsider-test.html (accessed November 26, 2012).

2. J. L. Schellenberg, *The Wisdom to Doubt: A Justification of Religious Skepticism* (Ithaca, NY: Cornell University Press, 2007), pp. 47–48.

3. Ibid.

4. Ibid.

5. Edward Tryon in *Nature* (December 1973), and Stephen Hawking in *Physical Review* (December 1983).

6. See Lawrence M. Krauss, *A Universe from Nothing: Why There Is Something Rather Than Nothing at All* (New York: Free Press, 2012).

7. Victor J. Stenger, *God: The Failed Hypothesis* (Amherst, NY: Prometheus Books, 2008), pp. 132–33. See also Stenger's *The Comprehensible Cosmos: Where Do the Laws of Physics Come From?* (Amherst, NY: Prometheus Books, 2006), supplement H.

8. David C. Sim, "How Many Jews Became Christians in the First Century?

The Failure of the Christian Mission to the Jews," *Hervormde Teologiese Studies* 61, nos. 1 and 2 (2005), available online at http://repository.up.ac.za/bitstream/handle/2263/13403/Sim_How(2005).pdf?sequence=3 (accessed December 27, 2012).

9. Gotthold Lessing, "On the Proof of the Spirit and of Power," in *Lessing's Theological Writings*, trans. and ed. Henry Chadwick (Palo Alto, CA: Stanford University Press, 1956), pp. 51–55.

10. Ibid.

11. John W. Loftus, "Christians Are Not Credible Witnesses So Christianity Is Not Credible Either," *Debunking Christianity*, http://debunkingchristianity.blogspot.com/2012/11/christians-are-not-credible-witnesses.html (accessed December 27, 2012).

12. "possibly_maybe," blog commentator, quoted by John Loftus in "Who Answers Prayers?" *Debunking Christianity*, http://debunkingchristianity.blogspot.com/2011/07/who-answers-prayers.html (accessed December 26, 2012).

13. See John W. Loftus, "What Would Happen If Christians Went on Strike?" *Debunking Christianity*, http://debunkingchristianity.blogspot.com/2012/05/what-would-happen-if-christians-went-on.html (accessed November 26, 2012), and "Again, What If Christians Went on Strike?" *Debunking Christianity*, http://debunkingchristianity.blogspot.com/2012/05/again-what-if-christians-went-on-strike.html (accessed November 26, 2012).

14. Randal Rauser, quoted in ibid.

15. Richard Carrier, *Proving History: Bayes's Theorem and the Quest for the Historical Jesus* (Amherst, NY: Prometheus Books, 2012), p. 61. See Carrier's book for further details.

16. Ibid., pp. 61, 62. For people who are interested in a Bayesian analysis of the Outsider Test for Faith, mathematician James A. Lindsay has done such an analysis in two blog posts. See James A. Lindsay, "Loftus's Outsider Test for Faith Viewed in HD with Bayes's Theorem," *God Doesn't; We Do*, http://goddoesnt.blogspot.com/2012/12/loftuss-outsider-test-for-faith-viewed.html (accessed December 27, 2012. He writes:

> The OTF has the goal of having someone consider their assumption of the prior probability that their religion is true more honestly against a broader perspective, greatly reducing the tendency of a biased believer inside a faith to overestimate the prior probability. The OTF will cause someone to lower their assumed prior probability to a more realistic value. (This is what I have called *a* here, usually labeled something like P(h|b) in math-speak.)
>
> The OTF has the goal of having someone consider how well the evidence (i.e. the universe) matches their religion's claims about it more honestly, greatly reducing the tendency of a biased believer inside a faith to overestimate the degree to which the assumption of truth of their religion

predicts the evidence presented by the world. The OTF will cause someone to evaluate the failure of their religion to explain reality more seriously, lowering this consequent to a more realistic value. (This is what I have called *t* here, usually labeled something like P(e|h,b) in math-speak.)

The OTF has the goal of having someone consider how well other explanations of the evidence would explain what is seen on the presumption that their religion is false. This number is hard to see honestly from within a religious framework and is likely to be underestimated by believers inside it, and the OTF will have the effect of reducing the tendency to underestimate this number.

See also James A. Lindsay, "A Bit More Clarity on Bayes's Theorem and Loftus's Outsider Test for Faith," *God Doesn't; We Do,* http://goddoesnt.blogspot.com/2012/12/a-bit-more-clarity-on-bayess-theorem.html (accessed December 27, 2012).

17. Dan Barker, *Godless: How an Evangelical Preacher Became One of America's Leading Atheists* (Berkeley, CA: Ulysses, 2008), p. 39.

18. Carl Sagan, *The Demon Haunted World: Science as a Candle in the Dark* (New York: Random House, 1996), p. 101.

19. Hector Avalos, *The End of Biblical Studies* (Amherst, NY: Prometheus Books, 2007).

20. See Ed Young, "Creating God in One's Own Image," *Discover Magazine,* November 30, 2009, http://blogs.discovermagazine.com/notrocketscience/2009/11/30/creating-god-in-ones-own-image/ (accessed November 26, 2012).

CHAPTER 10. WHY SHOULD ANYONE BELIEVE ANYTHING AT ALL?

1. Victor Reppert, "More Responses to the Outsider Test," *Dangerous Idea,* http://dangerousidea.blogspot.com/2009/03/more-response-to-outsider-test.html (accessed November 26, 2012).

2. Michael Shermer, *How We Believe: The Search for God in an Age of Science* (New York: W. H. Freeman, 2000), pp. 85–86.

3. Michael Shermer, *Why People Believe Weird Things: Pseudoscience, Superstition, and Other Confusions of Our Time* (New York: A. W. H. Freeman, 2002), p. 299.

4. George H. Smith, *Atheism: The Case against God* (Amherst, NY: Prometheus Books, 1989), pp. 96–98.

5. Ibid., p. 100.

6. Ibid., p. 101.

7. Ibid., p. 120.

8. Ibid., p. 121.

9. Norman L. Geisler and Frank Turek, *I Don't Have Enough Faith to Be an Atheist* (Wheaton, IL: Crossway Books, 2004), p. 26.

10. Words in quotes are from Malcolm Ruel, *Belief, Ritual, and the Securing of Life* (Boston: Brill, 1997), quoted in David Eller, *Introducing Anthropology of Religion: Culture to the Ultimate* (London: Routledge, 2007), p. 33.

11. Voltaire, *Philosophical Dictionary*, ed. and trans. Theodore Besterman (New York: Penguin Books, 2004), "Foi Faith," p. 208.

12. Mark Twain (Samuel Clemens), "The Entire Project Gutenberg Works of Mark Twain," ed. David Widger et al., Project Gutenberg, http://www.gutenberg.org/dirs/3/2/0/3200/3200.txt (accessed November 26, 2012).

13. Sam Harris, *Letter to a Christian Nation* (New York: Alfred A. Knopf, 2006), p. 67.

14. Richard Dawkins, "The Irrationality of Faith," *New Statesman*, March 31, 1989.

15. The following quotes are found in chapter 11, "The 'F' Word," in Matt McCormick's book, *Atheism and the Case against Christ* (Amherst, NY: Prometheus Books, 2012).

16. Victor J. Stenger, from the preface to his book *God and the Folly of Faith: The Incompatibility of Science and Religion* (Amherst, NY: Prometheus Books, 2012), pp. 25–30.

17. David Eller, *Natural Atheism* (Cranford, NJ: American Atheist Press, 2004), p. 133.

18. A. C. Grayling, *Meditations for the Humanist: Ethics for a Secular Age* (Oxford: Oxford University Press, 2002), p. 117.

19. Bertrand Russell, "Will Religious Faith Cure Our Troubles?" *Human Society in Ethics and Politics* (New York: Routledge, 2009).

20. Bertrand Russell, "The Existence and Nature of God," in *Russell on Religion*, ed. L. Greenspan and S. Andersson (New York: Routledge, 1999), p. 94.

21. W. L. Reese, *Dictionary of Philosophy and Religion: Eastern and Western Thought* (Atlantic Highlands, NJ: Humanities Press, 1980), p. 166.

22. Eller, *Natural Atheism*, p. 132.

23. Ibid., p. 143.

24. David Eller, *Atheism Advanced: Further Thoughts of a Freethinker* (Cranford, NJ: American Atheist Press, 2007), p. 398.

25. Ibid., p. 402.

26. Stephen Law, *Believing Bullshit: How Not to Get Sucked into an Intellectual Black Hole* (Amherst, NY: Prometheus Books, 2011), p. 75

27. Randal Rauser, comment on blog post by John W. Loftus, "A Reasonable Faith Is an Oxymoron," *Debunking Christianity*, http://debunkingchristianity.blogspot .com/2012/02/reasonable-faith-is-oxymoron.html (accessed November 26, 2012).

28. See Randal Rauser's post "John Loftus Challenges Me to Define Faith," March 10, 2012, *Randal Rauser*, http://randalrauser.com/2012/03/john-loftus -challenges-me-to-define-faith/ (accessed November 26, 2012).

29. Randal Rauser, comment on blog post by John W. Loftus, "An Open Challenge to Christians about Faith," *Debunking Christianity*, http://debunking christianity.blogspot.com/2012/03/open-challenege-to-christians-about.html   (accessed November 26, 2012).

BIBLIOGRAPHY

Antony, Louise M., ed. *Philosophers without Gods*. Oxford: Oxford University Press, 2007.

Ariely, Dan. *Predictably Irrational: The Hidden Forces That Shape Our Decisions*. Revised ed. New York: Harper Perennial, 2010.

Atran, Scott. *In Gods We Trust: The Evolutionary Landscape of Religion*. Oxford: Oxford University Press, 2002.

Avalos, Hector. *The End of Biblical Studies*. Amherst, NY: Prometheus Books, 2007.

———. *Fighting Words: The Origins of Religious Violence*. Amherst, NY: Prometheus Books, 2005.

Barbour, Ian. *Religion in an Age of Science*. San Franscico: Harper & Row, 1990.

Barker, Dan. *Godless: How an Evangelical Preacher Became One of America's Leading Atheists*. Berkeley, CA: Ulysses Press, 2008.

Berger, Peter L. *The Sacred Canopy: Elements of a Sociological Theory of Religion*. Garden City, NY: Anchor Books, 1990.

Berger, Peter L. and Thomas Luckmann, *The Social Construction of Reality: A Treatise in the Sociology of Knowledge*. Garden City, NY: Anchor Books, 1966.

Bering, Jesse, *The Belief Instinct: The Psychology of Souls, Destiny, and the Meaning of Life*. New York: W. W. Norton, 2011.

Bishop, John. "Faith." (2010), In *Stanford Encyclopedia of Philosophy*. Stanford University, 1997. Article substantially revised August 20, 2010. http://plato.stanford .edu/entries/faith/.

Boyer, Pascal. *Religion Explained*. New York: Basic Books, 2010.

Brafman, Ori, and Rom Brafman, *Sway: The Irresistible Pull of Irrational Behavior*. New York: Broadway Books, 2009.

Carrier, Richard. *Proving History: Bayes's Theorem and the Quest for the Historical Jesus*. Amherst, NY: Prometheus Books, 2012.

Chabris, Christopher, and Daniel Simons, *The Invisible Gorilla: And Other Ways Our Intuitions Deceive Us*. New York: Crown, 2010.

Cialdini, Robert B. *Influence: The Psychology of Persuasion*. New York: William Morrow, 1993.

Coyne, Jerry. *Why Evolution Is True*. New York: Viking, 2009.

Craig, William Lane. "Politically Incorrect Salvation." In *Christian Apologetics in the Post-Modern World*. Edited by T. P. Phillips and D. Ockholm. Downers Grove, IL: InterVarsity Press, 1995.

———. *Reasonable Faith: Christian Truth and Apologetics.* 3rd ed. Wheaton, IL: Crossway Books, 2008.

Dawkins, Richard. *The Greatest Show on Earth: The Evidence for Evolution.* New York: Free Press, 2009.

DeRuvo, Fred. *The Anti-Christian Bias of Ex-Christians and Other Important Topics.* Scotts Valley, CA: Adroit, 2009.

Eller, David. *Atheism Advanced: Further Thoughts of a Freethinker.* Cranford, NJ: American Atheist Press, 2007.

———. *Natural Atheism.* Cranford, NJ: American Atheist Press, 2004.

Eller, Jack David. *Cultural Anthropology: Global Forces, Local Lives.* London: Routledge, 2009.

Epstein, Greg. *Good without God: What a Billion Nonreligious People Do Believe.* New York: Harper Collins, 2009.

Everitt, Nicholas. *The Non-Existence of God.* New York: Routledge, 2004.

Feldman, Richard, and Ted Warfield, eds. *Disagreement.* Oxford: Oxford University Press, 2010.

Feyerabend, Paul. *Against Method.* 3rd ed. New York: Verso, 1993.

Fine, Cordelia. *A Mind of Its Own: How Your Brain Distorts and Deceives.* New York: W. W. Norton, 2008.

Finke, Roger, and Rodney Stark, *The Churching of America, 1776–1990: Winners and Losers in Our Religious Economy.* New Brunswick, NJ: Rutgers University Press, 1992.

Flannagan, Matthew. "A Review of 'The Christian Delusion: Why Faith Fails.'" *Philosphia Christi* 13, no. 1 (Summer 2011): 231–36.

Flew, Antony. *God, Freedom, and Immortality: A Critical Analysis.* Amherst, NY: Prometheus Books, 1984.

———. *The Presumption of Atheism.* Amherst, NY: Prometheus Books, 1976.

Garcia, Robert K., and Nathan L. King. *Is Goodness without God Good Enough: A Debate on Faith, Secularism, and Ethics.* New York: Rowan and Littlefield, 2009.

Geisler, Norman L. "From Apologist to Atheist: A Critical Review," *Christian Apologetics Journal* 6, no. 1 (Spring 2007): 93–109.

Geisler, Norman L., and Ronald M. Brooks, *Come, Let Us Reason: An Introduction to Logical Thinking.* Grand Rapids, MI: Baker Academic Books, 1990.

Geisler, Norman L., and Frank Turek. *I Don't Have Enough Faith to Be an Atheist.* Wheaton, IL: Crossway Books, 2004.

Geisler, Norman L., and William D. Watkins. *Worlds Apart: A Handbook on Worldviews.* 2nd ed. Grand Rapids, MI: Baker Book House, 1989.

Grayling, A. C., *Meditations for the Humanist: Ethics for a Secular Age.* Oxford: Oxford University Press, 2002.

Greenspan, Lois, and Stefan Andersson, eds. *Russell on Religion.* New York: Routledge, 1999.

Hallinan, Joseph T. *Why We Make Mistakes.* New York: Broadway Books, 2009.

Hanna, Mark M. *Biblical Christianity: Truth or Delusion?* xulonpress.com, 2011.

Harris, Sam. *Free Will.* New York: Free Press, 2012.

———. *The Moral Landscape: How Science Can Determine Human Values.* New York: Free Press, 2010.

Harrison, Guy P. *50 Popular Beliefs That People Think Are True.* Amherst, NY: Prometheus Books, 2012.

———. *50 Reasons People Give for Believing in a God.* Amherst, NY: Prometheus Books, 2008.

Hecht, Jennifer Michael. *Doubt: A History.* New York: Harper Collins, 2003.

Hick, John. *An Interpretation of Religion: Human Responses to the Transcendent.* New Haven, CT: Yale University Press, 1989.

Horton, Michael. *Christless Christianity: The Alternative Gospel of the American Church.* Grand Rapids, MI: Baker Books, 2008.

Irwin, William, ed. *The Matrix and Philosophy: Welcome to the Desert of the Real.* Chicago: Open Court, 2002.

Jenkins, Philip. *The New Faces of Christianity: Believing the Bible in the Global South.* Oxford: Oxford University Press, 2006.

———. *The Next Christendom: The Coming of Global Christianity.* 2nd ed. Oxford: Oxford University Press, 2007.

Keller, Timothy. *The Reason for God: Belief in an Age of Skepticism.* New York: Riverhead Books, 2008.

Krauss, Lawrence M. *A Universe from Nothing: Why There Is Something Rather Than Nothing at All.* New York: Free Press, 2012.

Kurtz, Paul, ed. *Science and Religion: Are They Compatible?* Amherst, NY: Prometheus Books, 2003.

———. *The Transcendental Temptation.* Amherst, NY: Prometheus Books, 1991.

Law, Stephen. *Believing Bullshit: How Not to Get Sucked into an Intellectual Black Hole.* Amherst, NY: Prometheus Books, 2011.

Lessing, Gotthold. *Lessing's Theological Writings.* Edited and translated by Henry Chadwick. Stanford, CA: Stanford University Press, 1956.

Lewis, C. S., *The Abolition of Man.* New York: Collier Books, 1947.

Loftus, John W., ed. *The Christian Delusion: Why Faith Fails.* Amherst, NY: Prometheus Books, 2010.

———, ed. *The End of Christianity.* Amherst, NY: Prometheus Books, 2011.

———. *Why I Became an Atheist: A Former Preacher Rejects Christianity.* 2nd ed. Amherst, NY: Prometheus Books, 2012.

Loftus, John W., and Randal Rauser, *God or Godless? One Atheist. One Christian. Twenty Controversial Questions.* Grand Rapids: Baker Books, 2013.

Long, Jason. *The Religious Condition.* New York: iUniverse, 2008.

Malcom, Norman. *Dreaming.* New York: Routledge & Kegan Paul, 1976.

Marcus, Gary. *Kluge: The Haphazard Evolution of the Human Mind.* New York: Mariner Books, 2009.

Marshall, David. *The Truth Behind the New Atheism.* Eugene, OR: Harvest House, 2007.

Martin, Michael. *Atheism: A Philosophical Justification.* Philadelphia: Temple University Press, 1990.

———, ed. *Cambridge Companion to Atheism.* Cambridge: Cambridge University Press, 2007.

———. *The Case against Christianity.* Philadelphia: Temple University Press, 1991.

Martin, Michael, and Ricki Monnier. *The Improbability of God.* Amherst, NY: Prometheus Books, 2006.

McCormick, Matthew S. *Atheism and the Case against Christ.* Amherst, NY: Prometheus Books, 2012.

McGrath, Alister E. *Science and Religion: An Introduction.* Oxford: Blackwell, 1999.

McKim, Robert. *Religious Ambiguity and Religious Diversity.* Oxford: Oxford University Press, 2001.

McRae, Mike. *Tribal Science: Brains, Beliefs, and Bad Ideas.* Amherst, NY: Prometheus Books, 2012.

Moreland, J. P. *Christianity and Science: A Philosophical Investigation.* Grand Rapids, MI: Baker Book House, 1989.

Moreland, J. P., and William Lane Craig. *Philosophical Foundations of a Christian Worldview.* Downers Grove, IL: InterVarsity Press, 2003.

Newsom, Carol A., and Sharon H. Ringe, eds. *Women's Bible Commentary: Expanded Edition.* Louisville, KY: Westminster John Knox Press, 1998.

Niebuhr, H. Richard. *Christ and Culture.* New York: Harper & Row, 1956.

Petty, Richard E., and John T. Cacioppo, *Attitudes and Persuasion: Classic and Contemporary Approaches.* Dubuque, IA: William C. Brown, 1981.

Plantinga, Alvin. "Pluralism: A Defense of Religious Exclusivism," Carnival Sage. http://www.carnivalsage.com/articles/plantinga-alvin-pluralism-defense-of-religious-exclusivism.html.

———. *Warranted Christian Belief.* Oxford: Oxford University Press, 2000.

Rauser, Randal. *The Swedish Atheist, the Scuba Diver, and Other Apologetic Rabbit Trails.* Downers Grove, IL: InterVarsity Press, 2012.

———. *You're Not as Crazy as I Think: Dialogue in a World of Loud Voices and Hardened Opinions.* Colorado Springs, CO: Biblica, 2011.

Reese, W. L. *Dictionary of Philosophy and Religion: Eastern and Western Thought.* Atlantic Highlands, NJ: Humanities Press, 1980.

Riskas, Thomas. *Deconstructing Mormonism: An Analysis and Assessment of the Mormon Faith.* Cranford, NJ: American Atheist Press, 2011.

Sagan, Carl. *The Demon Haunted World: Science as a Candle in the Dark*. New York: Random House, 1996.

Schellenberg, J. L. *The Wisdom to Doubt: A Justification of Religious Skepticism*. Ithaca, NY: Cornell University Press, 2007.

Schick, Theodore, Jr., and Lewis Vaughn. *How to Think about Weird Things: Critical Thinking for a New Age*. 6th ed. Boston: McGraw-Hill, 2010.

Scholz, Susanne. *Sacred Witness: Rape in the Hebrew Bible*. Minneapolis: Fortress Press, 2010.

Sennett, James F, ed., *The Analytic Theist: An Alvin Plantinga Reader*. Grand Rapids, MI: Eerdmans, 1998.

Shermer, Michael. *The Believing Brain: From Ghosts and Gods to Politics and Conspiracies—How We Construct Beliefs and Reinforce Them as Truths*. New York: Times Books, 2011.

———. *How We Believe: The Search for God in an Age of Science*. New York: W. H. Freeman, 2000.

———. *Why People Believe Weird Things: Pseudoscience, Superstition, and Other Confusions of Our Time*. New York: A. W. H. Freeman, 2002.

Shook, John R. *The God Debates: A 21st Century Guide for Atheists and Believers (and Everyone in Between)*. Malden, MA: Wiley-Blackwell, 2010.

Sinnott-Armstrong, Walter. *Morality without God?* Oxford: Oxford University Press, 2011.

Sire, James W. *The Universe Next Door*. 5th ed. Downers Grove, IL: InterVarsity Press, 2009.

———. *Why Should Anyone Believe Anything at All?* Downers Grove, IL: InterVarsity Press, 1994.

Smart, Ninian. *Worldviews: Crosscultural Explorations of Human Beliefs*. 3rd ed. Upper Saddle River, NJ: Prentice Hall, 2000.

Smith, George H. *Atheism: The Case against God*. Amherst, NY: Prometheus Books, 1989.

Smith, Huston. *Why Religion Matters*. New York: HarperSanFrancisco, 2001.

Stark, Rodney, and William Sims Bainbridge. *The Future of Religion: Secularization, Revival, and Cult Formation*. Berkeley: University of California Press, 1985.

Stenger, Victor J. *The Comprehensible Cosmos: Where Do the Laws of Physics Come From?* Amherst, NY: Prometheus Books, 2006.

———. *God: The Failed Hypothesis—How Science Shows That God Does Not Exist*. Amherst, NY: Prometheus Books, 2007.

———. *God and the Folly of Faith: The Incompatibility of Science and Religion*. Amherst, NY: Prometheus Books, 2012.

Stone, David Reuben. *The Loftus Delusion: Why Atheism Fails and Messianic Israelism Prevails*. Raleigh, NC: Lulu.com, 2010.

Sweeney, Julia. *Letting Go of God.* Indefatigable, 2006, 2 compact discs.

Swinburne, Richard. *Faith and Reason.* 2nd ed. Oxford: Oxford University Press, 2005.

Talbott, Thomas. "The Outsider Test for Faith: How Serious a Challenge Is It?" http://www.willamette.edu/~ttalbott/Loftus%20OTF2.pdf.

Tarico, Valerie. *Trusting Doubt: A Former Evangelical Looks at Old Beliefs in a New Light.* Independence, VA: Oracle Institute, 2010.

Tavris, Carol, and Elliot Aronson, *Mistakes Were Made (but Not by Me): Why We Justify Foolish Beliefs, Bad Decisions and Hurtful Acts.* Orlando: Harvest, 2007.

Thargard, Paul. *The Brain and the Meaning of Life.* Princeton, NJ: Princeton University Press. 2010.

Wade, Nicholas. *The Faith Instinct: How Religion Evolved and Why It Endures.* New York: Penguin, 2009.

Walsh, Brian J., and J. Richard Middleton. *The Transforming Vision: Shaping the Christian World View.* Downers Grove, IL: InterVarsity Press, 1984.

Weitnauer, Carson, and Tom Gilson, eds. *True Reason: Christian Responses to the Challenge of Atheism.* Englewood, CO: Patheos, 2012.

Williams, Bernard. *Descartes: The Project of Pure Enquiry.* Revised edition. New York: Routledge, 2005.

Zuckerman, Phil. *Faith No More: Why People Reject Religion.* Oxford: Oxford University Press, 2011.

———. *Society without God: What the Least Religious Nations Can Tell Us about Contentment.* New York: New York University Press, 2010.

INDEX OF NAMES

INDEX OF SUBJECTS

Specific discussions of certain subjects are indicated by **bold** page numbers